ecpr PRESS

I0094612

Europeanised or European?
Representation by Civil Society Organisations in EU Policy Making

Sandra Kröger

ecpr PRESS

© Sandra Kröger 2016

First published by the ECPR Press in 2016

The ECPR Press is the publishing imprint of the European Consortium for Political Research (ECPR), a scholarly association, which supports and encourages the training, research and cross-national co-operation of political scientists in institutions throughout Europe and beyond.

ECPR Press
Harbour House
Hythe Quay
Colchester
CO2 8JF
United Kingdom

Typeset by Lapiz Digital Services

Printed and bound by Lightning Source

British Library Cataloguing in Publication Data

A catalogue record for this book is available from the British Library

HARDBACK ISBN: 978-1-785522-32-1
PAPERBACK ISBN: 978-1-785522-48-2
PDF ISBN: 978-1-785522-45-1
EPUB ISBN: 978-1-785522-46-8
KINDLE ISBN: 978-1-785522-47-5

www.ecpr.eu/ecprpress

If you are interested in European representation, you may like

Between Nationalism and Europeanisation
Nevena Nancheva
Nevena Nancheva tells a small story from the periphery of Europe. Looking at
two post-communist Balkan states – Bulgaria and Macedonia – she explores
how their narratives of national identity have changed in the context of
Europeanisation and EU membership preparations.
Paperback ISBN 9781785521430

More in the ECPR Press Monographs series
Consultative Committees in the European Union: No Vote — No Influence?
(ISBN: 9781910259429)
Diana Panke, Christoph Hönnige and Julia Gollub

*Why Centralisation? Concept, Theory and Comparative Evidence from Sub-
National Switzerland*
(ISBN: 9781785521294)
Sean Mueller

Situating Governance
(ISBN: 9781907301681)
Antonino Palumbo

Democratic Reform and Consolidation: the Cases of Mexico and Turkey
(ISBN: 9781907301674)
Evren Celik Wiltse

Please visit www.ecpr.eu/ecprpress for information about new publications.

Contents

Acknowledgements

First of all, I would like to acknowledge the generous support of the project of which this book is the result, by means of a Marie Curie Intra European Fellowship within the 7th European Community Framework Programme (FP7-PEOPLE-2010-IEF). Without the Fellowship, which brought me to Exeter for the first time, the research underlying this book would not have been possible. In this context, I would like to thank my friend and colleague Dario Castiglione for being my mentor and for always being available to help, give advice and support, and discuss the evolving project. I would similarly like to thank Fiona Raffael for the amazing administrative support she gave me from well before the Fellowship started until its end. Next, I am indebted and would like to thank all the interviewees who accorded some of their precious work time to me. Their voices are very much at the heart of this study, and I do hope that I have done them justice and that this book might also be of interest for their work. I would also like to thank Ben Boulton and Alexandra Ostendorf for their help with the transcriptions of the interviews as well as Hans Kirschner for his help with the statistical data. I was then able to finalise the analysis and the drafting of the manuscript thanks to a Fellowship at the Hanse Wissenschaftskolleg in Delmenhorst (Germany, just south of Bremen). I am very grateful for the Fellowship also because it allowed my partner and me to spend a great year together in Germany, as well as my seeing colleagues and friends in Bremen and spending a good amount of time with my mother to whom I am forever indebted for having offered to move from Berlin to Bremen for the time of the Fellowship to look after my cat Loulou. I would also like to thank a number of colleagues and/or friends who have made this book possible by way of supporting the proposal through references or giving critical feedback to different aspects of it: Dominika Biegon, Dawid Friedrich, Thorsten Hüller, Anne Jenichen, Beate Kohler, Claus Offe, Heiko Pleines, Sonja Puntscher Riekmann, Sabine Saurugger, and Arndt Wonka. More than anyone else, I need to thank my partner Richard Bellamy for the numerous discussions we have had about different aspects of the research and the manuscript which have helped me a great deal to improve the work - thank you so much. But also, for all the mental support and encouragement you have given me throughout the years which has often kept me going. Last but not least, I am grateful to the team from ECPR Press with which it was great to work during the review and publication process. Again, their in-house feedback as well as the feedback by the two anonymous reviewers greatly helped me improve the manuscript.

List of Abbreviations

AGM – Annual General Meeting

BAG FW – Bundesarbeitsgemeinschaft der Freien Wohlfahrtspflege

BUND – Bund für Umwelt und Naturschutz Deutschland

CAP – Common Agricultural Policy

Copa-COGECA – Committee of Professional Agricultural Organisations - General Confederation of Agricultural Cooperatives

CSO – Civil Society Organisation

DG – Directorate-General

DGB – Deutscher Gewerkschaftsbund

DNR – Deutscher Naturschutzring

DRK – Deutsches Rotes Kreuz

EAPN – European Anti-Poverty Network

ECI – European Citizen Initiative

EDF – European Disability Forum

EEB – European Environmental Bureau

ENAR – European Network Against Racism

EP – European Parliament

EU – European Union

FEANTSA – European Federation of National Organisations Working with the Homeless

MEP – Member of European Parliament

MP – Member of Parliament

NABU – Naturschutzbund Deutschland

NAK – Nationale Armutskonferenz

NFU – National Farmers' Union

NGO – Non-governmental Organisation

OMC – Open Method of Coordination

RSPB – Royal Society for the Protection of Birds

WTO – World Trade Organisation

Introduction

Understanding the role played by civil society organisations (CSOs) is central to the study of contemporary democracies, both at the national and the supranational level. CSOs have become important actors in agenda-setting and in the design, implementation and monitoring of public policies. Both in the European Union (EU) and also more globally, CSOs have also been granted a democratising role, not least because of the absence or at least deficiencies, in supranational contexts, of traditional representative actors.

By and large, though, scholars have conceptualised CSOs in terms of participatory or associative theories of democracy. Little scholarly attention has been paid to the topic of political *representation* by CSOs, either in general or in the EU in particular (Kohler-Koch 2010: 101). However, CSOs engage in interest *representation,* and they do so in the context of *representative* democracies. Therefore, political *representation* is the key to studying the democratic credentials of CSOs. This study seeks to contribute to closing this research gap. It will empirically investigate how CSOs engage in political representation, and use the multi-level system of the EU and its search for more democracy as its example. Concluding, it will use the empirical findings to discuss whether CSOs can compensate for the alleged failure of traditional forms of democratic representation in the EU, and more specifically, whether they are capable of a) reducing the institutional deficit of the EU by enhancing the representation of a broad range of interests or even of b) reducing the structural deficit of the EU by contributing to the building of a European demos. Finally, this study is also interested in whether or not being involved in EU policy making perhaps reduces the democratic potential of CSOs.

To study political representation by CSOs in the EU implies being situated at the intersection of two research agendas: a) the reconfiguration of political representation within contemporary democracies, and b) the further democratisation of the EU, both of which I will now address in turn.

The reconfiguration of political representation

Since the revolutions in what was to become the United States of America and in France, democracy has been linked to representation. Political representation is generally perceived as the means for safeguarding the political equality of citizens, by giving every individual potentially affected by a decision the same opportunity to influence this decision. In this context, representative democracy has been understood as a more or less tight principal-agent relationship, as a way of establishing the legitimacy of democratic institutions and of creating institutional incentives for governments to be responsive to citizens (Castiglione and Warren 2008). In this context, the 'standard model', so to speak, is defined by the formal moments of authorisation and accountability, when voters periodically elect representatives who meet in parliament and are in some way accountable to the voters.

The political egalitarianism on which the institutions of modern representative democracy rest is today challenged by a number of diversification processes. We are witnessing an increasing number of non-governmental, private actors and agencies claiming representative functions, thereby contributing to a proliferation of *actors* involved in representation as well as *loci* where representation occurs. This development has specific consequences for political parties, which are no longer the only mediators between the citizens and the state. Elected politicians are losing their monopoly over political representation, not least because trust in political parties is declining in Western democracies. Declining electoral turnout, the widespread fall in party-identification and membership, the weakening of the capacity of parties for symbolic integration and political aggregation as well as the difficulties they face in sustaining effective governments are indicative of a generalised crisis of political representation and intermediation through partisan channels (Mair 2006; Manin 1997).

Furthermore, we can observe the spread of representative functions across different geographical *levels*. Nation-states have started to delegate tasks up- and downwards, so that political representation, accountability and democratic legitimacy are no longer tied to one single jurisdiction, something that the term 'multi-levelness' seeks to capture. Indeed, European integration and wider processes of globalisation seem to undermine the traditional notions of 'demos' and 'sovereignty' which lie at the heart of modern concepts of representative democracy; to the point that some have spoken of the lack of usefulness of the category of national 'sovereignty' altogether (Goodhart 2007). These and other diversification processes are contributing to the dilution of traditional representative politics (Warren and Castiglione 2004) and to the development of 'new frontiers' of representation (Urbinati and Warren 2008: 402). Leading authors have argued that as a result of their impact representation can no longer be restricted to electoral representation and to representation in the nation-state alone, for such a conceptualisation fails to mirror political reality (Rehfeld 2006; Lord and Pollak 2010).

However, as yet no particular attention has been given to CSOs and their contribution to political *representation*. As I noted, CSOs have been associated with participatory and associative conceptions of democracy rather than with representative democracy. Recently, however, some scholars have tried to enlarge the concept of political representation so as to open it to non-electoral forms and to forms beyond the nation-state, in particular (Kohler-Koch 2010; Kröger 2013; Lord and Pollak 2010; Mansbridge 2003; Rehfeld 2006; Saward 2009). A central move in this development has been the theoretical abandonment of any necessary identity of represented and representative. This acknowledgment of the non-identity of represented and representative allowed a change of perspective in representation theory. It no longer need involve 'making present' that which is absent (Pitkin 1967) but can focus instead on the character of the representative *relationship* (Plotke 1997). What happens in between the formal moments of authorisation and control has moved centre stage (see Mansbridge 2003; Urbinati 2006). This understanding of representation naturally places greater emphasis on non-electoral forms of representation that occur between and besides electoral processes. In sum, we are witnessing changes in the reality of political representation as well as in its conceptualisation, and the present study engages critically with this development.

The further democratisation of the EU

The second research agenda to which the present study links is the further democratisation of the EU. The EU has been struggling with an alleged democratic deficit since the early 1990s. The deficit arises because the EU as a whole has so far not developed the kind of thick identity that allows for mutual trust and solidarity between citizens who recognise each other as members of the same polity (Offe 1998). As a consequence of this fundamental barrier to democratic politics, the EU has not seen the development of the intermediary structures that allow for representative government, such as the media and political parties, in the same ways as they evolved in Member States. European news is still delivered through national channels of communication and thereby filtered by what are perceived as national interests. European parties, in turn, have kept their organisational and electoral bases in Member States and European elections continue to be perceived as second-order elections – with ever-lower turnouts – in which national governments are rewarded or punished on the basis of their domestic record. The institutional consequence of the lack of a European demos is the lack of democratic channels of representation and an elected government; as a consequence, the EU has a limited ability to engage in partisan, majoritarian politics.

In this situation, functional representation has been perceived by some as a possible equivalent to electoral representation, offering a welcome source of legitimacy-generation that can compensate for the lack of legitimacy generated through the standard model of representative democracy at the EU level. They have hoped that an increase in the involvement and participation of CSOs in EU policy making could be a means for democratising EU politics, by bringing the political system closer to the citizen and *vice versa*: thereby acting as a 'transmission belt' between Brussels and EU citizens (Nanz and Steffek 2004) or even as the cornerstone of a polity-building project (Eriksen and Fossum 2000). Indeed, the idea of representing specific publics via a 'partnership' with relevant 'stakeholders' has become a guiding theme of the EU in the last twenty years (Kohler-Koch and Finke 2007; Saurugger 2010). Empirically, the European Commission has actively engaged in the promotion and development of societal representation at the EU level, something reflected in the much debated '2001 White Paper on Governance', in which the Commission argued that 'its legitimacy today depends on involvement and participation' (European Commission 2001: 11).

The main focus of the related research has been on what CSO involvement contributes to deliberation, participation and the emergence of a public sphere in the EU (Della Sala and Ruzza 2007; Friedrich 2011; Hüller 2010, Kröger 2008a; Steffek and Nanz 2008). From these studies, we have a fairly good understanding of the involvement of CSOs in EU policy making. However, we hardly have any information about a number of other questions: which conceptions of representation do CSO actors have and who do they represent? What are the organisational structures and processes by which CSOs organise representation in the EU? To what degree are CSOs Europeanised? Who are CSOs addressing when they engage in political representation in EU affairs? Does the institutional environment of the EU affect the activities of CSOs and their interest representation strategies? What are the incentives and disincentives for CSOs to engage with EU policy making? Examining these questions will not only give us a better understanding of the issues involved, it will also allow us to discuss what type of political representation the related practices embody, and what can and should be their legitimate role in EU policy making.

There are a number of innovations in this study. First, a striking aspect of the two literature streams laid out above has been that they have co-existed in parallel rather than mutually influencing one another. The general political science literature on representation has not much informed the study of representation in the EU, particularly not the study of CSOs in the EU, and likewise EU studies have not strongly influenced the more general political science literature on representation. This study seeks to have these two streams interact.

Second, and a bit likewise, EU studies themselves have been divided in so far as CSOs are concerned. The literature on interest groups in EU studies tends to either address the EU level or the domestic level, but rarely ever links those levels. Because of the missing link, between the governance levels, related research generally does not capture who gets actually *represented* in EU policy making, something the present study sets out to do. If we want to know whether CSOs can work against the institutional or the social deficit in the EU, then we need to know who it is they are actually representing, and this can only be done by looking at the different governance levels. This study and the way it has been conceived thus seeks to contribute to closing this gap in the literature.

Third, and related, *representation* has by and large been a missing category in the literature concerned with CSOs in the EU (but see Kohler-Koch 2010; Smismans 2009; Steffek *et al.* 2008; Trenz 2009). Studies interested in democratic theory have by and large related CSOs to participatory, associative or deliberative democracy. In contrast, this study considers that CSOs and their contribution to EU policy making ought to be embedded in a representation framework (*see* Chapter 1.2 and Chapter 2.3.1). Adopting such a framework will allow for two things. First, it will allow to pose different questions to those asked, by and large, by the existing research and therefore to discover new evidence. Second, it will allow to better discuss which contribution CSOs make and can make to *representative* democracy in the EU.

Fourth and finally, this study mainly relies on qualitative data, even though it also uses quantitative data to a limited degree. This stands in contrast to much of the research on interest groups and the way they Europeanise, which tends to be quantitative and is therefore likely to miss important aspects of interest representation in the EU. By contrast, in this study understanding how actors think of political representation, and the way they construct it across levels of governance, is central (*see* Chapter 2.2). Let me now turn to the structure of this book.

The first chapter will set the scene of the topic by addressing the theoretical debates linked to both research agendas, that is, the reconfiguration of political representation and the democratisation of the EU. On the way, the research questions that have guided this study will be linked to these debates. The chapter will start by briefly reviewing the intellectual history of democratic representation and the central norms of what is known as the 'standard model' of representation (*see* Chapter 1.1). It will then move on to discuss the different ways in which scholars have sought to link democratic representation to non-electoral processes, not least representation by CSOs (*see* Chapter 1.2). This will also provide the opportunity to differentiate between democratic representation, legitimate representation and representation *tout court*. Finally, the chapter moves on to the debate about the potential role of CSOs in the EU (*see* Chapter 1.3). I firstly lay out the different channels of representation in the EU and how CSOs can and do engage with them. I then show how CSOs have been linked to the democratic deficit debate in the literature – namely by working against an *institutional* deficit or a *social* deficit ('no demos') – or how they could additionally be linked to it, namely as feeling the effects of the EU by way of a *domestic* deficit.

In Chapter Two, I will lay out the research design of this study. I begin by briefly reminding the general context of the overall research question (*see* Chapter 2.1). The next section develops the methodological approach of this study which is abductive (*see* Chapter 2.2). This is followed by the discussion of three models of representation by CSOs which form the basis of the case choice, namely representation of 'members', of a 'cause' and of 'weak interests' (*see* Chapter 2.3). In the next section, the research questions which had emerged from the theoretical discussions in Chapter One are developed in greater detail (*see* Chapter 2.4) before I move on to detail the methods used and the material these methods generated (*see* Chapter 2.5).

In Chapters 3–5, I will present the results of the empirical research, from agricultural CSOs (Chapter Three) over environmental CSOs (Chapter Four) to anti-poverty CSOs (Chapter Five). These chapters will each have the same structure.

The first section will give a brief introduction to the policy field and its actors in which the respective organisations work. It will also provide the details of the interviews conducted in each of the three cases.

The second section of the empirical chapters will address the *understanding* of representation by the actors involved. What, in their view, *is* representation? Do they see themselves as representing a constituency or an issue? Do they perceive themselves as lobbyists or do they favour a more participatory approach that includes a more interactive role perception? When do they think representation is achieved? And, not least, how do actors conceive of the legitimacy of their activities – is it thought to be generated through input by relevant constituencies or through output via expertise and/or achieved policies?

In the third section, I am interested in the *practices* of representation within CSOs rather than, as in the previous section, in what actors *understand* by representation. I will be looking a) at how the different groups involve their constituencies in the decision-making and internal governance of the organisation, and b) at how far they mobilise a potentially larger constituency. That is, how far do they widen their mobilisation for some of their activities – do groups reach out to a larger public, do they seek to enlarge their constituency, or do they mainly focus on their existing constituency? Overall, this section will allow me to see how representative CSOs are of their constituencies, and also, how the practices of internal governance relate to the more general understandings of representation addressed in the previous section.

The fourth section will show the different ways in which CSO actors seek to represent their constituencies in EU policy making. I will first briefly consider the degree of Europeanisation of the different groups. The main part of this section will focus on the addressees of CSOs in EU policy making as well as the strategies CSOs use to address them. Special attention will be given to how far groups try to organise themselves under the aegis of European umbrella organisations. This is in order to evaluate whether groups themselves see an added value in co-operating with groups from other Member States. Only if this was the case could it be taken as an indicator of a contribution to a European demos, as discussed in parts of the interested literature. If groups were only co-operating with other groups from the same Member State, this would suggest that national differences between them, even within the same policy field, would remain too strong for stronger European co-ordination. In a next step I examine whether being involved in EU policy making has an impact on CSOs. This is relevant as it can indicate whether being involved in EU policy making distances the organisations from their constituencies in one way or another. The empirical chapters each close by addressing incentives and disincentives, for CSOs to get involved with the EU, as well as the priorities in their EU-related work, as perceived by the actors themselves, thereby providing clues for explaining their engagement with the EU.

Chapter Six will first sum up and comparatively discuss the empirical findings (*see* Chapter 6.1). This will particularly involve discussing what type of political representation the practices of representation described in Chapters 3–5 embody, how Europeanised they are and which strategies CSOs use when engaging in EU affairs. Concluding, I will use the empirical evidence to discuss the larger question of whether or not CSOs can compensate for the alleged failure of traditional forms of democratic representation in the EU, as discussed in the literature around the institutional and social deficit in the EU (*see* Chapter 6.2).

Chapter One

The Contribution of CSOs to Legitimate Representation in the EU

For many observers, there is a lack of democratic representation in the EU, if for different reasons. Some commentators have argued that given the deficiencies of traditional representative institutions at the EU level, perhaps civil society organisations (CSOs) could step in and compensate for what mainly political parties in the European Parliament, but also national politicians in the Council of the EU, struggle to achieve. They might be capable of a) reducing an *institutional* deficit by enhancing the representation of a broad range of interests or even of b) reducing a *social* deficit by contributing to the building of a European demos. This study is interested in whether or not CSOs can live up to either – or even both – of these roles, or, whether on the contrary, being involved in EU policy making perhaps reduces the democratic potential of CSOs. To address these larger questions, it empirically explores a number of research questions which are developed in the course of this chapter, and are laid out in more detail in the next chapter. Doing so, it aims to bring together what has hitherto been separated, i.e. broader theories of representation on the one hand and studies of the EU's democratic deficit on the other.

To develop the research agendas in which this study is embedded, I will first review the development and key features of the 'standard model of representation' which I associate to democratic representation (*see* Chapter 1.1). In a next step, I will review arguments that challenge the 'standard model' in light of different diversification processes, particularly the diversification of actors (*see* Chapter 1.2). The discussion will eventually allow me to differentiate between representation *tout court*, *legitimate* and *democratic* representation, with legitimate representation being what mostly interests me in the context of this study. Finally, I will turn to the specific case of the EU and discuss which roles have been associated to CSOs in the context of its much debated democratic deficit, i.e. to work against the institutional deficit by participating in European governance, or to work against the social deficit by contributing to the creation of a European demos (*see* Chapter 1.3). On the way, I will associate the mentioned debates to a number of research questions which have guided the empirical analysis. In the present chapter, the aim is to link those questions to the theoretical debates surrounding them whereas in the next chapter, I will go into them in more detail.

1.1 What is democratic representation?

Conceptually and empirically, the link between representation and democracy is not self-evident (Pitkin 1967: 2). In fact, historically, representation was considered to be *in opposition* to democracy (Rancière 2006: 298). These days, most scholars agree that representation is a necessity for democracy: 'Representation is not an unfortunate compromise between an ideal of direct democracy and messy modern realities. Representation is crucial in constituting democratic practices' (Plotke 1997: 19; Hobson 2008: 451; Urbinati 2004, 2006). This is not the place to settle this dispute. Instead, I will provide a short history of the development of representative democracy, reminding the reader of its constitutional features and thereby providing the ground against which I will subsequently discuss more recent developments in representation theory which, not least, have sought to link CSOs to democratic representation.

The American and French Revolutions offered the intellectual and political context in which democratic government came to be envisaged and institutionalised as representative government (Urbinati 2004). James Madison argued that through representative institutions democracy could be extended over a much greater territory and population than had previously been thought possible. He thought that representative, as opposed to directly participatory, institutions provided more continuity and stability, as representative bodies are less likely than the people to act on sudden changes of opinion. Through electoral engineering, a representative government will aim at a general good that encompasses the interests and preferences of many, more reliably than if all individuals in the people were polled directly. In France, Abbé de Sieyès considered the establishment of representative government as the 'true object of the revolution' (Hobson 2008: 453). For him, representation was a means of reactivating democracy in the context of territorial nation-states.

What is it, then, that makes us appreciate democratic representation? It is that which makes it an expression of political equality. Democratic representation transfers the equal moral worth of people into law-making and politics. Scholars generally agree that each individual is of equal moral worth, a position that ultimately dates back to the tradition of natural law and social contract theory as developed by Hobbes, Locke and Rousseau. They all postulated that individuals, in their natural condition, possess equal rights, as also mirrored in the categorical imperative of Kant, which defended the equality postulate of universal human worth, later one of the guiding themes of the French Revolution, along with freedom and fraternity.

What we today call the 'standard model' of representative democracy is the institutional translation of the principle of political equality. The substantive equal worth of all citizens translates into citizenship rights that guarantee the right to participate in public law-making and to control decision-makers. All those who are bound by collective decisions are entitled to an equal say in their making; and collective public actions should be grounded on processes inclusive of those affected (see, e.g., Habermas 1992; Dryzek 2000; Young 2002). Giving all citizens the equal right and ability to control their life through collective decisions is realised through, first, regular, free and fair elections. Elections authorise political leaders and make them responsive and accountable to the electorate. For the limited time-span of an election cycle, political authority is delegated to elected representatives based on the voting act that follows the rule of one-person-one-vote, thereby translating the norm of political equality. Electoral outcomes are respected by those not represented in the constituted government because they are the result of equal, fair and free election, by the people. Normatively, electoral cycles imply that power is conditional and that its abuse can be penalised.

The second way in which representative democracy is realised is through the representative government that follows from the results of elections, which aggregates social interests into a political programme. In this context, parties are a means of organising voters and linking them to politicians and policies. Parties compete for a majority by putting forward a manifesto that aggregates voters' preferences into a political programme with maximum electoral appeal (Auel and Benz 2005: 375). Democratic legitimacy is created through competition between parties, contributing to forming political awareness, offering political alternatives and expressing the will of citizens. The above described institutional translation of the 'standard model' is what Hanna Pitkin addresses under 'formalistic' representation. Formalistic representation refers to the formal mechanisms of authorisation and accountability, to the establishment of representative institutions and a representative government. It is concerned with the institutional and social passage from personalised representation to parliamentary representation. So conceived, representative democracy has been understood as a way of establishing the legitimacy of democratic institutions and has been shown to be a practically feasible and normatively justifiable version of democracy (Mill 1861, chapter three).

Crucially, democratic representation has traditionally been seen as consisting of a vulnerable relationship between authorisation and accountability. This relationship has been described as follows:

'1. Political representation involves representative X being authorized by constituency Y to act with regard to good Z. Authorization means that there are procedures through which Y selects or directs X with respect to Z. Ultimate responsibility for the actions or decisions of X rests with Y.

2. Political representation involves representative X being held accountable to constituency Y with regard to good Z. Accountability means that X provides, or could provide, an account of his or her decisions or actions to Y with respect to Z, and that Y has a sanction over X with regard to Z.'
(Castiglione and Warren 2008: 7)

A focus on authorisation entails that the actions of the agent(s) can be ascribed to the principal and that the represented are bound by such acts. The focus on accountability is, instead, concerned with the reverse aspect of representation: how and to what extent representatives can be made accountable to the represented. Authorisation is thus the conferral of authority, the act by which a representative obtains his status as representative, while accountability means the responsiveness of the representative to the represented, as well as the ability of the represented to punish their representative for failing to act in accordance to their wishes.

The way the relationship between the represented and the representative works has been the object of much debate. In Hanna Pitkin's view, the autonomy of both the represented and of the representative should be safeguarded. Representatives should act in ways that safeguard the capacity of the represented to authorise and to hold their representatives accountable *and* uphold the capacity of the representative to act independently of the wishes of the represented. Scholars have traditionally thought of this problem in terms of the *delegate* and the *trustee* models of representation. *Delegate* conceptions of representation, commonly associated with the American anti-Federalists, require representatives to 'stand for', that is, to follow their constituents' preferences. A delegate seeks to defend the interests of his or her constituency as defined by this constituency. The delegate model perceives of politics as power conflict over diverging interests and is primarily interested in the control of power. *Trustee* conceptions of representation require representatives to 'act for', that is, to follow their own judgment about the proper course of action. The trustee aims at the good of the whole, as judged by the representative after deliberating with other representatives, acting not in the light of foreseeable sanctions but on the ground of civic virtue. The trustee model conceives of politics as deliberation about the common good and is primarily concerned with the exercise of self-rule (Rehfeld 2009).

After having elucidated the 'standard model' of representation and its historical development, I will now turn to how it has been challenged since the 1990s and, more specifically, which arguments link representation to CSOs rather than just to Parliaments and political parties.

1.2 Linking CSOs to representation

For some time now, some scholars have argued that the 'standard model' of representation may no longer be adequate, if it ever was. On the one hand, they observe empirical diversification processes of different kinds – of arenas, of geographic levels, of issues, and, not least, of actors. In consequence, it has been argued that representation is a much more diverse phenomenon than that found in elected legislatures, that it is realised by a variety of actors and takes places in more instances and spaces than through elections and in parliament (Rehfeld 2006; Saward 2006; Trenz 2009; Urbinati and Warren 2008; Warren and Castiglione 2004). On the other hand, scholars make more normative arguments about why the 'standard model' might never have achieved political equality in the first place. I will address both types of arguments subsequently and thereby show how CSOs have been and can meaningfully be linked to representation.

Turning to the empirical changes first, it seems fairly safe to say that Parliaments and political parties have lost their exclusivity in representative politics. Conventionally, parties integrated and mobilised the citizenry; they articulated and aggregated interests and translated these into public policy; they recruited and promoted political leaders; and they organised parliament and the government. Parties aimed to combine government for the people with government by the people and they combined key representative functions with key procedural ones (Mair 2006). It is now widely acknowledged that parties have shifted away from their representative functions towards a focus on procedural functions, moving from society to the state, a process 'by which parties and their leaders separate themselves from the arena of popular democracy' (Mair 2006: 48). Indeed, a number of scholars have argued that the centrality of parties for the mediation of social interests may be historically circumscribed to a certain period (Manin 1997). Empirical evidence, in any case, suggests that citizens are increasingly disengaging from the arena of conventional politics (Mair 2006), as evidenced in a steady, decades-long decline in electoral turnout; declining party membership and identification; greater volatility in voter preferences and, hence, electoral outcomes; greater difficulty in obtaining and sustaining majority support for governments; and a decrease in trust in politicians, parties and political institutions in general (Schmitter 2009).

At the same time, there is an increasing range of more or less institutionalised, more or less organised actors, such as neo-corporatist actors, CSOs, social movements, local short-term initiatives, citizen juries and self-acclaimed or declared experts. CSOs and social movements, in particular, seem to have profited from the declining attraction of political parties. They are increasingly recognised as important for the survival of democracies and this trend holds in particular at the EU level, where the inclusion of CSOs has been seen as a means of democratising the EU further (Kohler-Koch and Finke 2007, *see* Chapter 1.3). The extent to which all these actors increasingly influence public policies or play a central role in implementing policies corresponds to the extent to which the division between formal and informal representation has been blurred.

These developments have strongly, theoretically, been echoed by those who argue that representation is not just about elections, but also that which happens in between elections (Disch 2011; Rehfeld 2006; Trenz 2009; Saward 2006; Urbinati 2006), thereby analytically opening the door to non-electoral forms of representation.

This strand of the literature therefore focuses on the *relationship* between the representatives and the represented. It is held that represented and representatives communicate through a variety of media and forums, including the press, opinion polls, internet campaigns, associations, events, etc. A functioning public sphere is key for representation to take place legitimately for it constitutes the space where representative claims can be made, accepted or rejected. Elections are still the fundaments of this universe, but, not all instances of representation are electoral, and this is also where functional representation comes in. CSOs are seen as one important way for citizens to become represented in the political process.

Theoretically, this shift in representation theory was possible because representation is no longer seen as a defective substitute for direct democracy but as the condition that renders political freedom possible. For example, Plotke (1997) contends that 'representation is democracy', while Iris M. Young (2002) argues that representation is 'positively desirable'. Representation is no longer seen as hindering autonomy or self-rule, and therefore of reproducing *Fremd-Herrschaft*, as Rousseau once claimed. Instead, representation is now conceptualised outside the logic of identity of the represented and the representative: it recognises the difference between the two. An implication of the shift of perspective is that civil society is no longer the bearer of the democratic project of self-rule, as had been the case in deliberative and communitarian theories. Instead, it is integrated into an understanding of representative democracy based on difference, in which representative institutions set the framework in which non-electoral representation can unfold by means of more informal political processes. By acknowledging the non-identity of represented and representative, we witness a change of perspective in representation theory. It is not the 'making present' of that which is absent (Pitkin 1967) anymore that is of central interest, but the character of the *interactive* representative *relationship* (Plotke 1997; Saward 2006). The existential difference between represented and representative means that representation is always a matter of interpretation and judgment. In consequence, what happens in between the formal moments of authorisation and control in terms of communication and action is moving to centre-stage (Young 2002; see also Mansbridge 2004), leading some to speak of a 'constructivist turn' in representation theory (Disch 2011).

The most comprehensive attempt, perhaps, to adapt the concept of representation to contemporary practices comes from Jane Mansbridge. Mansbridge argues that democratic representation should not be conceived as a monolithic but as a multiform concept that includes a variety of forms: promissory, anticipatory, gyroscopic and surrogate representation (Mansbridge 2003). *Promissory* representation happens when the representatives focus on what they promised to do during the electoral campaign. This model of representation is 'promissory' in that representatives are rewarded by voters if they fulfil their electoral promises and punished if they do not. This corresponds to a traditional principal-agent model which is built on electoral authorisation and accountability.

Anticipatory representation occurs when representatives focus on what they think the represented will approve in the next elections. It focuses on the ongoing deliberative process between representatives and represented. On the one hand, citizens communicate their views via the media, opinion polls, interest groups, events, etc. On the other hand, the representatives in spe try to influence the preferences of the represented by offering their arguments and justifications, implying that accountability in this model goes beyond elections and also occurs in deliberative ways between elections. Anticipatory representation has gained in importance with the development of information systems (public opinion polls), which allow the representative to be aware of the preferences of future voters and can therefore try and manipulate them.

Gyroscopic representation occurs when representatives look within their personal background to derive interests and principles. Here, the behaviour of representatives is, to some degree, predictable in advance, based on their observable characteristics (personal reputation, character and so on). One selects a representative with similar policy preferences, whom one trusts will stay committed to his or her known principles, whose way of behaving and preferences are predictable, and with whom, therefore, no ongoing communication is needed. Once the representative has gained the support of an individual, engagement in regular deliberation with this person is no longer necessary as the representative is trusted by the citizen to work in accordance with shared preferences. In this model, passivity and tacit support of and by the represented are the rule. In case the represented wishes to change policy, (s)he will not seek to influence the representative, but change the representative (s)he supports (Mansbridge 1999: 644). The way representation through CSOs works will often be gyroscopic. Citizens chose to support a given CSO because of what they do and are known for and judged trustworthy, not necessarily in order to get involved themselves. If the CSO starts behaving in a way that the supporter does not support, (s)he terminates membership and (perhaps) joins another CSO that is judged more trustworthy.

Surrogate representation occurs when representatives represent constituents outside their particular constituency (district, party and so on), that is, constituents with whom they do not have any electoral relationship (such as monetary or value-driven surrogacy). It seeks to act for those who cannot vote for the representative but nevertheless are concerned by a specific issue, such as air pollution or climate change. It comes about by the representative choosing their represented by committing themselves to a specific cause. The often cited example of Bono, who suggests he is speaking for the poor of Africa, is a case in point.

According to Mansbridge, all four forms of representation are ways in which citizens can be legitimately represented within a democratic regime, yet none of the latter three forms (necessarily) operates through the formal mechanisms of authorisation and accountability. With these four forms of representation, Mansbridge shows that representation is more than a relationship between elected officials and constituents and that it is more than a simple, territorially based principal-agent relationship. What is more, Mansbridge has even defended a 'case against electoral accountability' (Mansbridge 2004).

Representation as a dynamic political process also figures prominently in the work of Nadia Urbinati (2006), who argues for understanding representation as *advocacy*. Urbinati identifies two main features of advocacy: 1) the representative's passionate link to the electors' cause and 2) the representative's relative autonomy of judgment. She argues that the significance of political representation lies in the perpetuation of public debate about competing political programmes and in the ongoing 'making present' of the represented in choices about public policies. Deliberation, therefore, is a crucial moment of the representation relationship, which she understands as continuous and agonistic rather than rational and consensus-oriented; it is a circular and mutual process between representative institutions and society, which cannot be reduced to the formal act of electoral authorisation. This understanding of representation almost inevitably places greater importance on informal forms of influence and representation, which occur between and besides electoral processes, not least those involving CSOs, social movements or the media (2006: 28–9).

The perspective that perhaps takes the focus on the *relationship* between represented and representative the furthest is the one developed by Michael Saward. He understands representation as *claims-making*, a constantly changing social dialogue in which different actors make claims to audiences which discuss, reject or amend them (Saward 2006). Saward insists on the dynamic nature of the relationship and on the performative (rather than the institutional) side of representation, in which both represented and representative play active roles. His work is grounded on three assumptions. First, representation is not a relationship at precise moments but must be thought of as a continuing process that evolves over time. Second, the core of representation is the practice of making a claim to be representing. Crucially, there is no constituency prior to representation but the represented is 'constituted and defined and understood *within* the process of political representation itself, and not somehow apart from or prior to it' (Saward 2005: 181). Whereas people with certain characteristics exist, it is only through representation that they become a group (Saward 2005: 185). Representatives constitute constituencies by creating and offering descriptions and images of them and present themselves as their representatives (Saward 2006: 300–1). When a claim to represent a specific constituency is accepted by the relevant audience to which it is addressed, then the claim is legitimate. A functioning public sphere is a key prerequisite for representation to take place and to take place legitimately. Even though the claims-making approach shifts the focus to the representative, both represented and representative are involved and constructed in the process of representation, which Saward understands as a 'two-way street' (Saward 2006: 301). Third, constituents and representatives need not be members of electoral districts or elected parliamentarians, respectively. As will have become clear, the concept of claims-making is not embedded in a theory of *democratic* representation. Instead, it is mainly concerned with representation as a *social* phenomenon.

What all of these different approaches share is that representation to them is more than just electoral representation and more than just the formal moments of authorisation and accountability. By mainly focusing on how the representation relationship works between and beyond elections, they open much conceptual space for more informal forms of representation, including those of CSOs. I will now turn to the two main normative arguments that have challenged the 'standard model' of representation which both also open the conceptual space for representation by CSOs.

First, some authors criticise that the 'standard model' would exclusively be interested in procedural equality, but not in substantive equality which would equally be required for fully legitimate representation. Substantive equality refers to a certain level of equality in outcomes, which in turn will allow citizens to make better use of their procedural rights. This involves attending to structural obstacles that result in de facto inequalities of opportunity (Phillips 1995: 37–8). To address this issue, a number of feminist and multiculturalist theorists have developed the idea of *descriptive* representation. *Descriptive* representation can contribute to realising political equality if it brings weak interests into the political process that otherwise would not be represented (Young 2002; Phillips 1995; Williams 1998; Mansbridge 1999; Dovi 2002).

To make up for systematic biases in electoral representation, representative institutions should be more descriptive in regard to certain social characteristics that are systematically under-represented though politically relevant. The background analysis to this demand is that the electoral process and public deliberation more generally are biased towards the more educated parts of society. Groups with a history of marginalisation have structurally unequal possibilities to gain representation and influence policy making, including being elected, putting their concerns on the political agenda, or gaining public visibility. This inequality can be reduced by deliberately increasing the share of representatives who are members of these groups; i.e. deliberate differences (less equality) on the formal, procedural input side can result in fewer differences (more equality) in the outcomes.

One of the main political theorists who have argued in favour of the representation of marginal groups is Iris M. Young (Young 2002). Young maintains that most societies are dominated by a set of discourses and social perspectives that represent the views of dominant social groups (Young 2002: 144–5). According to Young, individuals who are 'close in the social field have a similar point of view on that field and the occurrences within it, while those who are socially distant are more likely to see things differently' (Young 2002: 136). In order to avoid essentialism, it is argued that a 'social perspective' has a different meaning from, for instance, an 'interest'. A social perspective consists of a set of 'questions, kinds of experience and assumptions, with which reasoning begins' (*ibid.*). People might share a social perspective yet have different interests, because they reason differently and have different goals. The representation of marginalised groups and their social perspectives also brings their experiences and situated knowledge, that is, perspectives commonly not heard, into the political debate. Politicians who make decisions based on a limited selection of social perspectives risk making decisions that are 'more likely to perpetuate injustices or take imprudent action' (Young 2002: 145).

In sum, the specific social perspectives that people have influence their political views and choices. It needs a person with a particular background and therefore a certain social perspective to represent others of the same social group. Unless disadvantaged people themselves are more consistently present in policy making, it may not be possible to push the issues necessary to overcome their disadvantage sufficiently high up the political agenda. Bringing structurally and historically disadvantaged peoples and views into the political process may lead to fairer outcomes and improve the situation of the people concerned. *Descriptive* representation therefore helps to address issues of equity and exclusion. This seems necessary because representative institutions are at present not sufficiently inclusive. Political equality thus is understood as requiring substantive equality, not only procedural equality, and has a distinct goal, namely, a fairer and more just society (Young 2002; Kymlicka 1995; Philipps 1995; Williams 1998; Mansbridge 1999; Dovi 2002).

While the argument for descriptive representation has mainly been developed in regard to electoral representation, it is not difficult to see that it can also be related to non-electoral representation. Given the structural under-representation, in Parliaments, of disadvantaged groups, a case can be made that those CSOs who defend their cause should have privileged access to policy making in order to assure that their interests are also represented in legislative acts and political programmes. The argument becomes even stronger when the disadvantaged themselves are active in CSOs and try to promote their own cause.

The second normative argument against the 'standard model' of representation relates to the latter's aggregate view of political preferences which would not capture the multitude of identities and preferences that citizens have. According to this strand of the literature, citizens have multiple identities which coexist but do not get represented to the same degree (if, at all) by political parties. For example, a person could have leftist economic preferences and conservative moral preferences; another person might be homosexual and have conservative moral preferences; still another might like the environmental friendly policies of green parties but not their progressive moral positions. In addition, many people are parents, grandparents, students, workers, artists, believers, etc., and many of the identities and preferences that come with these different roles will often get under-represented when voting for a political party at election time. Also, preferences evolve over time and in interaction, and that cannot sufficiently be captured by electoral representation either.

An approach that in particular focuses on this aspect is that of 'discursive representation'. Anchored in deliberative democracy, discursive representation suggests that representatives should represent *discourses* rather than peoples (Dryzek and Niemeyer 2008) and be authorised through rational public discussion. The approach assumes that it is not people *per se* that matter but their views and interests. According to John S. Dryzek and Simon Niemeyer, people are not undivided 'wholes' but carry with them a multitude of identities and views that cannot adequately be represented through one vote. They suggest it 'is important that all these discourses get represented. Otherwise, the individual in his or her entirety is not represented' (Dryzek and Niemeyer 2008: 483). The various discourses that people endorse are more important than the people who endorse them, which is why counting is not important or even wrong. However, Dryzek and Niemeyer concede that discursive representation cannot offer a complete theory of democracy. Its role is to supplement other institutional mechanisms (*ibid.*: 489). While electoral and discursive representation are essential in nation-states, discursive representation is particularly required in politics beyond nation-states (*ibid.*: 491). This is so because supranational or global institutions do not adequately represent the totality of the relevant views. Discursive representation can render intergovernmental institutions more democratic by forcing them to justify their actions in light of different discourses.

Also from this normative perspective, CSOs are deemed useful when it comes to representing different aspects of citizens' identity, as citizens can give support to different groups.

From the above discussion as for what will follow, no individual theory or hypothesis will be tested (*see* Chapter 2.2 for the methodology adapted in this study). Instead, the focus is on the perceptions of the involved actors themselves. In regard to their understanding of representation, I wanted to know:

Which conceptions of representation do CSO actors have and who or what do they represent?

The increasing influence of CSOs has obviously also been met with criticism by other scholars. A first argument is that CSOs are not representative of the body politic as a whole but, at best, only of particular group interests and values (Papadopoulos 2010). As such, they do not live up to the principle of political equality (Rehfeld 2005). Second, while CSOs' claims would often be justified in universal terms, in practice, such justifications would frequently be undermined by a single-issue focus (Vedder 2003). Third, CSOs can and often do disproportionally advantage those who are educated, well resourced and well connected. Overall, then, functional representation would be part of a trend towards an advocacy democracy, in which 'the formal egalitarian dimension of the "one man, one vote" principle disappears' (Papadopoulos 2010: 1043; Näsström 2010).

Fourth and not least, it is often unclear on behalf of which constituencies CSOs speak, leaving it open whether they are in any sense representative at all or purely self-authorised (*cf.* Collingwood and Logister 2005). Whereas this study is not concerned empirically with the three first listed arguments, it is interested in how CSOs organise representation, in the EU. For CSOs, authorisation and accountability might work either in similar or different ways. For one, there are many CSOs who are member-based in the sense that the CSO's aim is to defend the rather narrow interests of its (paying) members. This is often, but not exclusively the case for sectoral CSOs. In such cases, e.g. trade unions, representation often follows a similar electoral path as traditional electoral representation, implying that representatives are elected by the represented for a defined period of time and with a more or less concise mandate. Even CSOs which do not defend the narrow sectoral or professional interests of their members are often member-based in the sense that registered members will (mostly) define the political agendas and elect their representatives. Where there are no regularised means of authorisation such as elections, authorisation can grow from the ability of groups to attract supporters. Such a support can take different forms: membership, petitions, voices, donations, public visibility, etc. Likewise, the existence of internal democratic mechanisms, including elections, can provide mechanisms of accountability. Where there are no elections of representatives, accountability can work through public justification, transparency, exit, or 'horizontal policing' by groups and media (Goodin 2003). In short, I wanted to know:

What are the organisational structures and processes by which CSOs organise representation?

Addressing this question will help us to discuss whether we are dealing with CSOs which are largely self-authorised and broadly not connected to a larger public, which are increasingly professionalised and ever less detached from whatever constituency, or whether we are dealing with CSOs which have institutionalised democratic procedures for will-formation. It will similarly help us to evaluate whether their contribution to democratic representation in the EU is legitimate (see below).

Indeed, there are all sorts of representation (Saward 2009). Representation need not necessarily be political, let alone democratic. Therefore, it is important to differentiate between different kinds of representation. This will also allow a discussion of whether, and if so how, the kind of representation we find in CSOs can contribute to democratic representation in the EU. I will therefore differentiate between representation *tout court*, legitimate representation and democratic representation.

Representation is not *per se* democratic; democratic representation is only one form of representation amongst others (Rehfeld 2006: 2; Saward 2009). Constructivist approaches such as those discussed above help to show that political representation is more than the formal process of authorisation and accountability and that representation is an interactive relationship. At the same time, these approaches are in danger of reversing the representative relationship, to the point that the represented seem to exist only by virtue of the representative, thereby reversing the principal-agent relationship (Severs 2010) and de-coupling the representative claim from democratic institutions. Constructivism does not necessarily offer a normative standard for assessing the democratic character of representation, therefore. Also, specific acts of self-authorisation cannot be called legitimate representation since claims-makers can be entrepreneurs and seek to create constituencies or interests – to what purpose is not always clear. Indeed, in these cases, more often than not, democratic structures will be lacking and there will be no direct interaction with those the representative claims to represent; the so-called 'representative' may only care for their own private interest; here, there is neither authorisation nor accountability. In such cases, the agent engages at best in acts of representation *tout court*, though exactly of what or whom often remains unclear.

Legitimate representation is normatively superior to representation *tout court* in that it derives from a societal mandate, and it requires a link to a social constituency which needs to be actively involved in the development of policy positions. It is normatively inferior to democratic representation in that on its own, it cannot achieve, even in theory, the norm of political equality (see below). Three kinds of such legitimate representation by CSOs, which could potentially work in favour of democratic representation, can be imagined: firstly those which represent *members* who are democratically involved in the decision-making of the organisation by way of chains of delegation; secondly those which represent a '*cause*', which, in contrast to human constituencies, cannot represent itself; and thirdly those which represent *weak interests* that are structurally under-represented in electoral representation (*see in more detail* in Chapter 2.3).

Indeed, operating on different terms than the standard model of representation does not free CSOs from the requirement of some sort of authorisation and accountability by their respective constituencies if their contribution to policy making is to be legitimate. As discussed above, authorisation and accountability might – though does not have to – take different forms than in electoral representation. In some cases, they might follow a similar electoral path as traditional electoral representation, implying that representatives are elected by the represented for a defined period of time and with a more or less concise mandate. In others, authorisation might work through attracting a large group of supporters, and accountability by these supporters staying and expressing approval of policies or exiting and thereby indicating disapproval; or it can work through public justification or 'horizontal policing' by groups and media (Goodin 2003). Either way, output legitimacy is insufficient for legitimacy if the outputs have not been considered in terms of how they 'resonate with the constituencies' substantive values ... and interests' (Schmidt 2013: 11). Only when the constituent parts of the organisation have 'the opportunity to reflect for themselves, speak of their factual immediacies and defend their judgments, can they bring to light the specifics that need to be perceived and recognised' (Maia 2012: 435).

Such a position reflects the recent shift of representation theory towards a focus on process and throughput and on the interaction between the represented and the representative (see above). What happens in terms of communication, public debate and (inter)action between the represented and the representative moves centre-stage and an *ongoing* interaction between the claims representatives are making and the subjective experiences of the represented, and the mutual adjustment of both, are central to the representative relationship.

In the context of the multi-level system of the EU, in which 'the legitimising criteria of input and output are largely split between the EU and national levels of governance' (Schmidt 2013: 9), interaction between the representatives and represented is even more important. Input legitimacy alone is insufficient, since it does not ensure that the interests of the constituencies are not being deterred or corrupted on the way to output legitimacy. It is therefore essential to address the national constituencies of supranational representation in order to assess whether these are actually being represented and whether the representation is therefore legitimate.

Finally, there is *democratic* representation (see the discussion in Chapter 1.1). Democratic representation, which is the institutionalisation of the norm of political equality, can a) only stem from the functioning of the overall system of political representation (Pitkin 1967) and b) must necessarily pass via Parliaments in which representatives are elected on the basis of one-person-one-vote. In the process, elected representatives, parliamentary groups and parties ensure the aggregation of interests into competing political programmes. These programmes generally seek to cover the full range of issues, whereas elected governments, in theory anyway, are called upon to represent the whole of the citizenry. CSOs, on their own, cannot achieve the same degree of political equality as these mechanisms and actors, and for three reasons.

First, it is not CSOs' aim to be representative of the *body politic* as a whole. They seek to represent particularistic interests and values, even though their claims are often justified in universal terms. Therefore, even when internal democratic structures are in place, CSOs are only accountable to a specific constituency and not to the entire citizenry, thereby replacing citizens in a normative perspective by holders in a functional perspective. Second, CSOs often do not work on the basis of electoral models, with the implication that it is difficult to assess whether they are even representative of the constituency they claim to represent or whether they are purely self-authorised and therefore also not controlled. Third, given that not all interests organise and mobilise themselves equally, the entire range of interests is not represented (equally), with the better educated and resourced better off through interest representation. In electoral representation, the mechanism of one-person-one-vote (re)weights power in the direction of political equality and thereby achieves outcomes that differ from the private distribution of power in society, at least in theory. In the absence of such a mechanism, access to power is ruled by ownership of resources, not by possession of an opinion worthy of equal consideration. The consequence of the three points above is that there is a triple bias in group representation by CSOs, which acts against their ability to promote the norm of political equality on their own.

However, this need not mean that groups cannot help the more representative actors to uphold the standard of political equality in the different phases of policy making, and particularly so in the EU's multi-level system. Indeed, we have seen in the discussion above that democratic representation is more than the formal processes of authorisation and accountability. Ongoing public debate about competing political programmes between and beyond elections is crucial for democratic representation because it allows interaction between the represented and the representatives and for the former to influence the choices about public policies of the latter, and CSOs have a valuable role to play in this process.

First, they can support political competition between political parties. Without political competition, there cannot be government and opposition and therefore no democratic control of government. Political competition requires at least two political parties, offering alternative political programmes that give expression to disagreements that exist across the electorate. However, we know from empirical research that *de facto*, not all parts of the electorate and related interests are represented equally in Parliaments. This may be the case because, for example, the less well-off and less well-educated tend to use their voting rights less than the better-off and better-educated; or because existing MPs are not interested in or willing to take a position on issues that are of interest to only some parts of the electorate. In such situations, CSOs can bring issues to the table that would otherwise be neglected or they can introduce a perspective on an issue that is not represented by MPs, and thereby widen political competition.

This links to a second valuable role that CSOs can have, which is to contribute to publicity, particularly in the context of the EU. Publicity exists when office-holders and administrations act in a transparent manner so that citizens can assess whether their interests are being represented. It includes both access to relevant information as well as the presentation of arguments about policies in public debate (Hüller 2007). Public debate is crucial for democratic legitimacy, as it is in debate that all the relevant reasons, their benefits and shortcomings, as well as political alternatives can be exchanged and discussed in a transparent manner. By informing their members / supporters about policy developments in the EU and by campaigning about some of them, CSOs provide a fair degree of publicity of EU affairs.

Third, CSOs have an important role to play when it comes to public control, and again particularly so in the EU context. Since the publicity of EU affairs, but not only, is often restricted, (public) control is proportionally diminished. In such a situation, CSOs have a vital role to play when it comes to holding office-holders to account and assuring that misbehaviour is penalised.

After having discussed the history and features of democratic representation as well as how representation has been and can be linked to CSOs, we will now turn to the specific role some have associated to them in the context of the EU.

1.3 The contribution of CSOs to the EU's system of representation

As is well known and hardly contested anymore, the EU suffers from a democratic deficit. Disagreements however prevail over the nature and the concrete features of the deficit. This is not the place to review the enormous literature on the democratic deficit in the EU. Instead, I will only focus on those scholars who have diagnosed an institutional, social, or domestic deficit of the EU and show how CSOs have been or can be related to the respective diagnosis. Before I do, I will briefly lay out the EU's various channels of representation.

1.3.1 The various channels of representation

Representation is a central concept in the way in which the EU understands its democratic legitimacy. Title II on 'Provisions on Democratic Principles' of the Lisbon Treaty highlights two key principles: 'political equality', in Article 9, and 'representative democracy', in Article 10. These provide the self-proclaimed democratic 'meta-standards' of the EU (Lord and Pollak 2010: 126). As Article 10 spells out:

> 2. Citizens are directly represented at Union level in the European Parliament. Member States are represented in the European Council by their Heads of State or Government and in the Council by their governments, themselves democratically accountable either to their national Parliaments, or to their citizens.

3. Every citizen shall have the right to participate in the democratic life of the Union. Decisions shall be taken as openly and as closely as possible to the citizen.

4. Political parties at European level contribute to forming European political awareness and to expressing the will of citizens of the Union.

In addition, Article 11 stipulates that European institutions shall give citizens and associations 'the opportunity to make known and publicly exchange their views in all areas of Union action' and to maintain a regular and open dialogue with them. It also introduces the European Citizen Initiative, whereby a group of at least a million EU citizens may petition the European Commission to take further actions that fall within its competence.

Therefore, the Lisbon Treaty distinguishes between an electoral, a territorial, a functional and a direct channel of representation. In fact, since its foundation, the EU has sought to achieve the political equality of its citizens through parliamentary, territorial *and* functional representation (Rittberger 2009). However, it has not clarified the relationship between these different channels. Moreover, political equality in the Lisbon Treaty refers to two different political subjects, individuals and states, which involve different normative goals and related distributions of rights and obligations (Kröger and Friedrich 2013b). I will now look at each of these channels in turn and briefly describe how CSOs can access them in principle.

The territorial channel of representation

The territorial channel of representation materialises through the Council of the EU and the European Council.[1] The European Council brings together heads of state or government. It does not legislate but 'defines the general political directions and priorities' of the EU (Treaty of the European Union (TEU) Article 15 para. 1). The Council of the EU meets in diverse sectoral configurations, bringing together the respective ministers of national governments (Naurin 2014). It is the main European legislator, even though most laws are now passed under the co-decision procedure with the EP. Even though qualified majority voting (QMV) is formally the default for decision-making, in practice the Council operates through consensus wherever possible. The double-majority rule for QMV, which requires the assent of 55 per cent of Member States representing at least 65 per cent of the population, is designed to ensure that decisions balance the interests of large and small states, by preventing the former from imposing a decision on the latter and *vice versa*.

The European Council is quite removed from interest group lobbying. It only meets every six months and is therefore less important for day-to-day policy making in the EU. The Council of the EU, in contrast, would seem highly relevant to lobbying, given that all legislative proposals are discussed and

---

1. And, to a lesser degree, through the Committee of the Regions (Piattoni 2012). However, given its low political salience in EU policy making, it will be left out here.

negotiated in it. However, the Council has proven to be a rather secretive body, with the administrative body that prepares its meetings, the Committee of Permanent Representatives (Coreper), a non-accessible committee. There is no official way to get the names of the people involved, not even the chair, and no means to submit documents directly to the Council or to access its documents easily (Butler 2008). There is, therefore, no formal avenue by which groups can lobby the Council. As a result, it is rarely lobbied in Brussels by interest groups. Instead, domestic interest groups tend to address their concerns to their governments in their respective capitals (Butler 2008).

The channel of electoral representation

The electoral channel works via national parliaments (NPs) and via the European Parliament (EP) and the parties that campaign for the respective elections. NPs do not have direct influence over the European agenda and the executive is generally strengthened while the controlling powers of the opposition are weakened. Not surprising, then, is the emergence of a 'deparliamentarisation' thesis in the 1990s (Raunio and Hix 2000). The thesis seeks to capture the transfer of policy making powers to the EU and the resulting loss of power and influence of domestic parliaments as well as the strengthening of executives in EU policy making, resulting in informational asymmetries between the legislature and the executive (Auel and Benz 2005: 373; Raunio and Hix 2000: 145). As a result, national parliaments have no direct control over European policy making and 'suffer from a lack of authoritative power over transnational policymaking' (Schmidt 1999: 25). Instead, executives have become the 'gatekeepers' in EU policy making. National parliaments have, therefore, often been called the main 'losers' of European integration (Maurer and Wessels 2001).

Since the Lisbon Treaty entered into force, NPs are mentioned in the main text of the Treaty for the first time, thereby continuing a trend going back to the Maastricht Treaty and the debate on the EU's democratic deficit that have seen the empowerment of NPs in EU affairs as one possible mechanism for tackling this issue. Most notably, Article 12 now details the basic rights and functions of NPs in EU matters and introduces an 'Early Warning Mechanism' (EWM) that assigns national legislatures the right to scrutinise proposed EU decisions and initiatives for compliance with the principles of subsidiarity and proportionality. Furthermore, NPs can have a collective legislative influence in that a majority of them may force, by way of a so-called 'Orange Card', an early vote on an EU legislative proposal in the Council and the EP. They are also now involved in the evaluation of measures taken within the area of freedom, security and justice (Articles 70, 85, 88), may block Treaty changes under the simplified revision procedures (Article 48) and must be informed of new applications to join the EU (Article 49). NPs have therefore become actors in their own right in EU policy making. CSOs typically lobby members of Parliament either in their capital or in their respective constituency.

Contrary to NPs, the EP does not possess the right to initiate legislative proposals which originate in the European Commission. However, and also in contrast to NPs, the EP has gained hugely in legislative power with co-decision procedures with the Council of the EU now being the rule rather than the exception. With increased legislative powers, the EP has also become more interesting for interest groups over time. Being directly elected by national voters, the members of the EP (MEPs) are more open than, for example, the Commission, to national interests, in addition to professional and diffuse interests, making them an attractive target for lobbyists. This is particularly the case for the heads of the Standing Committees and the rapporteurs who draft policy dossiers. But the Parliamentary Intergroups can also be interesting for CSOs, given that the latter often provide the secretariat for these Intergroups (Butler 2008). The EP therefore seems much more open to CSOs than the Council of the EU, with a mutually beneficial relationship between MEPs and CSOs 'where MEPs have the opportunity to be kept informed while NGOs have the chance to exert some influence' (Butler 2008: 578).

The channel of functional representation

Functional representation has traditionally mainly addressed the European Commission. As the initiator of legislation and its role in agenda-setting, the Commission is the most important contact partner of interest groups (Kröger 2008a). There is now a distinct system of interest representation in place in Brussels (Coen and Richardson 2009; Fairbrass and Warleigh 2013; Greenwood 2011). Mostly, scholars have been interested in issues of access and influence and in explaining why either of these exists or not (Klüver 2012), however with inconclusive results.

The Commission is under-staffed and therefore dependent on external expertise (Bouwen 2002; Broscheid and Coen 2003). A substantial part of European legislation touches upon new areas with a quite complex character and the European institutions are keen on gaining expert knowledge. The interactions between the Commission and CSOs are thus structured by the informational needs of the former and their concern to avoid overload, on the one hand, and the goal of interest groups to influence legislation on the other (Bouwen 2002; Broscheid and Coen 2003). But also, the Commission is working towards more system-integration (Cram 1993, 2007), not least by consulting CSOs and thereby supposedly lending its proposals greater legitimacy. The Commission consults with CSOs in different ways. As regards official consultations, these are (sometimes) carried out in the context of impact assessments. Furthermore, there can be 'open' consultations and, according to the Principles and Minimum Standards for Consultation of Interested Parties, they should be clear, easy to follow and public. These days, they are often organised as online consultations. However, there is 'no requirement to actually conduct such "open" consultations in the first place' (Butler 2008: 567). Next to the impact assessments and the 'open' consultations, the Commission also engages in a 'structured' dialogue with

CSOs, mainly materialising in the forms of yearly meetings between individual Directorate-Generals and the respective CSOs. However, precisely which groups are invited to these meetings does not seem to be defined by a clear set of rules. Overall, it is therefore 'not clear on what basis a particular DG will decide which body to consult with' (Butler 2008: 570). To have direct interlocutors in Brussels, the Commission has, additionally, actively promoted and cultivated Euro-groups of all kinds (Bouwen 2007; Neuhold 2005).

The channel of direct representation

The direct channel of representation as expressed in the European Citizens' Initiative (ECI) is the fourth channel of representation. It is also the most recent channel, introduced with the Treaty of Lisbon and in force since April 2012. Its legal basis is set out in Article 11, para. 4 of the 'Treaty of the European Union' and in Article 24, para. 1 of the 'Treaty on the Functioning of the European Union'. By way of an ECI, European citizens can invite the European Commission to propose legislation on matters about which the EU has competence to legislate. The ECI has to be backed by at least one million EU citizens, coming from at least seven out of the twenty-eight Member States. Once officially registered, the organisers of the ECI have one year to collect signatures. After that, the Commission examines the initiative and decides whether to take action or not. If it decides to put forward a legislative proposal, the normal legislative procedure is in place and, if adopted, becomes law. CSOs also play a role in the context of the ECI as those are typically organised and supported by larger CSOs (Greenwood 2012).

Overall, then, the EU differs markedly from national political systems in its mix of electoral, territorial, functional and direct representation (Bartolini 2005; see also Martensson 2007). Given its multiple channels of representation, which tend to exist in parallel rather than following one single logic of representation, with different procedures, mandates and forms of accountability, scholars have found it impossible to speak of a single system of representation in the EU. Instead, they have preferred to speak of 'multi-level governance' (Marks 1993: 392), or of 'compound' representation (Benz 2003). It is this 'compoundness' which blurs responsibilities and works against transparency that many citizens and scholars alike feel is at the heart of the democratic deficit of the EU. Still, those who think that the EU suffers of a democratic deficit – of course there are also those who dispute this diagnosis (Moravcsik 2008; Majone 2006) – can be divided into three groups, with each of them focusing on a different aspect of the overall deficit. Each of these research streams will be discussed in the following, noting along the way how the present study addresses related aspects.

1.3.2 CSOs and the institutional deficit of the EU

This view argues that there is a mismatch between policies increasingly operating at the EU level while politics still mainly operates at the national level. It is therefore argued that democratic government should move more consistently to the EU level, in particular to the EP, so as to be responsive and accountable at the level at which policy decisions are taken. What is the background against which such reform proposals are formulated?

Despite the steady growth of the area of competence of the EP (Dinan 2014; Kohler 2014), it is argued that important caveats remain. Above all, the main function of a democratic parliament, that of initiating laws, is still not within the powers of the EP. Also, crucial and highly distributive policies, such as taxation or security and defence, are still not fully incorporated into the co-decision procedure. Another main problem is the elections to the EP and the way parties are organised therein. European elections are largely conceived of as second-order elections (Reif and Schmitt 1980). Voters 'tend to see the elections primarily as an opportunity to sanction unpopular national governments' (Hurrelmann and de Bardeleben 2009: 231). However, as long as European elections are to some significant degree 'second-order', the link between citizen and representative is very weak and public control of EU policies is accidental and not systematic. Worse, the EP even becomes part of the democratic deficit because MEPs are not sufficiently authorised for what they do (because of the second-order problem). Additionally, candidates do not offer European programmes and voters are not guided by European preferences. The Euro-parties are epiphenomena of national political parties, rather than full parties, and unable to fulfil the aggregative functions of parties (Lord 2010). Furthermore, a central arena for executing the control (accountability) function is the parliamentary plenary itself and the struggles between opposition and governmental majority therein. The functioning of the EP, however, is still dominated by an informal 'grand coalition' between the two largest groups in the EP, the European People's Party and the European Socialist Party. A consequence is that the 'big moments' of politics, clashes between the governmental majority and its opposition, are absent. This makes it difficult for citizens to detect alternative political programmes. Voting therefore is neither an evaluation of rival programmes for a forthcoming EP nor an appraisal of the relative performance of parties in an outgoing EP. Thus, both *ex ante* and *ex post* mechanisms of public control seem to be lacking. Finally, the crucial function of sanctioning a government is restricted. Neither the intense hearings, in the context of appointing new Commissioners, by the EP of nominated EU Commissioners nor the EP's ability to issue a vote of no confidence with regard to the whole EU Commission are entirely convincing exercises of this function. The EP's lack of competence to elect a European government, makes one of the most important, publically visible powers of parliaments non applicable, namely contestation over leadership (Føllesdal and Hix 2006: 554).

Central functions of electoral representation at the EU level are therefore only rudimentarily developed or are lacking *tout court*. In other words, there is no electoral connection between citizens and their representatives and therefore a disconnection between European citizens' preferences and EU decisions. In essence, therefore, the democratic deficit lies in the impossibility of a majority exercising its power, holding representatives to account and influencing policy decisions (Mény 2002: 9).

In response, scholars who perceive the democratic deficit as being an institutional deficit encourage the further politicisation and political integration of the EU (Føllesdal and Hix 2006; Mény 2002). Most of the proposals focus on the EP (Føllesdal and Hix 2006; Crum and Fossum 2009) and the direct election of a European president (Hix 2002; Hobolt 2014). The lack of a European-wide party system and the absence of a clearly recognisable parliamentary opposition at the EU level are perceived as the greatest hindrances to the development of European democracy (Føllesdal and Hix 2006). Accordingly, a reform of the European party and electoral system is supported, so that European elections would become first-order elections. The idea is that with increasing competition at the EU level, voters will become more aware of what their MEPs are doing in the EP, and therefore be more interested in having a say come the next elections. In short, it is held that if the flaws and omissions in the institutional design of the EU could be corrected, the democratic deficit would disappear.

Other proposals to improve the institutional democratic deficit focus more on governance architectures (Schmitter 2007; Sabel and Zeitlin 2008), deliberation (Eriksen and Fossum 2002) and organised civil society (Ruzza 2007). In governance-led approaches, hierarchical decision-making by government makes way for more cooperative forms of policy making. The governance approach is guided by the functional belief that those who are affected possess relevant knowledge to improve policy decisions and that the engagement of private actors adds to efficient and effective problem solving. From this perspective, CSOs are co-producers in governance. Empirically, this rationale became visible with the White Paper on European Governance (COM 2001) and its notion of 'good governance'. One of its expectations was that the inclusion of CSOs would contribute to more effective problem-solving, by involving the relevant partners early on, by pooling experiences and ideas, by collectively searching for the best solution and by securing loyalty to decisions through the involvement of the actors in the process: all of which would help to overcome problems of implementation. The Commission obtains expertise at low cost, which CSOs, in the hope of obtaining political influence, are generally happy to provide. Here, participation was functionally defined, according to the value and resources that actors can bring to the policy process (Schmitter 2002: 62–3). This rationale was reflected in the broad definition of CSOs that the Commission adopted, which encompasses practically all non-state actors: 'Civil society includes the following: trade unions and employers' organizations ("social partners"); nongovernmental organizations; professional associations; charities; grass-roots organizations; organizations that involve citizens in local and municipal life with a particular contribution from churches and religious communities.' (COM 2001: 14).

Other approaches to the institutional deficit are more normative (Eriksen and Fossum 2002; Ruzza 2007). They perceive of political outcomes arising from bargaining between elites as inherently problematic for wider legitimacy. Particularly in the context of the EU with the discussed deficiencies of the traditional representative actors which leave little room for citizens to participate in will-formation and political contestation, CSOs have a contribution to make to input legitimacy as a complementary layer to outlets of representative democracy. The idea is that CSOs could function as 'transmission belts' that bring the interests and values of citizens to the EU (Nanz and Steffek 2004; Rumford 2003: 32).

Empirically, this perspective was also reflected in the White Paper on European Governance, which equally mentions the importance of participation by European citizens through CSOs. Indeed, rather than speaking of interest groups, it referred to civil society twenty times (Smismans 2009). This shift implied a more normative approach to consultation practices, as CSOs, other than interest groups, were here credited with democracy-enhancing potential. The Discussion Paper on non-governmental organisations (European Commission 2000) also acknowledged the contribution CSOs can make to legitimate European governance. It referred to different democratising functions of CSOs, and clearly included a view of CSOs as representatives of European citizens. The Discussion Paper argued that although the decision-making process in the EU is 'first and foremost legitimised by the elected representatives of the European people', CSOs can also make a contribution in fostering participatory democracy at the EU level (European Commission 2000: 4). CSOs are seen to represent the views of specific groups of citizens, to reach out to the disadvantaged and to provide a voice for those not heard through other channels (European Commission 2000: 5).

Whether or not CSOs respond to these calls, is of course a different matter, and one that has been addressed mainly by the literature on interest groups in the EU, be it in regard to their presence in Brussels or be it in regard to their Europeanisation. Overall, it seems that a broad range of interests is represented in the Commission consultations even though the consultative practices of the Commission have been characterised as corporatist (Obradovic and Vizcaino 2006; Sánchez-Salgado 2007). There is a broad variety of access venues, ranging from informal meetings between Commission officials and CSO representatives to institutionalised formal committee meetings with a sound Treaty base. These access venues tend to be similar if not the same across policies and DGs. Access tends to be strongly linked to the preparatory phase of policy making (Obradovic and Vizcaino 2006). Inclusion in the monitoring and evaluating phases of policy making is a clear exception to the rule, thereby supporting the impression that the Commission is mainly interested in societal inputs in order to support its own proposals (Broscheid and Coen 2003).

Not all CSOs decide to be present in Brussels and many, indeed, are not concerned with the EU at all, at least not explicitly and directly. For others, it is their daily business, often with important consequences for their organisational life and aims. The Europeanisation literature has been interested in related questions – to what degree, and why or why not, do groups Europeanise their activities, that is, become engaged with EU affairs or not (Beyers 2002, 2004; Kendall 2010)? An often-cited definition of Europeanisation sees it as:

> ... processes of (a) construction (b) diffusion and (c) institutionalisation of
> formal and informal rules, procedures, policy paradigms, styles, "ways of doing
> things" and shared beliefs and norms which are first defined and consolidated

in the making of EU public policy and politics and then incorporated in the logic of domestic discourse, identities, political structures and public policies (Radaelli 2003: 30).

Interest groups have not been at the centre of the Europeanisation literature so far. One reason may be that the processes and effects of Europeanisation are by definition indirect for these actors, given there is no legal obligation or incentive to comply with EU directives. Still, the EU does create new lobbying and funding opportunities for domestic actors and therefore changes the opportunity structure for exerting political influence (Kitschelt 1986; Tarrow 1994). According to Tarrow (1994: 85), political opportunities are 'dimensions of the political environment that provide incentives for people to undertake collective action by affecting their expectations for success or failure'. One could expect that CSOs might want to use these new opportunities in one way or another, and perhaps combine them creatively in order to engage in two-level games (Putnam 1988). Accordingly, the empirical research will address the following questions:

To what degree are CSOs Europeanised?

In a next step, we want to know who CSOs are actually addressing when engaging with the EU. Do they mainly focus on policy-makers and administrations where bargaining takes place outside of public scrutiny and therefore opt for 'access' ('insider') strategies, addressing one or several of the European institutions described in Chapter 1.3.1? Or do they primarily opt for 'voice' ('outsider') strategies in the public arena, that is, seeking to influence decision-makers through press conferences, media campaigns and the mobilisation of their constituency and citizens more generally (Beyers 2004: 213–4; Eising 2007)? If the latter (at least as well), this could also work in favour of the creation of a European demos (see below). We therefore ask:

Who are CSOs addressing when they engage in interest representation in EU affairs and with which strategies?

From what we know, Europeanisation does not happen automatically and evenly (Matteo and Dür 2012), and we can differentiate broadly between two sets of arguments to explain why they do or do not Europeanise. One set focuses on the institutional *environment* of the organisations, the other on the organisations *themselves*. In the case of the former, legislative activity is obviously a strong incentive to get involved in EU affairs whereas the absence of legislative activity is a disincentive to get involved (Hooghe and Marks 2001: 122 and 128–9; Constantelos 2004: 1028). Another external explanatory factor that the literature has used to explain the degree of Europeanisation is the so-called degree of fit or 'misfit'. According to this view, it is the degree of fit or misfit of domestic institutions broadly conceived with European institutions and policy making that determines the specific kind of Europeanisation (Börzel and Risse 2003; Duina and Blithe 1999; Eising 2007; Grote and Lang 2003; Risse, Green Cowles and Caporaso 2001; Schmidt 1999). Related research identifies the degree of fit between the institutions of both levels and then typically assumes that a high degree of fit implies a low degree of adaptational pressure and *vice versa*. The difficulty with this approach is that there are different views about the characteristic features of both domestic institutions and the European political system, leading scholars to categorise them differently and therefore to have different expectations about the domestic adaptational pressure. These different categorisations suggest that the degree of fit or misfit is difficult to evaluate, unless the degree of abstraction is so high that it hardly could be used for empirical research.

A second group of authors focuses on the kind of access groups enjoy at the domestic level. In federal or pluralist environments that are characterised by high levels of inclusion of interest groups in policy making, groups are expected to have good access to government, parliament and administrations. Accordingly, it is hypothesised that they will seek to realise their political goals through lobbying domestically and therefore not Europeanise. For statist environments, in contrast, which are characterised by the exclusion of intermediary structures and the denial of good access points for CSOs, it is hypothesised that the latter will seek to compensate for the lack of domestic access at the EU level and therefore Europeanise (Beyers 2002; Saurugger 2007). It is plausible to assume that those actors who can reach their goals domestically do not have a great incentive to Europeanise themselves. This is more likely to be the case in intergovernmental policies. However, there seem very few policy fields for which this still is the case today, and for (at least partly) integrated policies the corresponding hypothesis has more limited explanatory power. Other commentators suggest that there might be a prolongation of access (*'Verstärkungsthese'*), that is, that good domestic access would translate into good European access whereas the absence of domestic access would lead to poor European access (Eising and Kohler-Koch 2005: 46, see also Cram 2001). Indeed, it is likely that, more often than not, CSOs will be multi-level players who will address either or both levels as they see fit, in order to exert influence.

Other scholars focus more on the organisational characteristics of CSOs. Mostly, this has meant looking at the material resources an organisation has (Eising 2007). Being active at the domestic *and* the European level or transnationally is obviously demanding in terms of material and human resources. But resources can also be understood in terms of the expertise or the size of the constituency an organisation has – both of which can potentially lend legitimacy to its claims (Dür and Mateo 2012). For example, by being active on European issues, domestic interest groups strengthen their domestic position because this enables them to provide crucial information to domestic public officials. It has been suggested that when having to decide how to invest the available resources, groups have to choose between the 'logic of membership', dedicating resources to activities that strengthen their membership base, and the 'logic of influence' (Schmitter and Streeck 1999), dedicating resources to 'defend specific interests *vis-à-vis* decision-makers' (Dür and Mateo 2012: 972). The assumption has been that resource-poor groups will reserve the large share of their resources for their membership and therefore cannot afford to engage in EU affairs, whilst the well-endowed groups have the resources to engage in both logics and also to lobby European institutions rather than exclusively domestic ones (Dür and Matteo 2012). Furthermore, what groups opt for is not only related to their resource-endowment, however, but also to the kind of constituency they have – some are very narrow (business and certain kinds of professional organisations); others are quite diffuse and heterogeneous ('cause' organisations). While the former have a well-defined constituency, with clear material gains and losses related to legislation and are therefore comparatively easy to organise, the latter lack these attributes. The consequence is not only that they have more collective action problems (Dür and De Bièvre 2007) but also that they need to invest more resources in maintaining, mobilising and, ideally, expanding their constituency through membership-related activities, with the effect of leaving less resources for lobbying activities. Again, there seems to be a tension between the logic of influence and the logic of membership (Greenwood 1997: 16–17; Beyers 2004: 216). And yet, recent evidence seems to put in question this expectation to some degree, in that no clear relationship between resources and lobbying by CSOs was found (Mahoney 2008: 198; Baumgartner *et al.* 2009). Addressing why CSOs get involved with the EU or not, the empirical research explores the following question:

What are the incentives and disincentives for CSOs to engage with EU policy making?

1.3.3 CSOs and the social deficit of the EU

Another branch of authors perceives of the democratic deficit not as being institutional, but as being social. This is known as the 'no-*demos*' thesis (Höreth 1999). According to this perspective, the EU lacks the fundamental features of nation-states that enable citizens to collectively govern themselves: a *demos*, a public sphere for debate and therefore an authoritative channel of representation. Because there is no *demos* and no shared identity, not least due to the absence of a shared language, the necessary intermediary structures are lacking (Grimm 1995; Kielmannsegg 2003). These intermediary structures – political parties and a media-based public sphere – are necessary preconditions for integrating different political, economic and social interests into a democratic political process (Scharpf 1999: 187), in that they mediate between politicians and citizens. The institutional consequence of the lack of a *demos* and intermediary structures is that there is not a single centre of authority which would allow for common debate and political control and therefore for democratic politics. In sum, citizens from such a perspective cannot be represented at the EU level because there is no common *demos*.

However, not all scholars sharing the 'no-*demos*' view are sure it cannot be overcome. Either, they contend that the EU ought not to be compared against the standards of national democracies and seek to identify other parameters for legitimate European governance (Cheneval and Schimmelfennig 2012; Sabel and Zeitlin 2008). Or they argue that the EU is in a state of deep transformation, a process of polity and social constituency building (Fossum and Trenz 2006; Trenz 2009) which leads to the creation of a *demos*-equivalent outside the framework of the nation-state (Eriksen and Fossum 2000). Similar accounts set their hopes on the creation of a common public sphere, to be constructed through a vibrant civil society, be it in more or less organised forms, in Brussels or transnationally. Why should a democracy-building process not also be possible at the supranational level, if given enough time? After all, national democracies are the results of long historical processes as well (Habermas 2001). A political community in-the-making in turn requires trust: trust in the reciprocity of the rule-conforming behaviour of others and in mutual solidarity (Putnam 1993: 182–3). Civil society and its organisations are hoped to be able to foster and maintain the mutual trust required for the mutual interdependence among Europeans and the polity-building project. The inevitable ingredients of such a process are a vibrant European public sphere, the Europeanisation of the national demoi and the construction of a common European interest, all of which should be fostered by CSOs.

Empirically, this rationale found its expression in 'The Commission and Nongovernmental Organizations: Building a Stronger Partnership', in which the goals of consulting CSOs were first outlined: participatory democracy; representation of the views of citizens in the EU; contributing to policy making and project management; and contributing to European integration: 'By encouraging national CSOs to work together to achieve common goals, the European CSO networks are making a vital contribution to the formation of a "European public opinion" usually seen as a pre-requisite to the establishment of a true European political entity' (European Commission 2000: 13). This rationale matches the Commission's own agenda of ever more integration (Bauer 2002; Greenwood 2007; Smismans 2004). By consulting diverse actors, the Commission can claim more legitimacy for its own proposals. The European Commission has therefore actively engaged in a systematic attempt to promote and develop 'societal representation' at the EU level which it can consult (Bellamy and Castiglione 2010; Kohler-Koch and Finke 2007; Kröger 2013; Saurugger 2010).

To some degree the aspects that this literature addresses in regard to CSOs are addressed by some of the empirical questions that were formulated in Chapter 1.3.2. E.g., it is difficult to imagine how CSOs could perform a demos-creating function if they were hardly Europeanised or did not engage with EU policy making at all. Similarly, that section addresses whether CSOs recur to 'voice' strategies which address a larger public, not least through the media – an obviously crucial element of the constitution of a European public sphere. Additional insights into whether or not CSOs contribute to EU demos-building are also gained by addressing who CSOs address when engaging in interest representation. Are they mainly addressing national actors to pursue their goals or also European actors? And, particularly, how much do national CSOs work with and through their European umbrella organisations? If they do, then this can be seen as a willingness or even desire to cooperate with CSOs from other Member States and to find common ground with them, though of course the motivations to do so might differ between groups. Finally, this study addresses which activities (lobbying, networking, funding, information and exchange, services, protest, contributing to democracy) are most important for CSOs when engaging with the EU. It thereby gains an additional sense of why CSOs get engaged with the EU – is it mostly rent-seeking or does it go beyond lobbying *strictu sensu*?

1.3.4 CSOs and the domestic deficit of the EU

Finally, to some scholars, the democratic deficit is mainly domestic. To them, the EU's democratic legitimacy is 'borrowed' legitimacy, borrowed from its Member States. Therefore, it is important that democracy be defended 'back home' (Bartolini 2005; Offe 1998; Schmidt 2006). From this perspective, the *locus* of democracy is the nation-state and it cannot be reproduced at the EU level, given the lack of a *demos* and of common representation of that (lacking) *demos*. Worse, the European integration process in fact seems to undermine the capacities of its Member States to remain democratic.

This position has been defended most prominently by Fritz Scharpf (1999, 2009). He argues that the range of available policy options is restricted in favour of a conservative bias at the EU level, due to the joint-decision trap, which implies that decisions will be based on the lowest common denominator. Further, he claims that the progressive realisation of the internal market, due to the effect of supremacy of EU law and its direct effect, is increasingly constraining citizens in the range of their democratic choices, not least the choice for a welfare state. 'Negative integration', from this perspective, undermines democracy,[2] which entails commitments to de-commodification from the market necessary for functioning democratic citizenship. Structurally, then, these problems cannot be overcome because of the lack of a European public sphere and, of course, the 'no-*demos*' problem.

While not always as concerned with the repercussions European integration has on national welfare states as Scharpf is, a number of authors are similarly concerned with the potentially damaging effects of European integration on domestic democratic politics – and on national parliaments in particular. Parliaments have a public mandate from voters to legislate and to control the executive. *De facto*, their institutional core consists of the government (which controls the agenda and formulates policy proposals), the parliamentary majority (which accepts or rejects these proposals), and the parliamentary opposition (assuring public deliberation, the generation of political alternatives and control). Democratic legitimacy is created through the competition between the different

---

2. Similarly, Stefano Bartolini (2005) has argued that European integration would undermine national democracy by undermining the boundaries between nation-states. In contrast to Scharpf, however, he focuses more on the weakening of shared identities and cultural loyalty.

parties who form the majority and the opposition, publicly offering different programmes to the electorate and being accountable for their actions.

In the context of the EU, though, the domestically rather clear role-distribution becomes blurred. Neither the national parliaments nor the national governments have direct influence over the European agenda. Governments hardly ever have electoral authorisation for specific EU policies nor can they or the parliaments initiate legislation. Meanwhile, the opposition and the parliaments' powers of exercising accountability more generally are weakened. Not surprisingly then, the 1990s witnessed the emergence of a 'deparliamentarisation' thesis (Raunio and Hix 2000). This thesis seeks to capture the transfer of policy making powers to the EU and the resulting loss of power and influence of domestic parliaments – and with them those of the electorate, which exercises these functions indirectly through its representatives – as well as the strengthening of executives in EU policy making, which results in informational asymmetries between legislatures and executives (Auel and Benz 2005: 373; Raunio and Hix 2000: 145). As a result, national parliaments have no direct control over European policy making and 'suffer from a lack of authoritative power over transnational policymaking' (Schmidt 1999: 25). Instead, executives have become the 'gatekeepers' in EU policy making. National parliaments have, therefore, often been called the main 'losers' of European integration (Maurer and Wessels 2001; see also Bellamy and Kröger 2014).

So far, the potentially negative impact of the EU on domestic political systems has mainly been addressed in regard to NPs, courts, governments and political parties, and less so in regard to CSOs. However, this need not mean that the EU cannot have detrimental effects on the capacity, of CSOs, to legitimately represent a constituency or an issue. The limited research that exists in this direction has concerned itself with the issue of the professionalisation, of CSOs, in response to being active at the EU level. Indeed, given the institutional differences between EU policy making and domestic policy making, one might expect CSOs to be affected in some way or other by their engagement with the EU. Given the European Commission is the main addressee of lobbying efforts by interest groups, I more specifically focus on how the Commission might be influencing CSO's strategies and activities. This might occur in two main ways, i.e. through its consultation regime and through the practicalities of EU funding.

In regard to the former, if CSOs want to be capable of influencing the Commission, they need to be able to react quickly, 'on demand', which might prevent them from thoroughly consulting their members. In particular, if representation corresponds to a mandate by members and relies on structures of internal democracy, then the normally allocated period of eight weeks for consultation is clearly insufficient (Ruzza 2005: 22). These requirements will structure the work organisation of the liaison offices in Brussels, which will become ever more specialised and professionalised in the context of their lobbying activities (Maloney 2009) while possibly losing contact with the grassroots level of their organisations. Officials of the CSOs themselves do not seem to be too troubled by this development: 'While ideally it would be good to get people involved … my role is not to encourage the most participatory governance, but to ensure the best results for the environment' (Senior officer, European Environmental Bureau, quoted in Sudbery 2003: 91–2). In order to be heard, CSOs also possibly adopt consensus-seeking strategies and positions, and seek to avoid conflict (Beyers and Kerremans 2007), thereby possibly deviating from what their members at grassroots level would opt for.

Another potential way of influencing the activities of CSOs is through funding (Greenwood 2007). European funding schemes and the expenditure for NGO activities have constantly risen since the 1970s and the Commission 'spends approximately 1 per cent (1bn) [euro] on funding groups and almost the entire (300) citizen interest group universe (excluding Greenpeace) mobilized at the EU level receives some EU funding' (Maloney 2008: 77), with some EU umbrella organisations receiving up to 90 per cent of their total funding from the Commission. How does giving money to CSOs influence them in ways that distort their capacity to represent legitimately? The money, to put it in a nutshell, is not provided unconditionally (Maloney 2008):

> One of the most visible methods governments employ to guide activity is government contracts. By deciding what projects are to be funded and who will be responsible for bringing the projects to fruition, institutions guide policy debates and wield considerable control over interest activity (Mahoney 2004: 444).

Calls for proposals lay out in detail what sort of activities are eligible for funding, thereby excluding other activities which CSOs may want to pursue. They privilege those CSOs which are ready to use the dominant EU-speak as well as the dominant approaches to specific policy areas over more critical ones. Many of the supported actions consist of seminars, workshops, information diffusion and/or awareness-raising activities, to name the most current ones. These activities clearly do not prioritise the original activity of each and every CSO; instead, they prioritise the setting-up of transnational networks and, through them, 'European ways' of doing things. Another requirement for attracting EU money, intended to work in favour of network-building, is that CSOs increasingly have to be part of a transnational co-operation partnership (Sánchez-Salgado 2007: 257–8). While the Commission was at first somewhat vague about what was meant by these partnerships, it now clearly sets out their format and their specific characteristics. This implies that CSOs must find potential partners both within and outside the EU, which takes time away from their other activities while leaving the added value of the emerging transnational partnership open.

In sum, representation by CSOs is located in a specific institutional environment, and we may expect it to be influenced by the latter. CSOs 'may be trapped by the need to adapt to the "logic of influence" prevailing in Brussels' (Kohler-Koch, Quittkat and Buth 2008: 6). Keeping a close contact to their constituencies may take second place to the more functional objectives of being part of the policy making process and to the kind of professionalisation this requires (Klüver and Saurugger 2013). The research therefore asks:

Does the institutional environment of the EU affect the activities of CSOs and their interest representation strategies?

This chapter has set out the theoretical debates surrounding democratic representation in general and representation by CSOs in particular. It has similarly laid out the specific institutional context of the EU in which representation from different perspectives has found to be deficient and shown how CSOs have been or can be associated to each of these perspectives. On the way and finally, it has linked the different debates to research questions which have guided the empirical research.

Chapter Two

Research Design

In this chapter, I will start by restating the research agenda and the overall research question of this study (*see* Chapter 2.1). In a next step, I develop the methodological approach (*see* Chapter 2.2). I then focus on political representation by CSOs and show why the analysis of CSOs in the EU requires a representation framework. I differentiate between three kinds of representation which form the basis of the case choice (*see* Chapter 2.3). Based on this framework, I then proceed to detail the different research questions (*see* Chapter 2.4) before concluding by presenting the methods used to address them (*see* Chapter 2.5).

2.1 The research agenda and overall research question

As explained in the introduction, the present study is located at the intersection of two research agendas, that is, the (re)configuration of political representation in Western democracies and the role CSOs (can) play therein on the one hand, and the democratic deficit of the EU and potential ways of alleviating it on the other.

The (re)configuration of political representation is considered in the context of two trends. First, European integration and wider processes of globalisation challenge the principle of territorial representation on which nation-state democracy is founded. Second, elected representatives are losing their monopoly on political representation because trust in representative institutions and their agents is declining in Western democracies. Declining electoral turnout, decreasing party membership and party-identification, growing volatility in voting behaviour and hence in electoral outcomes and greater difficulties in obtaining and maintaining a majority to form a government are all indicative of a generalised crisis of political representation and intermediation through parties and traditional representative institutions (Mair 2006; Manin 1997). More fundamentally, some scholars object that traditional representative politics as organised by parties is, in some structural sense, exclusive (Taylor 2010; Young 2002; Urbinati 2000). Therefore, it has been argued that political representation can no longer be restricted to electoral representation in the nation-state (Kymlicka 1995; Mansbridge 2003; Plotke 1997; Rehfeld 2006; Saward 2006; Young 2002).

The EU, in turn, has been struggling with a democratic deficit ever since at least the early 1990s. The deficit arises because the EU as a whole has so far not developed the kind of thick identity that allows for mutual trust and solidarity between citizens who recognise each other as members of the same polity (Offe 1998). The lack of a European *demos* implies that the EU's system of representation does not offer a clear division of competence between the different levels and actors of governance; moreover, there is no direct chain of authorisation linking the citizen to an EU government (Scharpf 2009), with an important consequence being the lack of political parties offering political alternatives in the same public sphere and which would be mirrored in shared media. European news is still received through national channels of communication and thereby filtered by what are perceived as national interests. European parties, in turn, have kept their organisational and electoral bases in Member States and European elections continue to be perceived as second-order elections – with ever-lower turnouts – in which national governments are rewarded or punished for what is perceived as national politics.

In this context, functional representation has been perceived by many as a response to both challenges, that of the crisis of traditional representative institutions and that of the democratic deficit of the EU. As regards the first challenge, both organised and unorganised civil society have attracted considerable support from the larger public in many European countries. From a more theoretical perspective, it has been argued that functional representation can contribute to bringing weak interests into the political process, thereby helping to address issues of equity and exclusion (Young 2002). Others have placed the emphasis on the representation of discourses through non-electoral representation, suggesting that some discourses and ideas are less well represented by traditional representative actors than others, particularly on a supranational or global level (Dryzek and Niemeyer 2008; O'Neill 2001).

As regards the second challenge, functional representation in the EU has, by many, been perceived as an additional source of legitimacy-generation, given the lack of democratic legitimacy through the standard model of representative democracy at the EU level. 'Partnership' with relevant 'stakeholders' as a means of representing additional publics has, therefore, become a guiding theme of the EU in the last twenty years (Kohler-Koch and Finke 2007; Saurugger 2010). In particular, the European Commission has actively engaged in a systematic attempt to promote and develop societal representation at the EU level, something reflected in the much-debated White Paper on Governance (2001), in which the Commission argued that 'its legitimacy today depends on involvement and participation' (European Commission 2001: 11).

Ever since the White Paper, the involvement of CSOs in EU policy making has been on the research agenda. We now have a fairly good understanding of the involvement of CSOs in EU policy making as well as of the Commission's consultation regime (Kröger 2008a) and of different models of political representation by CSOs more generally. What we lack is a linkage between the more general political science literature on representation by CSOs on the one hand, and empirical research into the concrete practices of interest representation by CSOs in the EU on the other. Therefore, this study is empirically investigating how CSOs engage in political representation in the EU, and uses the empirical findings to discuss whether CSOs can compensate for the alleged failure of traditional forms of democratic representation in the EU. More specifically, it asks whether they might be capable of a) reducing an institutional deficit by enhancing the representation of a broad range of interests at the EU level or even of b) reducing a social deficit by contributing to the building of a European demos. This study is interested in whether or not CSOs can live up to either – or even both – of these roles, or, whether on the contrary, being involved in EU policy making perhaps reduces the democratic potential of CSOs. In a next step, I will now detail the methodology with which the related research questions have been addressed.

2.2 An abductive approach and a subjective perspective

In this section, I will lay out the methodological approach of this study. Siding with Friedrichs and Kratochwil, I will argue that 'the time has come for a pragmatic turn in research and methodology' (Friedrichs and Kratochwil 2009: 702). *Pragmatism* rejects ontological realism (the assumption that there is an objective world that exists independently from its observer) and the correspondence theory of truth (propositions are true when they match reality and there are clear-cut yes and no answers to everything). Pragmatism helps to acquire useful, meaningful and reliable knowledge for theoretical and practical purposes; it also helps to formulate questions that cannot be formulated in advance of the research itself (Kratochwil 2007). Instead, the research design evolves in the course of the research process, as do concepts. They help to orientate the research and are modified during the process. There is no clear temporal differentiation between design and implementation as both influence each other mutually. Pragmatism as a research strategy does not imply that in the absence of a universally valid and timeless truth, 'anything goes' or that everything becomes relative, deprived of all norms. Instead, the field of study is a co-operative intellectual practice, with a tradition of historically produced norms, rules, conventions and standards of excellence that remain subject to critical debate, and with a narrative content that gives meaning to it (Friedrichs and Kratochwil 2009).

There are two methodological implications. First, a pragmatic study cannot be a deductive one: 'If it is true that the subject is always implicated in the constitution of the object, then there can be no direct testing against reality' (Kratochwil 2007: 3). In the present study, a deductive design would not work because of the *sui generis* structure of the EU and the unclear locus of political authority in it as well as the fluid character of non-electoral representation. Exactly *what* the EU is – whether an intergovernmental organisation, a supranational polity, or anything in between these two – is likely the most contested issue in EU studies and partly beyond. Empirically, power is no longer concentrated and arranged hierarchically but dispersed across different levels of governance and sub-systems of policy making. Different levels, actors and forms of policy making influence each other without it necessarily being clear in which directions these influences go and of what nature they are. In addition and partly related, there also is no consensus on which should be the criteria by which the EU and its politics and policies should be assessed – those we know from the domestic context or different ones, and if the latter, then which criteria? In such a situation of multi-level governance, which is characterised by multiple uncertainties about where the power centre is and by which criteria politics should be assessed, empirical research requires new approaches that accommodate this specific context and is best advised to not engage in theory-testing. Therefore, the purpose of this study is not to test any theory, but to use different concepts as analytic tools in studying representation by CSOs in the context of the EU multi-level system.

A pragmatic study is also not necessarily an inductive one, in that its goal is not to arrive at conclusions that can be generalised, and in part for the reasons just listed. The goal, therefore, is not to arrive at authoritative conclusions about interest representation in the EU, but rather to explore the different usages, understandings and practices of this term (Wedeen 2004: 281), in the context of multi-level politics in the EU. To achieve this, an abductive research strategy is chosen:

> The typical situation for abduction is when we, as social scientists, become aware of a certain class of phenomena that interests us for some reason, but for which we lack applicable theories. We simply trust, although we do not know for certain, that the observed class of phenomena is not random. We therefore start collecting pertinent observations and, at the same time, applying concepts from existing fields of our knowledge. Instead of trying to impose an abstract theoretical template (deduction) or 'simply' inferring propositions from facts (induction), we start reasoning at an intermediate level (abduction) (Friedrichs and Kratochwil 2009: 709).

This study can furthermore not be an inductive study which seeks to generalise from the empirical findings because of the specific perspective it takes, i.e. that of CSO representatives. The research has been designed so as to elucidate how far CSOs conceive of their role as interest representatives in the EU. It does not compare or contrast these perceptions with either the experiences of the grassroots constituencies of those CSOs or those of politicians or other involved actors – it exclusively looks at the perceptions of CSO representatives, at how these representatives themselves construct representation, and identifies the meanings it has for them.

It might seem that the reason for adopting such an approach could be to probe the concept of claims-making as developed by Michael Saward. That is not the case. A pragmatic reason for this choice is that there exists a fair amount of quantitative data on the Europeanisation of interest groups, whereas missing from much of the scholarship are micro-sociological accounts that explore the questions of how CSO actors perceive of their activities and why they assign relevance to the EU – or not (but see Heidemann 2012). One way of getting at actors' perceptions of interest representation and of the EU lies in a 'subjective' approach (Crotty 1998) whereby the views of actors become the analytical focal point. This study therefore adds to the existing picture of interest representation and Europeanisation by and of CSOs and complements other research rather than competing with it.

Conceptually, the reason to choose such an approach is rooted in the premise that 'opportunity is, ultimately, what people make of it' (Kurzman 2004: 117) and thus ultimately grounded in well-established principles of social constructionism (Harris 2007), the relevance of which to European studies has been documented (Checkel 2001; Christiansen *et al.* 1999). From a social constructivist perspective, social structures and human behaviour do not exist independently of their context and their interpretations by the actors involved. Instead, it is through language and the way actors interpret their environment that institutions and actions acquire meaning (Pitkin 1967: 9–11). Social meanings 'are not learned by pointing to an object, but rather by speaking the words and responding to speech in the context of their use' (Wedeen 2004: 281). The inevitable implication of a constructivist perspective is that the social meanings that actors give to their behaviour become the focus of analysis.

Political representation is a highly context-dependent and dynamic process, the nature of which strongly depends on the involved actors' interpretations of their roles, particularly in non-electoral representation where, other than e.g. for national Parliaments and parliamentarians, there is no legal obligation to engage with the EU. In such a context, what CSO actors think of the EU and how they perceive of their role becomes crucial to understand their engagement with the EU – or the lack thereof. Also, only if we address actors' perceptions and views about the EU will we be able to see whether or not the Europeanisation of CSOs also implies that their actors are interested in EU democracy. This is crucial to know in order to relate to the social deficit literature (*see* Chapter 1.3.3). Additionally, without such an interest and there being a sense of being part of a European demos, their institutional participation in EU policy making would also appear rather fragile.

Providing thick descriptions of actors' experiences does not imply that nothing can be explained. They can help explain why, for example, some interest representation strategies might work better than others for the relevant actors (Wedeen 2004: 285). Indeed, limited objectivity, and thereby explanation, is possible – even within the constructivist tradition (Bevir and Rhodes 2006) – and explanation is grounded on the meaning actors give to their actions. However, such an explanation is limited to the particular time and space, based on a subjective interpretation and, as such, is provisional whereas generalisations must be avoided.

The consequence of taking such an approach is that the focus of the empirical chapters will very much be on how actors interpret their role, rather than how I interpret it. My analysis of their reflections can mainly be found in the closing chapter, which follows the empirical chapters, though it obviously to some degree structures the account in the empirical chapters as well.

That this study adopts an abductive research strategy does not preclude the usage of some limited quantitative data. Presenting quantitative data can help readers gain a sense of how representative and widespread particular instances are. This addresses a common concern about the reporting of qualitative data, i.e. that the writer only choses to report findings that are in line with his/her own view of things, or that undue attention has been paid to rare events, at the expense of more common ones. Data triangulation – the mix of different data – is instead a technique for providing multiple perspectives on a problem, with discrepancies between data sources being themselves findings (Seale 1999). That said, the quantitative data used in this study has been generated by the same actors which have generated the qualitative data – once through questionnaires, once through interviews. Therefore, this quantitative data also contains the subjective interpretations, by actors, of the related questions, and no broader truth claims will be based on it. The more specific methods used in this study will be addressed at the end of this chapter.

So, what are we talking about when talking about 'civil society organisations'? In principle, all civil voluntary and non-state organisations are relevant to this study. There are two reasons for this, one conceptual, one empirical. Conceptually, CSOs are, in this study, perceived to have a complementary role to democratic representative institutions, rather than standing on their own and being able to provide for democratic representation. As such, there is no need to associate a heavy normative burden with them, as is often the case in participatory or associative democratic theories. They are not capable of securing political equality in the same way representative institutions can and this should therefore not be expected of them (see the discussion in Chapter 1.2). This is sometimes forgotten in accounts in which the term civil society mobilises a range of positive normative connotations that imbue it with democratising power. We also know that 'civil society' can also be quite 'uncivil' and that participation alone need not equal democratisation (Ruzza 2010). Indeed, there is 'nothing *intrinsically* democratic about "civil society organisations"' (McLaverty 2002: 310). What is more, 'in reality they often fall short of democratic principles' (*ibid.*: 314). Adapting a conceptually parsimonious definition of CSOs is, therefore, in line with the broader role they are perceived to have in this study. Hence, I shall define CSOs as groups characterised by three elements: organisation, political interests and informality (Beyers, Eising and Maloney 2008: 1106). Organisation refers to 'organised forms of political behaviour'; political interests 'refer to the attempts these organisations make to influence policy outcomes', rendering the study of these CSOs relevant to scholars of political representation; and informality 'relates to the fact that interest groups do not normally seek public office or compete in elections, but pursue their goals through frequent informal interactions with politicians and bureaucrats' (*ibid.*, 1106–7). Empirically, European institutions, particularly the European Commission and the European Parliament, use a broad definition of CSOs, providing an empirical incentive to work with the same broad definition as they do (European Commission 2001).

In a next step, I will detail the case choice, not without first having reminded the reader of why I situate CSOs in a representation theory framework (see also the discussion in Chapter 1.2).

2.3 Representation by CSOs

2.3.1 Why a representation theory framework for CSOs?

Associating CSOs with representation does not come naturally. Indeed, up to now, participation has been associated with civil society while representation was associated with parliaments and parties. Indeed, *representation* linked to CSOs has until very recently been a missing category in EU studies (but see Kohler-Koch 2010; Kröger 2012; Smismans 2012; Steffek, Piewitt and Rodekamp 2010; Trenz 2009). Only slowly are scholars starting to ask how far CSOs represent; what contribution they make in terms of representation in general and to EU policy making in particular; and under what conditions could that contribution be legitimate? There are a number of reasons for linking CSOs to representation, which I shall now lay out (see also the discussion in Chapter 1.2).

First, representation is a central concept in the way in which the EU understands its legitimacy. Indeed, the Lisbon Treaty specifies that the 'functioning of the Union is based on representative democracy' (Article 8, para. 1). While conceding a limited role to CSOs, it specifies governments, parliaments and parties as its main representative institutions. Certainly, that is also the kind of democracy we find in Member States. Therefore, representative democracy can be seen as a normative meta-standard of the EU (Lord and Pollak 2010: 126). But also, European institutions privilege representative institutions and actors over CSOs in reality (Kohler-Koch and Quittkat 2013). It would be of limited value to frame the contribution of CSOs to EU policy making in different terms from those set out by the operating Treaty. Similarly, the European Commission has started to place greater importance on the representativity of CSOs, thereby signalling that they, too, ought to be democratically governed and to some degree at least representative of a social constituency: 'With better involvement comes greater responsibility. Civil Society must itself follow the principles of good governance, which include accountability and openness.' (European Commission 2001: 15). CSOs must provide information about 'which interests they represent' and 'how inclusive that representation is' (European Commission 2002: 17). Nonetheless, the information that the Commission requests as an indicator of their representativeness, is provided by CSOs upon a voluntary basis. The Commission also does not exclude non-representative organisations from its consultations: 'Representativity, though an important criterion, should not be the only determining factor for membership of an advisory committee, or to take part in dialogue with the Commission. Other factors, such as their track record and ability to contribute substantial policy inputs to the discussion are equally important' (European Commission 2000: 9; see also European Commission 2002: 11–12).

Second, what these organisations bring into EU policy making *are* interests. They are not apolitical associations concerned with bowling but organisations that clearly *represent* interests in the political process and would like to see them *represented* in policy outcomes. Consequently, it is relevant to know who or what and how these groups actually represent, issues that have not received enough attention in the context of participatory or associative approaches.

Third, I side with those who argue that political equality is the normative core of democracy. Democratic theory scholars generally agree that we should regard each individual as of equal moral worth (see the discussion in Chapter 1.1). They believe that individuals possess equal human rights. Hence, all those who are bound by collective decisions are entitled to an equal say in their making and in controlling the rulers and the administration. Governments are democratic if they recognise the principle of political equality and thereby, at least in principle, treat all citizens and their interests with equal concern and respect. Addressing how far CSOs contribute to political equality of all citizens thereby becomes a crucial normative question.

2.3.2 Three kinds of representation by CSOs

As discussed in Chapter 1.2, I differentiate between representation *tout court*, *legitimate* representation, and *democratic* representation. The first is not desirable because it is not normatively demanding, given it does not require a stable link to a social constituency. The third is not achievable for CSOs alone, because it by definition needs the electoral mechanism of one-person-one-vote to support political equality as well as the institutional checks and balances we find in modern representative democracies. Therefore, this study is mainly interested in different forms of legitimate representation. For representation to be legitimate, there must be stable links between the represented and the representatives. In the context of the EU, this implies that there should be traces of involvement of the constituencies of European umbrella organisation in the development of policy positions (see research question number 4 in Chapter 2.4 below). From the discussion of the related literature in Chapter 1.2, three kinds of groups come to mind, which have three different kinds of constituency and therefore are likely to construct representation in different ways: 'members', 'cause' and 'weak interests' groups. All three of them have the potential to be legitimate forms of representation *and* contribute to democratic representation of the overall political system by supporting political equality (*see* Chapter 1.2).

a) 'Members' groups

Mirroring criteria of representative democracy, existing EU studies have suggested that the existence of democratic governance structures legitimises the contribution of groups to EU policy making, providing citizens with a regular opportunity to voice their preferences and take part in EU policy making (Altides and Kohler-Koch 2009; Steffek, Piewitt and Rodekamp 2010). Accordingly, empirical research has asked in what ways members can participate in the agenda-setting, will-formation and decision-making of the CSO to which they belong. 'Members', as I dub this kind of representation by CSOs, is available to constituencies that are human, capable of presence and voice. Members of such organisations are identical with the constituency whose interests are being advocated (Binderkrantz 2009; Halpin 2006; McLaverty 2002: 309–10). They therefore have a strong personal incentive to influence will-formation within CSOs as the success of their activities will (more or less) directly influence members' (economic) well-being. Member-groups will mainly focus on existing members because their constituency is structurally limited. They typically organise and mobilise sectoral interests, with (re)distribution effects that directly concern the members. As a result, such CSOs are typically well resourced, not least due to the membership fees. In this type of organisation, members typically participate in the group's activities and decision-making, authorising their representatives and holding them to account through electoral mechanisms. Member-groups therefore follow a classical principal-agent model of representation. For this kind of CSOs, I am looking at groups that are organised under the head of COPA-COGECA[1] in order to influence the Common Agricultural Policy (CAP).

b) 'Cause' groups

Some have argued that when thinking about a legitimate role for CSOs, we ought to think 'outside the box' of representative democracy. For example, CSOs could support democracy if they support causes that are in the public interest, but are not sufficiently represented otherwise and/or cannot represent themselves, such as the environment (Halpin 2006; Collingwood and Logister 2005). Their legitimacy derives from bringing into the political process perspectives overlooked by more traditional representatives but which are nonetheless important in the pursuit of the common good. Along those lines, one proposition has been that political representation does not have to be anchored in a people in order to be legitimate. Instead, 'discursive' representation suggests that representatives should represent discourses rather than peoples (Dryzek and Niemeyer 2008). It is not people *per se* that matter but their views and the interests they have. Indeed, some have argued that to ask 'who do you represent?' is not appropriate for CSOs (Peruzotti 2006: 52–3) and that one should ask instead 'what do you represent?' CSOs, from this perspective, would represent ideas and positions rather than constituencies and therefore engage in 'discursive' representation (Dryzek and Niemeyer 2008). Particularly in regard to supranational or global institutions which do not adequately represent all relevant views, discursive representation would be necessary and legitimate.

In this kind of CSO, accountability is more political than procedural as deliberation, review and public support replace voting as the main mechanism of democratic authorisation (Halpin 2006: 927). Whilst it also includes keeping those interested up to date, e.g. by means of regular newsletters and information on a website, accountability mainly works through public support (Collingwood 2006: 252; Hendriks 2009; Saward 2009). It grounds on generalised 'trust in expertise, reflexive capacities, moral integrity or simply advocacy' and on the

---

1. Committee of Professional Agricultural Organizations and General Confederation of Agricultural Cooperatives.

general resonance created within a wider audience (Trenz 2009: 12–13). These incentives have a disciplining effect as reputation is the most valuable resource of most CSOs. If supporters do not feel themselves represented any more, they can vote with their feet and exit (i.e. stop supporting the association). In order to prevent this, functional representatives tend to anticipate their supporters' views in the actions they take (Maloney 2008: 81). Often, members or supporters do not want to engage actively, but prefer chequebook membership, i.e. giving ideal and financial support (Maloney 2008: 75–7). In 'cause' organisations (Halpin 2006) as I will label these kinds of CSOs, the relationship between the represented and the representative therefore resembles *gyroscopic* representation (Mansbridge 2003): one selects a representative (or an organisation) with similar policy preferences, whom one trusts will stay committed to his or her known principles and with whom, therefore, no *ongoing* communication is needed. However, 'cause' groups do also need to communicate with the constituency, in order to assure that members and supporters are aware of their positions and activities. For this type of CSO, I am looking at interest groups that are organised under the umbrella of the European Environmental Bureau (EEB) in order to influence European environmental policy.

c) 'Weak interests' groups

The third kind of legitimate representation by groups is what I call 'weak interests'. In this case, there are human constituencies, such as the poor, socially excluded, children or prisoners, which generally do not enjoy the different sorts of social or political capital necessary to organise themselves. From a democratic theory perspective, the representation of weak interests is important insofar as weak interests are generally under-represented in electoral representation and that their representation contributes to realising political equality (Young 2002). An unresolved issue is who can or should legitimately represent weak interests. Those who argue in favour of 'descriptive' representation make a case for representation by people who resemble their constituency in some important way, for example, in class, gender, ethnic background or religion. As discussed in Chapter 1.2, the argument is that these specific identities and social perspectives influence people's political views and choices and that the representation of these has, so far, been systematically skewed in electoral politics. Unless disadvantaged people themselves are more consistently present in policy making, it may not be possible to push the issues necessary to overcome their disadvantage sufficiently high up the political agenda (Philipps 1995; Williams 1998; Mansbridge 1999; Dovi 2002; Young 2002). From such a perspective, 'descriptive' representation would only be legitimate if realised by someone who shares the specific feature of those who have been under-represented. Alternatively, and when applying the concept of 'descriptive' representation to functional representation, one might argue that groups which have a focus on a specific disadvantage can act as proxies for those who live with that disadvantage. At times, they try to involve the disadvantaged themselves in their political and other activities. For this type of CSOs, groups that are organised under the head of the European Anti-Poverty Network (EAPN) in order to influence European anti-poverty policy are addressed.

A word on whether these three kinds of groups are comprehensive of the interest-group population that engages with EU affairs or not. They probably are not. Reducing the interest-group population to only three ideal-types would not do justice to the variation one finds between groups. However, the cases are emblematic of the type of representation a given sort of group will employ. In that sense, they could act as proxies for other organisations – which are either sectoral or not; which are based on member involvement or less so; which represent a constituency or an issue. So these three cases can be used to make a more general argument.

I researched these three cases at the EU level, the national and regional levels (with additionally some local actors), both in the UK and in Germany. Indeed, to the difference of most scholars who focus on either the European *or* the national level, I argue that both levels (and more) need to be taken into account. First, the very existence of different levels of governance implies that processes of representation cannot be addressed at one level only (Thomassen and Schmitt 1999: 8). Second, it may be argued that a democratic deficit exists on both the national and the European levels (Follesdal and Hix 2006) and that understanding why is impossible if not including the different levels in the analysis. Legitimation must be reached at EU-level because 'political scrutiny and political control cannot be effective at a lower level than decision-making' (Thomassen and Schmitt 1999: 8). European law over-rides national law, European decisions and policies affect peoples' lives and values as well as national institutions such as Parliaments, the EU redistributes money and controls a significant amount of public funds, and it binds member states through international agreements to third parties. For these reasons, democratic legitimation is also needed at EU-level. Legitimation of EU policies however must also be produced at the national and regional level(s). The continued existence of national and regional identities points in a direction where EU legitimation grows out of but does not displace domestic legitimation processes. In consequence the (nation-)state that remains needs to be included in any analysis of democratic legitimation processes.

The UK and Germany were chosen so as to be able to detect in how far different political systems and political cultures might affect actors' understandings of representation and their interest representation strategies. The UK and Germany differ in important features that can, possibly, help us to understand CSO actors even better. The first important difference is their general stance and commitment towards EU membership. The UK has traditionally been a Eurosceptic nation. It reluctantly entered the EU only in the early 1970s and is, at present, debating withdrawal from the EU. Germany, in contrast, has traditionally been very pro-integration. Germany is one of the founders of the EU and ever since has encouraged European co-operation and further integration, even though, in the 2010s, both public and government opinion also seem to have moved in a more Eurosceptic direction.

Second, these states differ in their modes and structures of governance. The political culture of the UK emphasises hierarchical steering. The administrative structure has a unified centre of authority and governments operate by majority rule. It has been classified as being on the majoritarian end of the scale. Still, UK governments tend to strive for consensus with CSOs even though they have the capacity to exclude them from political processes (Cowles 2001). By way of example, in the social-policy field, the legitimacy of independent voluntary action was never seriously questioned, even at the high point of welfare-state building by Beveridge. More generally, the British political system is pluralistic in nature, implying competitive interactions between CSOs and weak roles for peak associations (Wonka 2009).

In Germany, in contrast, there is no strong administrative centre, individual ministries operate in a largely autonomous manner and coalition governments are the norm. Indeed, the political culture of Germany emphasises consensus-seeking, incorporating a wide spectrum of interests into a political system that is generally characterised as corporatist (Lijphart 1999), in which CSOs 'are integrated in a hierarchical associational system and interact in a coordinated fashion' (Wonka 2009: 182), implying a greater role for peak associations. This is not least so because of the more general dispersion of state powers in Germany, with its federal structure, resulting in a greater need for horizontal consultation. As a result, German associations have more access opportunities and, in part, even take over certain state functions (Schmidt 1999) as is the case for welfare-provision. It is mainly these two features that seem relevant for the present study and might help getting an even better understanding of the involved actors. Unfortunately, however, it turned out that much more German than British actors replied positively to the invitation for an interview (*see* Chapter 2.5). Therefore, comparisons between these two countries are possible only to a very limited degree.

I will now come back to the research questions I linked to the more theoretical discussion in the previous chapter. Doing so, I will not reiterate the theoretical debates in any depth, but focus on detailing how the research question was actually addressed and what the findings should allow to discuss in the concluding chapter.

2.4 The research questions

1. Which conceptions of representation do CSO actors have and who or what do they represent?

To begin with, it was important to get a sense of the understanding actors have of representation – who or what do they actually think they are representing? This might seem a straightforward question – one might expect the agricultural actors to say 'farmers' and the other actors 'the environment' or 'the poor' respectively. However, particularly for the latter two kinds of actor, answers are not always as clear-cut as one might think. Also, when do they think political representation is achieved – do groups seek to influence legislation or governmental policy programmes, or are they satisfied if they have influenced a discourse, or, less still, merely raised their voice?

Furthermore, I was interested in what actors think confers legitimacy to the kind of representation they are engaged in? In principle, there are three possibilities. First, actors may see legitimacy as primarily deriving from the input of the groups' constituencies, i.e. from having a large membership in the first place and from that membership being involved in collective processes of will-formation, authorising their representatives and holding them to account. This perspective focuses on input legitimacy and corresponds to a delegate model of representation which we might particularly find with members of 'members' groups. Another kind of input legitimacy that actors might draw upon is a broader social mandate as expressed in legislation. In Germany, for instance, legislation foresees that environmental CSOs are consulted when new environmental laws are being prepared. Along the same lines, social welfare provision is heavily constitutionalised in Germany, and its organisation and delivery are in fact shared between the state and welfare organisations. These are input-related sources that actors can refer to when seeking to legitimise their representation activities.

Second, actors may think of legitimacy as stemming from the output generated by their very involvement in policy making. This could be achieved by 'doing the right thing', either because of their expertise, experience on the ground or their faith, or by the outcomes of the political process (policies). Any of these bases provides them with good arguments for their work, and the 'better argument' leads to the ability to attract supporters (or members) via broad, public and regular communication strategies. From such a perspective, the supporters and members are not the source of legitimacy, they 'only' help the group to speak for the cause (Binderkrantz 2008: Halpin 2006; Hendriks 2009; O'Neill 2001). This perspective mirrors a gyroscopic model of representation and might be found in 'cause' groups, given that 'two central features of legitimisation – authorisation and presence – are absent' (O'Neill 2001: 494).

Third, actors may perceive of legitimacy as stemming from descriptive representation. As discussed above and in the previous chapter, descriptive representation originates in the representative sharing some specific feature with the represented – gender, sexual orientation, ethnic background, religion – or being poor – and therefore being in a better position to bring a specific perspective into a political process that representatives without the specific feature could not as well represent. Indeed, we may find this perspective in 'weak interests' groups if actors refer to involving the poor themselves in activities of representation and link that involvement to the legitimacy of the group's activities.

Finding the answers to these different questions will allow me to discuss whether the different actors see themselves as representing a constituency or an issue; whether they conceive of themselves as representatives or whether they are, rather, in favour of a more participatory approach; whether they see their primary role as lobbyists or whether they think of themselves as having some interactive role to play; and whether their understanding of political representation is reflected and coherent overall.

2. What are the organisational structures and processes by which CSOs organise representation?

All organisations have internal governance structures, rules that exist to govern the organisation. What I am here interested in are the structures that allow the members of a given organisation to participate in its organisational life. Given the different kinds of constituencies and perhaps different kinds of understandings of representation, one might expect these governance structures to operate in different ways, depending on the organisation, even though, of course, the legal framework is the same for all three kinds of organisation, for example, that they need to have an annual general meeting, a treasurer and so on. 'Organisational structures and processes', therefore, relates here to the set-up of structures that allow members to participate in the organisational life and, in particular, in its interest representation, and how these structures are used by the members of the different organisations.

In agricultural organisations, one could expect members to participate in the group's activities and decision-making, authorising their representatives and holding them to account through electoral mechanisms:

> Office holders are directly and at regular and not infrequent periods elected by the membership or positions rotate regularly around the membership, the policies of the organization are decided by, or are subject to the approval of, the membership, reliable information about what the association is doing and why is widely available to the members and members are involved in open, egalitarian dialogue or communication in the running of the organization (McLaverty 2002: 309–10).

In this kind of organisation, members have a strong personal incentive to influence will-formation within the CSO as the success of its activity will (more or less) directly influence members' (economic) wellbeing. Typically, delegation chains should exist across levels of governance and mechanisms should be in place that assure that what the higher level of governance does is linked to what the lower level(s) of governance and the members ask it to do.

One crucial difference between 'cause' and 'members' groups is that 'cause' groups represent issues rather than human beings. Therefore, those supporting the organisation are not those that the organisation advocates for, they are not immediately concerned by the results of the organisations' activities, not least as no (re-)distributional issues are at stake that directly involve them. They may therefore be less interested in influencing will-formation in the organisation; for them, it might be sufficient to support the abstract cause by affiliating with the organisation in some more or less direct way, for example, by donating money (Binderkrantz 2009; Maloney 2009) or by signing a petition or supporting a campaign:

> Public interest groups are simply misunderstood if seen as mass participatory arenas. Groups employ a range of sophisticated techniques such as direct mailing to recruit members, but once recruited, few members exhibit any active

participation besides the annual writing of a cheque for membership dues. In return for their support, members receive newsletters or magazines, but when it comes to policy making they have little influence (Binderkrantz 2009: 658).

Identifying the accountability processes of 'cause' groups is, due to the lack of a clearly identifiable constituency, inherently difficult. Are they exclusively accountable to universal ideas or to expertise or should their activities also be subjected to internal control mechanisms? In fact, we may also find in-built accountability mechanisms in these groups, such the potential distance between the values which 'cause' groups defend and their actual practices; the competition between groups with similar goals; or the effectiveness of these groups' lobbying. In all three cases, if they fail to achieve their main goal or there is a visible discrepancy between their actions and their members' and/or supporters' aims and values, support will vanish and internal resistance grow (Binderkrantz 2009). Thus, in the case of 'cause' groups, we might find different forms of accountability.

As regards the 'weak interests' groups, one might expect a combination of the above two logics, though in a modified way. We are likely to find members of such groups. However, these will likely not be the poor themselves. Unlike for the agricultural groups, the members are thus not those who directly benefit from success in interest representation. Instead, members are likely to be (service-delivery) organisations of organisations. These members will have a vested interest in influencing the will-formation of the organisation. At the same time, we may also find individual supporters of charities and service-delivery organisations who might be less interested in directly engaging in internal will-formation processes and be happy instead just to support the organisation by donations.

To address this set of issues, I was first interested in the ways by which topics arrive on the agenda and how position-finding occurs. Do members participate in agenda-setting and position-finding or are these processes mainly driven by factors outside of organisations' control and/or by a few policy officers in headquarters? In a next step, I wanted to find out where and how decision-making occurs and who is involved in the related processes. This will also inform us about the different forms of authorisation and control in place. Are there formal rules and mechanisms for decision-making, authorisation and control or do these processes mainly happen through more informal mechanisms, via soft pressure through members and peers, for example? Finally, I was interested in how far actors reach out to the larger public. This could be seen as reflecting the image of representation an organisation has – does it deem it important to reach out to the public or not?

By addressing these questions, I will not only be able to understand how much the different actors – members, supporters, staff – are involved in the internal governance of the respective organisations and how they relate to the public, but also to consider, in a second step, how these practices relate to the respective more general understandings of representation discussed under question 1.

Before investigating the different venues that groups use for interest representation in EU affairs, I want to learn more about the degree to which they are Europeanised. The next question therefore is:

3. To what degree are CSOs Europeanised?

Europeanisation has long been conceptualised as a one-way street, a top-down process whereby national institutions and actors adapt to a greater to lesser degree to decisions taken and norms defended in Brussels (see, amongst many others, Radaelli 2003: 30). These perspectives suggest that the European level can be seen as fixed, static, whilst change can be expected from national actors and institutions because only national environments would be developing and adapting. However, given the increasing interconnectedness of the different governance levels in EU policy making and the degree of integration in many policy fields, it appears increasingly difficult to separate conceptually the different levels of governance and the direction of their mutual influence. Instead, the domestic and the European levels influence each other mutually, in circular movements. This means that Europeanisation can occur at different levels of governance and can include actors at the different levels; we need to see how the different levels and actors influence each other.

I will here define Europeanisation as the extent to which CSOs in their activities take the EU into account. This may occur in different ways. First, it can imply seeking to influence EU policy, either via European umbrellas or national actors addressing that level directly or by lobbying the domestic administration and politicians (bottom-up). Second, it can mean referring to EU policies when seeking domestic policy change and lobbying the national government for that (top-down or transnational). This may include reminding governments of their obligation to transpose EU directives in a timely and correct manner or bringing new cases before the European Court of Justice. Third, Europeanisation can also mean that groups act 'according to European practices, which are practices specifically attributable to European institutions such as transnational partnerships or a specific strategy for collective action' (Sánchez-Salgado 2007: 255), or mutual learning processes. Since the early 1990s, giving a 'transnational dimension' to projects has become a compulsory element of EU funding, thereby forcing CSOs to co-operate with project partners outside of their own Member State and therefore to internationalise their activities. Overall and importantly, the degree of Europeanisation is likely to be influenced by the degree to which a given policy field has been harmonised.

To find out about their degree of Europeanisation, I asked actors how important they thought the EU was for their organisation and also whether it was a regular topic in their work. I have also looked at the organisations' websites and checked whether or not they reported about EU policies. If they did, that indicates the organisation holds that EU policies and informing members and supporters about them are important, and *vice versa*.

Turning to the ways by which CSOs engage with the EU, the next question is:

4. Who are CSOs addressing when they engage in political representation in EU affairs and with which strategies?

I am here interested in the addressees as well as the strategies of CSOs, when participating in EU policy making and trying to represent their respective interests. What I am *not* interested in are the outcomes of the related lobby strategies. I differentiate between channels that are located at the national and those located at the European level. This allows me to engage with those approaches to Europeanisation which see a relationship between the kind of access groups have domestically to those they seek to lobby and that which they have at the EU level, be it a reinforcing relationship or a compensating relationship (*see* Chapter 1.3.2).

It also enables a discussion of which lobbying strategies CSOs prefer – access (insider) or voice (outsider). Do CSOs mainly focus on policy-makers and administrations where bargaining takes place outside of public scrutiny and therefore opt for 'access' ('insider') strategies; or do they primarily opt for 'voice' ('outsider') strategies in the public arena, that is, seeking to influence decision-makers through press conferences, media campaigns and the mobilisation of their constituency and citizens more generally (Beyers 2004: 213–4; Eising 2007)? One might expect that CSOs which defend a diffuse cause and therefore represent a fragmented constituency will find it harder to overcome collective action problems and to mobilise their constituency. Therefore, and because of their lack of resources, diffuse CSOs typically find it much harder to organise and to be a credible threat to legislators than sectional groups. As a consequence, they might 'voice' strategies and go public and attract media attention in order to publicise their cause and use public mobilisation to exert political pressure. In contrast, sectional or professional organisations have clearly defined constituencies and memberships with precisely defined material interests, who endow them with the necessary resources to engage in effective lobbying. They therefore do not need to mobilise the public as much, can be expected to have less severe collective action problems and use their resources for 'access' strategies in order to secure the desired goods (Dür and Matteo 2012; Dür and De Bièvre 2007; Olson 1965). Also, it may be more difficult to present their special interests as legitimate to the larger public.

Whereas these distinctions seem to make sense in the first place, recent evidence questions the continued usefulness of the distinction between diffuse and professional interests and related expectations as regards their use of access or voice strategies. Instead, this research suggests that both kinds of groups use both strategies and combine them as they see fit (Pollack 1997; Warleigh 2000; Beyers 2004; Binderkrantz 2005), even though voice strategies are used more often domestically than at the EU level (Imig and Tarrow 2001), likely because of the lack of a public sphere and of a constituency at the EU level. It therefore seems difficult to make a reliable prognosis of groups' behaviour in regard to their interest representation strategies.

Finally, special attention will be given to how far groups try to organise themselves under the head of a European umbrella organisation – often, but not always mediated by a national umbrella. Particularly for groups which are not resource-rich, being a member of an umbrella can be an important way of connecting with EU affairs, of receiving information about EU policies and, likewise, of feeding information from the grassroots to the umbrella, and also of engaging in interest representation.

Looking at the links between European umbrella organisations and their national members is also important in order to assess the character of CSOs' contribution to EU policy making. As argued in Chapter 1.2, *legitimate* representation by CSOs, in the EU context, implies that there must be some communication about European policy processes and some involvement of constituencies in the development of policy positions on those processes, so that constituencies have the opportunity to consent to or reject specific propositions and positions. Only such constituency involvement will produce the internal legitimacy that is necessary for CSOs to be able to live up to the institutional and/or demos-enhancing roles that some of the literature has associated to them. Without such involvement, CSO representatives may simply be speaking for themselves or, worse, may refuse to take into account the views of those for whom they are supposedly speaking, both of which would be problematic as regards the legitimacy of the representation.

If the policy positions of European umbrellas or other CSO actors active at the EU level are not to be merely formal, the constituency-to-be-represented must a) be aware of those positions and b) accept them; and on a continuing basis, moreover, as acceptance can only ever be provisional. The minimum condition for this to be the case is that the constituencies actually entertain some links to the European actors, be it directly or by means of a national umbrella, which, in a second step, would be in touch with the European actors. Similarly, at the very minimum, the 'public' sphere that is necessary for political representation to be legitimate has to exist within the organisations themselves, implying active information about EU-related positions within the organisations. Finally, it demands that the constituencies have some degree of satisfaction with the work the European actors are performing in their name. All three aspects – links to the European umbrella organisation, information about EU positions and degree of satisfaction with the work of the European umbrella – will be addressed in the empirical research.

Looking at the involvement of domestic groups with their European umbrellas is also relevant for another reason: it allows us to appreciate whether domestic groups see added value in co-operating with groups from other Member States in order to influence EU policies. If this was the case, it could potentially be interpreted as a willingness to find common solutions to shared problems and as such be a contribution to a European *demos*. If groups only co-operate with other groups from the same Member State, it would suggest that national differences between them, even within the same policy field, are considered too important to engage in stronger European co-ordination. Addressing these issues will allow me to discuss the multiple ways CSOs engage with the EU.

Finally, what is of interest in this study is how far being involved in EU policy making affects the activities and strategies of CSOs. The related question is:

5. Does the institutional environment of the EU affect the activities of CSOs and their interest representation strategies?

Given the institutional differences between EU policy making and domestic policy making, one might expect CSOs to be affected in some way or other by their engagement with the EU. In particular, I am interested in whether there are any effects on the way CSOs relate to their constituencies and their ability to represent them legitimately. For example, can we observe that being engaged with the EU leads to a stronger focus by CSOs on 'access' strategies, given the lack of a public sphere at the EU level, which renders the use of 'voice' strategies rather ineffective? Is the balance interest groups strike between the logic of influence and the logic of membership affected by their engagement with the EU? As William Maloney put it: 'Why spend a great deal of organisational resources seeking and servicing members, when patronage permits fully focussed professional lobbying?' (Maloney 2008: 80). Given the European Commission is the main addressee of lobbying efforts by interest groups, I will more specifically focus on how the Commission might be influencing the ways they engage with the EU. This might occur in two main ways, i.e. through its consultation regime and through the practicalities of EU funding (see the discussion in Chapter 1.3.4).

Addressing this question will allow me to discuss if, and if so in which ways, being involved in EU affairs affects CSOs interest representation strategies, from which one might infer how it affects their relationship and interaction with their constituencies.

6. What are the incentives and disincentives for CSOs to engage with EU policy making?

In order to understand why groups Europeanise or not, it is necessary to develop our understanding of the incentive structure that the EU provides and the motivations that drive actors' behaviour further. As discussed in Chapter 1.3.2, there can be different kinds of incentives and disincentives for CSOs to become engaged with EU policy making and the same incentive or disincentive does not necessarily work in the same way for the three different groups. These potential incentives and disincentives refer to the institutional environment in which CSOs act on the one hand and their organisational characteristic on the other (*see* Chapter 1.3.2). As regards the institutional environment, incentives can relate to the legislative activity at the EU level (the expectation being that CSOs active in less integrated fields will rely more on domestic lobbying), the kind of access groups enjoy domestically (the expectation being that access is mutually reinforcing, i.e. those with good domestic access will also seek to gain and eventually achieve good European access) or the degree of fit or misfit. The latter explanation has so far focused on differences between the systems of interest intermediation at the domestic and the EU level. In this study, I shall expand the notion of 'fit' and 'misfit' so as to relate to differences more broadly conceived that actors perceive, between the EU political system and their domestic political system, and being politically active in either of them. This approach was adopted because it allows us to better find out which are the differences that really matter to actors and might keep them from becoming or remaining involved with the EU, rather than assuming *prima facie* that only differences in interest intermediation would matter to them. In a second step, I am interested in whether, as a consequence of perceived differences, actors find it is easier or more difficult to be heard at the EU level than at the domestic level. As a part of this question, it will be of interest how satisfied the actors are with the European Commission's consultation regime in general, and with its online consultations in particular. This is relevant as the Commission is not only the initiator of legislation in the EU, it is also the main addressee of CSO lobbying in Brussels. Happiness with the Commission's consultation regime may be a strong incentive to becoming involved with EU policy making whilst dissatisfaction with it may be a strong disincentive to do so.

As regards the organisational characteristics of CSOs, I am looking at resources (Eising 2007). Being active at the domestic *and* the European level or transnationally is obviously demanding in terms of material and human resources, and so the lack of resources is likely to constrain the Europeanisation of CSOs. Will groups privilege the logic of influence or the logic of membership (Schmitter and Streeck 1999)? Will they use their resources to 'strengthen their membership base' or will they use them to 'defend specific interests vis-à-vis decision-makers' (Dür and Matteo 2012: 972)? It could be expected that resource-poorer groups such as anti-poverty or environmental organisations reserve the larger share of their resources for their membership, rather than engaging in EU affairs. To the contrary, we can expect that well endowed groups have the resources to engage in both logics and also to lobby European institutions rather than exclusively domestic ones (Dür and Matteo 2012). What groups opt for is not only related to their resource-endowment, however, but also to the kind of constituency they have – some are very narrow (business and certain kinds of professional organisations); others are quite diffuse and heterogeneous ('cause' organisations). While the former have a well defined constituency, with clear material gains and losses related to legislation and are therefore comparatively easy to organise, the latter lack these attributes. The consequence is not only that they have more collective action problems but also that they need to invest more resources in maintaining, mobilising and, ideally, expanding their constituency through membership-related activities, with the effect of leaving less resources for lobbying activities. Again, there seems to be a tension between the logic of influence and the logic of membership (Greenwood 1997: 16–17; Beyers 2004: 216).

However, we should not expect that the incentive structure of the EU is such that actors will automatically adapt to it if they only have the necessary means and work under 'ideal' institutional circumstances. We also need to take into account ideational incentives and disincentives therefore. A group may have no legal or financial incentive to become engaged with the EU and also find it rather difficult, given the language barriers and geographical distance; and yet may still want EU engagement because it perceives the EU – or the integration process – as having an intrinsic value that is worth struggling for. *Vice versa*, another group may have sufficient resources to engage with the EU but refrain from doing so because its overall appraisal of the EU is more negative. In order to look into CSOs' more general appraisals of the EU, I am enquiring what positives and negatives actors see as coming from the EU. As a sum of all of the above factors, I finally address what actors find most important, in their engagement with the EU.

Addressing these questions will allow me to appreciate what supports CSOs' engagement with the EU, and what may hinder it, as well as their more intrinsic motivations to get involved with EU affairs, all of which will help to make better sense of the representation strategies they chose or chose not to pursue.

Once having addressed and discussed these questions comparatively (Chapter 6.1), I will come back to the broader picture of this study and use the empirical findings to discuss whether CSOs can compensate for the alleged failure of traditional forms of democratic representation in the EU (Chapter 6.2). Doing so and more specifically, I will ask whether and if so how much CSOs might be capable of a) reducing an institutional deficit by enhancing the representation of a broad range of interests at the EU level or even of b) reducing a social deficit by contributing to the building of a European demos, or, whether on the contrary and c) being involved in EU policy making perhaps reduces the democratic potential of CSOs. Let me now turn to the methods with which I am addressing these questions.

2.5 Methods

To address the research questions developed above, the study combines different methods, namely semi-structured interviews and questionnaires. Adapting the abductive and subjective approach described above obviously calls for qualitative methods in order to 'describe, decode and translate, and otherwise come to terms with the meaning, not the frequency, of certain more or less naturally occurring phenomena in the social world' (van Maanen 1983: 9). Semi-structured interviews allow the researcher to delve into the various interests, identities, motivations, and expectations that guide CSO actors in their interest representation activities in regard to the EU and to develop a proper understanding of the meanings these actors associate to these activities and the EU. Questionnaires, in this study, allow for a limited amount of data which is more easily comparable and helps readers gain a sense of how representative and widespread particular instances are. The quantitative data used in this study has been generated by the same actors which have generated the qualitative data. Therefore, this quantitative data also contains the subjective interpretations, by actors, of the related questions.

---

2.   A more detailed description of the samples of each case will be provided in the first section of each empirical chapter.

As a first step, the three European umbrella organisations identified above (*see* Chapter 2.3) as well as all their national members were contacted.[2] Once actors had agreed to be interviewed, questionnaires were sent to the interviewees. Questionnaires included both multiple-choice questions and closed questions. Issues that were addressed in the questionnaires are: profession-related information about the officer interviewed, basic information about the CSO in question, questions relating to the understanding of representation, to the representation strategies and addressees, and to funding and the potential effects of that funding and of being involved in EU affairs more generally (*see* list 3 in the appendix). The main source of data, however, is semi-structured interviews in which all questions were formulated in an open manner (*see* list 2 in the appendix). In total, sixty-one interviews were conducted, forty-two with German actors, thirteen with British actors and six with European actors (the distribution of interviews between the levels of governance can be found in the first section of each empirical chapter). All the interviews have been transcribed. Once transcribed, they were coded and analysed with the help of Atlas.ti. The third sources are the webpages of the organisations – all CSOs that I looked at had one indeed. The webpages were useful in order to see how groups interact with their constituency and with the larger audience – is there an intranet, to which degree do groups inform about their activities and policy positions, can one donate, volunteer or blog, do groups specifically address press, are there public events to which they invite the larger public, and if so, are these events closer to access (lobbying) or to voice (different forms of protest) strategies? This information was gathered as much as it existed from each website and was then used as quantitative data.

Chapter Three

Representation by Agricultural CSOs

At the start of this chapter, it seems useful to point out that in this chapter – as in the two following empirical chapters – it will mainly be the actors on the ground that will be given full attention. Whereas I have obviously structured the account and have added minimal information where this seemed necessary in order to understand what actors have said, I am not interpreting or analysing what actors say and do in this chapter, so as to keep their voices and my analysis clearly distinct. The analysis and discussion follows in Chapter Six.

3.1 The policy field and its main actors

Agricultural policy in the EU is a fully integrated policy. In its original form, the CAP had a threefold purpose: securing high prices on the EU domestic market, insulating European producers from international markets (the principle of community preference) and being a welfare policy for farmers (Garzon 2006; Grethe 2006; Phelps 2007). Self-sufficiency in food production was desired for political, economic and psychological reasons. Such independence was also designed to protect the EU from the not-always-predictable conditions of international trade. Increased productivity would help provide farmers with a reasonable standard of living and consumers with quality food at affordable prices and also prevent further migration to cities, preserving rural heritage. In order to reach these goals, a number of policy instruments were introduced. However, these instruments successively became very expensive and have generated unforeseen problems. The number-one problem is (over) supply (Grant 2007; Phelps 2007); the second is that farmers' incomes, on average, have failed to keep up, despite protection from the CAP, with inflation and the costs of living. While a high percentage of farmers in the EU have become dependent on the CAP as an income-protection scheme, the greater part of CAP money goes to big farms that do not necessarily need it. Third, factory farming has increasingly provoked the discontent of the larger public by its pollution, use of pesticides and lack of animal welfare. Soil, water and air quality are under strain as well as organisms and ecological systems. Fourth, the CAP not only produces unfair external effects, its interventionist nature also increasingly produces time-consuming trade conflicts dealt with in the framework of the World Trade Organisation (WTO).

The more these issues became politicised, the more they gave the CAP a bad image, leading to decreasing public support and thereby increasing the pressure for reform of the CAP. There have been four such reform attempts since the early 1990s: The MacSharry reform (1992), the Agenda 2000 reform (1999), the Fischler reform (2003) and the so-called Health Check (2008), which was yet another attempt to reform the CAP in response to a changing economic, social and political environment. All these reforms since 1992 'have tried to address the market imbalances created by the original policy instruments based on price support' (Garzon 2006: 510) and have changed the composition of CAP expenditure (Grethe 2006). The most recent reform was only just concluded in summer 2013. What actors note is that the policy field is subject to transformations:

> Agricultural policy has become more complex. The number of interest organisations has increased dramatically as has the political agenda. Also issues are much more global today. Today, agricultural policy needs to be discussed against the background of agricultural markets worldwide. This used to be different. We used to be able to have our own agricultural policy in the EU because the markets were insulated from the rest of the world. That is not the case anymore (interview 3).

Who are the main actors of the CAP and what is their role? The four central actors can be said to be the Council, the Commission, the European Parliament and agricultural interest groups. The Council of the European Union – in this context, the Agriculture and Fisheries Council AGRIFISH – is responsible for legislative activity and for allocating funding. The Council also holds its own committee, the Special Committee of Agriculture, which has advisory functions. The Council usually aligns closely with agricultural interests since the respective ministers generally come from a related background. It is broadly agreed that the AGRIFISH Council has been very reluctant to reform and has thus been a strong defender of the *status quo* (Kay 2000; Lynggaard 2004). The interests of EU Member States concerning the CAP budget and its priorities differ (Greer 2005; Grethe 2006; Phelps 2007). These differences stem from different preferences as to the role agriculture should have in society and, accordingly, how much state intervention there should be. By way of example, the UK is in favour of abolishing tariffs and all other measures that keep EU agricultural prices above world-market levels. Germany considers that the CAP is healthy and needs only some minor adjustments to strengthen it while France rejects market liberalism in food production and deems the CAP so effective that the policy should be exported to developing countries.

Formally, the Commission controls the agenda of the AGRIFISH Council. It enjoys the sole right to propose legislation and to implement legislative enactments; for the AGRIFISH Council to agree on something different from an initial Commission proposal requires unanimity or the consent of the Commission. The Commission also administers the actual funding of the CAP and assures that Treaty provisions and legislative measures are implemented correctly. The Commission protects agricultural interests, to a certain degree. However, more recently, the Directorate-General (DG) Agriculture and Rural

Development of the European Commission has shown a strong interest in reforming the CAP in order to make it more competitive and to be able to sell European products on the world market without subsidies. The above cited transformations that the policy field is undergoing is also mirrored in the involvement of an increasing number of DGs in the CAP:

> In previous years, you only had to deal with agricultural issues, it was DG Agriculture who dealt with agriculture. But now, because of the nature of agricultural policy, it includes much wider things – like climate change, the environment, like animal health and welfare. So that means that you have DG Environment more involved in policy making, you have DG EMPL more involved in policy making, DG Competition, also and DG Climate Action. So the work that we do is much broader than just agriculture and just the CAP – it's much, much broader than that. We have a much wider range of people that we need to talk to and people that we need to engage with, definitely. And that also includes the parliament (interview 12).

The role of the European Parliament has, with the Lisbon Treaty, moved to the co-decision procedure[1]. It is too early for a characterisation of the nature of the EP's role in the CAP but three actors do note that it has become more important: 'I think generally the role of the European Parliament has increased significantly. And obviously your interaction with MEPs has to increase on the back of that' (interview 10).

Finally, a broad range of agricultural interest groups seek to influence the development of the CAP. The largest association of interest groups is the Comité des Organisationes Professionelles Agricoles (COPA), an interest group defending large-scale farming in particular. COPA members account for about half the membership of the Commission's advisory, management and regulatory committees that exist for each of the CAP product regimes. Interest groups within COPA generally seek to organise a common approach so that conflicts can be avoided (Nedergaard 2006). Some scholars find that their influence is not as strong as commonly assumed (Kay 2000) and, in particular, has diminished in recent years due to structural diversification and to increasing pressure from public opinion (Phelps 2007: 319). Nedergaard argues that an analysis of the political decision-making process is necessary in order to understand why farmers invest as much in lobbying. While economic profit-seeking in the market is generally not successful, political profit-seeking through interest representation generally pays off (Nedergaard 2006).

Three German actors stress the increased political role of environmental groups, something they perceive negatively. The most neutral actor observes that 'the number of interest representatives in the field has diversified', implying that the 'political addressees are confronted with a larger spectrum of views, which one obviously has

---

1.   In the co-decision procedure, the Council of the European Union and the EP act as equal legislators.

to take into account in one's own interest representation' (interview 4). Others are less balanced in their evaluation of the increased importance of environmental groups:

> In part one can talk to them, others are simply too fundamental and fanatic, and trying to talk is almost not worth the effort. We try time and again, even if we notice that we are not getting anywhere. What perhaps has changed is that our governments consider other societal groups much more, amongst which environmental groups, engage in exchanges at roundtables in common committees and seek to develop joint strategies and solutions. This has gained in importance and will continue to do so. In how far it is a success I doubt. Actually it is an increasing strain on work with little success in total (interview 1).

Overall, actors from agricultural groups tend to think that the environmental groups 'don't necessarily always make our lives easier' (interview 6), and therefore 'we regard them rather as being a problem. But they are there' (interview 6). An increased presence of diverse interests is also noticed in Brussels. Whilst in Germany, this tends to be perceived as a negative, one official working in Brussels comes to a more positive evaluation: 'In general, the number of interests in Brussels has grown in the last years. This is something that you see a lot – really everything and everyone is represented. So when we are talking about being part of the democratic process, this is a very good development' (interview 14).

Against this background, agricultural groups today seek to defend their interests. Before we look at their understanding of representation and then into their concrete practices of representation, let us have a look at the actors I interviewed. These comprise 14 actors in total – two from the European umbrella organisation, one representative of the British farmers' office in Brussels, one representative of the main German umbrella organisations' office in Brussels, one representative from a smaller German national umbrella organisation, two regional representatives from two different regional farmers' organisations in the UK; and seven regional representatives from organisations of seven different regions in Germany.

Graph 1: Agricultural actors interviewed

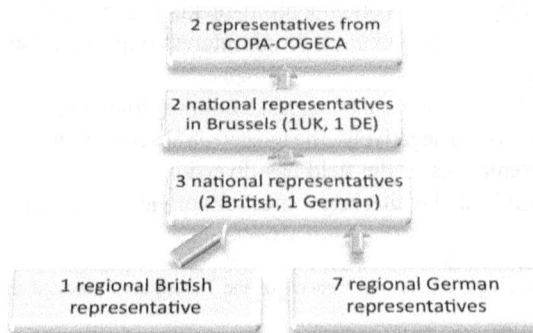

2 representatives from COPA-COGECA

2 national representatives in Brussels (1UK, 1 DE)

3 national representatives (2 British, 1 German)

1 regional British representative

7 regional German representatives

3.2 Actors' understanding of representation

As developed in Chapter Two, I shall now address a number of issues that relate to the understanding of representation by the involved actors, such as: what is representation in their view? Do they see themselves as representing a constituency or an issue? Do they perceive themselves as lobbyists or do they favour a more participatory approach that includes a more interactive role perception? This question also relates to the issue of when actors think representation has been achieved – do groups seek the maximum output, influencing legislation or governmental policy programmes, or are they satisfied if they have influenced a discourse or, even less ambitious, merely made their voices heard? Finally, how do actors conceive of the legitimacy of their activities – is it thought to be generated through input from relevant constituencies or through output via expertise and/or achieved policies?

3.2.1 Representation of people or of an issue?

Actors in agricultural groups responded 100 per cent that, in their view, representation was about representing members and their interests. This suggests that they clearly see themselves as representing a constituency rather than an issue, with no variation between levels of governance: 'I see myself as representing the members' (interview 9). It means that 'someone bundles the interests of the different members and then represents them vis-à-vis the public and politics' (interview 11), representing members' interests 'before the regional government, the federal government, and all the way to Brussels' (interview 7). It seeks to assure that 'the interests that you represent are being voiced in the relevant channels. So in our case it's making sure that the representation of farmers and co-operatives – that we make sure that their voices are being heard in the right places' (interview 14). However, and as we shall see in more detail below, while actors clearly understand themselves to be representatives, they also point out that they are only acting as proxies of the represented and that they always had to try to convince others and justify themselves before elections in their respective organisations (interview 1). Overall, then, the general picture of how these actors understand the role of a representative can be summed up as follows: 'I think that it's our job to make sure that the politicians and the people making decisions on policy that impacts on farmers, it's our job to let them know what farmers want and what farmers think' (interview 12). As a consequence of this understanding of representation, representatives do not seem concerned with taking into account interests other than those of farmers. At most, the interests of 'people living in rural areas' are also taken into account (interview 6).

Conceiving of themselves as representatives of members' interests is highly correlated with actors' understanding of their role in politics, which is that of lobbying in their members' best interests and, indeed, the 'implementation of their legitimate interests' (interview 2), 'having access to the decision-makers in the hope of influencing policy' (interview 11) and 'making sure that we get our views on specific issues known at the decision-making level, particularly in a European context' (interview 10). Actors point out repeatedly that they work for an entrepreneurial association and that 'our members are businessmen who need as open as possible a framework of regulation in order to decide about their economic activities' (interview 2). 'And what our members demand of us, let's say the majority of our members since we are organised democratically, that is what we advocate. Pure lobbyism' (interview 7).

3.2.2 Achievement of representation

The understanding of representation as representatives engaged in lobbying also correlates with actors' views on when representation is achieved. For 78.6 per cent, this is the case when legislation is influenced to the advantage of farmers: 'The goal is achieved when our demands are implemented by the legislator' (interview 2). Indeed, representatives of farmers tend to have a demanding view of representation, which, according to most of them, 'would be achieved when there is a specific proposal that is implemented in a way that agrees with our position' (interview 10) or at least mirrors farmers' views and demands 'as far as possible' (interview 6).

Whilst not losing sight of the goal of influencing legislation, some of the interviewees have a more process-oriented view of when representation is achieved – namely, never fully:

> Representation is an on-going process. I don't think it ever stops. I think that it's a question of making sure that you're working with the policy-makers, even before they're making proposals. I think it's important to discuss with people who formulate policy what they're trying to achieve and then try to give suggestions as to how they might achieve it, almost before anything is written on paper. Because once it's on paper, it's difficult to change. So I see representation as a continuing process' (interview 11).

This process starts with the first conversation, 'never has an end' (interview 1) and therefore is a continuing process which 'is never done' (interview 9).

There are also three interviewees (21.4 per cent) – two of whom are based in Brussels and one in a leading position at the national level – who consider that representation is achieved when one has made one's voice heard – whether or not that in the end influences legislation. According to such a perspective, one should:

> make a distinction between achieving [representation] and successful achievement. Because of course the representation has been furthered if you make sure that in all parts of the process you are making voices heard and are making sure that the interests of the farmer are clear for the decision-makers.

And then of course you have to make the distinction between whether or not you are successful in the end or not. So when do I think it's achieved? In principle if the decision-makers have heard what the concerns and the requests are, then in principle representation is achieved. And then of course in the end it is up to decision-makers themselves to decide how they go further (interview 14).

Similarly, another actor argues that:

representation of interests already happens in the moment in which I articulate positions. Whether and to which degree this is being mirrored in a legislative proposal, that is the result, but not the representation of interests. The representation of interests foregoes the result in my view. That is an on-going process, the articulation of interests. The articulation of interests is at the same time their representation (interview 4).

3.2.3 Legitimacy generation of representation

What actors think confers legitimacy to their activities is a central element of their understanding of representation. In principle, there are two possibilities. Either actors may see legitimacy as primarily deriving from the input of the groups' constituencies. Or they may think of legitimacy as stemming from the output generated by their very involvement in policy making. This could be achieved by 'doing the right thing', either because of their expertise or their faith, or by the outcomes of the political process (policies).

In the case of agricultural groups, the issue of legitimacy-generation as perceived by the actors is very clear. According to them, legitimacy is conferred on their representatives by the democratic structure and the mandate given by their members:

We have a totally democratic structure, starting with the voluntary membership. Our complete structure rests on this voluntary membership, including fees. We don't receive any money from the state, from some other sponsors or some industry. One becomes a member and pays the fee according to the rules. Everything else works with elections, steering committees of districts, of regions, federal steering committee, all that is being elected regularly. On the basis of rules there are elections, for the representation in committees, and I think that provides sufficient legitimacy because the members are voluntarily in them and because the committees and the representation result from free and fair elections, and that's decisive (interview 6).

Legitimacy thus derives from the voluntary character of the associations and from the democratic mandate that those working in committees on different levels and doing the representation have, implying that 'when we represent positions, then it's the result of democratic work in the different committees which we have at different levels' (interview 9).

Another, related, yet distinct, point that a number of interviewees mention, is how a high level of membership of their organisations confers legitimacy on them, for example, up to 90 per cent in Germany (interview 6). Seen from this perspective, representation by agricultural groups is legitimate because almost all farmers are organised in them. The same kind of reasoning is apparent in the statement of an English representative: 'The membership gives legitimacy. Not all farmers in England and Wales belong to the NFU. But by far the majority belongs. So it is an overwhelming majority of farmers that farms the overwhelming majority of land that gives credence and legitimacy to the representation' (interview 11). Both points, the high level of organisation of farmers and the democratic mandate of their representatives through free and fair elections come together nicely in the response given by a representative based in Brussels:

> I think we are legitimate because people want us to speak on their behalf. And because we are a professional organisation that has always represented members and growers. And the other reason why I think we are legitimate is that all of the decisions are actually made by our members. So our policy positions have been put together by our council who is elected by our members. So because it's farmers who make the decisions on what we do and say, nationally and in the EU, that makes us legitimate (interview 12).

3.3 Organisational structures and practices of representation within CSOs

In this section, I am interested in exploring the *practices* of representation within CSOs rather than, as in the previous section, what actors *understand* by representation. Obviously, practices can be quite different from the more abstract understanding actors have of a certain issue, given there is a multitude of competing actors in the political arena and also a number of more structural, institutional and legal constraints on actors' behaviour and the realisation of their organisational goals. More concretely, I will be looking at, first, how the different groups involve their constituencies in the decision-making and internal governance of the organisation. This will involve addressing how issues get on to the agenda of organisations in the first place; how and where position-finding then occurs; how far members – or, possibly, constituencies that are not members – are involved in the authorisation and control of their respective representatives and what forms authorisation and control take; and how far existing constituencies are mobilised for activities beyond the internal governance of the organisation. Second, I will be asking how far interest groups mobilise a wider potential constituency, that is, the larger public, for some of their activities – do groups reach out to a larger public and involve it in some of their activities? Do they seek to enlarge their constituency, or do they mainly focus on their existing constituency? Overall, this section should allow us to see how representative CSOs are of their constituencies.

3.3.1 Internal governance processes: agenda-setting, authorisation and control

How do issues get on to the agenda?

How do issues get on the agenda of agricultural groups? A large majority of the interviewed actors is convinced that agenda-setting is mostly (71.4 per cent) or entirely (7.1 per cent) government- or environment-driven. Some actors find that agenda-setting is mostly (14.3 per cent) or entirely (7.1 per cent) driven by members. More often than not, it is natural disasters or politics that force issues on the agenda of agricultural organisations:

> Often, our priorities are dictated by outside processes like, for example, government priorities or European priorities, e.g., you may have seen the news last night, there was a lot of talk about a drought. That is a very important issue for our members. So that is something that we have to prioritise that is out of our control (interview 12).

Similarly, there are:

> of course things which have to be decided very quickly, such as the EHEC-crisis last summer [2012] or the Dioxin-crisis. In such cases, we have to deal with issues for which we cannot take half a year to organise our will-formation. In such cases, things have to be done quicker, in consultation with the respective regional steering committees (interview 3).

The same can happen at the EU-level when something unforeseen arrives from the DG Agriculture and Rural Development that needs immediate handling (interview 13).

Besides politics and natural catastrophes, another external factor is mentioned, namely the press and thereby the broader public: 'In some way it's also the press that defines it...the society, e.g. take the debates about the protection of the environment, the saving of energy and such things, whatever is being discussed by society. That means the society also defines it' (interview 9).

In reality, it's likely to be a mixture of demands from members and government-led initiatives as well as natural conditions. One regional actor puts it like this:

> Of course much comes from below, from the grassroots, when members get active and let us know we have to do something about a topic. On the other hand, the policy officers in our house of course get information through different channels, from the EU, federal and regional level, about

agricultural policies. And then the respective policy officer will deal with that (interview 5).

Similarly, at the EU level:

in one way you have of course the agenda of the Commission and of EU politics that are on-going, something like the reform of the CAP – that's something that's put on the agenda so it's clear that we have to deal with this. But on the other side it's members coming from the Member States saying 'this is currently really a problem or this is coming up – you have to do something about it.' So then it's the members who are indicating what they want to discuss and they want COPA-COGECA to lobby on these things (interview 14).

Whether topics arrive on the agenda from outside the organisation or from within – as well as the urgency of the topic – they can influence how the further position-finding process unfolds. Are there traces of both bottom-up and of top-down position-finding processes as the foregoing discussion would lead us to expect? I will show below that there certainly are. Also, there are clearly democratic structures in place which are used from the local level all the way up to the European level; no important policy position is developed without an input from the members and nor could it be adopted without having consulted the members over the different governance levels. What actors from agricultural groups report about these processes is therefore very harmonious across the levels. So, what are the structures that are used to govern farmers' interests?

Structures and processes of developing policy positions, of authorisation and control

Farmers are organised throughout the governance levels, 'starting at the local level, then the district, then the county. So mostly one would contact the chairman at the county level who would take the issue to the regional organisation' (interview 2). At each of the levels, there are elected representatives – farmers – who 'meet regularly in panels, in committees, in working groups with experts, leading to results which will then be presented, discussed again, until the entire thing develops into a proposition, position, statement' (interview 1). Every time, before an issue reaches the higher level of governance, a decision must be taken by the steering committee of the lower level that the issue should be taken to the higher level, 'and with which substance and to which level' (interview 2). In every instance, these committees are made up of delegates from the lower level of governance.

As part of the governance structure, there are 12–13 technical committees on different topics which meet 4–5 times a year. Farmers with specific expertise are the (delegated) members of these committees. Farmers are elected and delegated into these committees for four years. So, 'when there is a need to develop a policy position, then a proposal is developed by our experts. To this goal, we have committees which are proportionally set up from the different counties of the region. And they debate, give recommendations, and then it's the steering committee that decides' (interview 1). There is a 'legal committee where classical legal issues are being discussed' (interview 3). The other committees are 'organised according to different commodity sectors. So there's a horticulture sector, poultry, livestock, crops, environment. So each sector will look at what policies are likely to come up and see how they will impact on each sector' (interview 11). There is of course also a committee for milk, 'where only milk issues will be discussed. For all kinds of sectors, there are technical committees in our organisation, in which we have experts of the regional organisations which normally are farmers, so members who try to bring in their experiences' (interview 3). These technical committees exist both at the regional and at the national level:

> So each region will have its own. If we take livestock, for example, which will cover cattle and sheep, each region will have its own livestock board, and the livestock board is made up of elected members from each county. So, for example, in the West Midlands we've got five counties. So the West Midlands livestock board will have two members from each county and then they will elect the chairman. And then the national livestock board consists of all the different chairmen from each region. So that's how the representation works (interview 11).

Once a technical group has found a position on an issue, this is then co-ordinated with the boards of other technical groups:

> So for example, if a policy issue came up from Brussels on poultry – the president, deputy president and vice president would all be informed about that. But the poultry board would ultimately be the board that deals with that issue because it ultimately affects poultry members. And they have approval from the council to do that as well. So if an issue came up on cereals, for example, exactly the same would happen. The three top people would be told and they would be informed and would be aware of the situation but it's ultimately the cereals board who would decide our policy position on that with the approval of the council. ... And the reason it's approved by council and the presidents is to ensure that it doesn't contradict a decision from another group, from another board (interview 12).

So, before a political statement can be made by anyone at a higher level of governance, first 'the expert committee has to deal with the topic, and then it goes in the next higher board, e.g. the steering committee. If the technical committee has not expressed itself, then the next higher governance level ... cannot express itself on the topic. That is always the basic structure that needs to be followed' (interview 9).

Once a technical committee has expressed itself, the position will be discussed by the steering committee and eventually be adopted – or sent back to the technical committee if some issue needed further exploration. Once a position has been found, it will be adopted by the majority of the regional steering committee, even though 'usually we don't have positions that we vote on. Usually we use compromise and advocacy. We don't generally vote on positions, we take a position and justify it and try and make sure that it is robust' (interview 12). The steering committee will vary in size, depending on the size of the region. It will mainly consist of the chairmen of the district organisations as well as of experts (farmers) of the regional commodities (interview 8). Once the regional committee has adopted a position, it becomes 'the position of the regional organisation' (interview 8). It can be passed on to the federal level where again it will be discussed and eventually adapted by members who proportionally come from the different regions – 'that is a democratic process in our organisation, following the bottom-up principle, from the bottom to the top' (interview 7).

The same process is in fact repeated at the European level where the same technical committees exist, in line with the different commodity sectors:

> Here we have the working parties again. I always like to call them the backbone of the organisation because this is actually where the expertise comes in. Those working parties, which have an expert from each of the Member States, they will look at the proposal from the Commission or the communication from the Commission, what's coming up and what do we think should be the COPA-COGECA position on this? (interview 14).

At the European level, there are about forty of these technical committees which each meet two or three times a year. Once they have agreed on a position, it:

> will go to the next stage, which is the policy co-ordination committee. All the different positions will come through this policy co-ordination committee, which is held every month. And they will look – in this committee – at whether our views in the different working parties are coherent (interview 14).

The co-ordination committee is made up of one person per member organisation plus staff from COPA-COGECA. Once the co-ordination committee agrees on a position, it is transferred to the board, which consists:

> of the presidents of all the organisations. And all the presidents from the different organisations will be coming together there. And they will take the final decision on the positions ... And in the end it's the members again who can say 'we want this' or 'we don't want this' – they can decide (interview 14).

Besides the steering committees and the technical committees, there are further ways in which position-finding is organised. The annual general meetings (AGMs) are highly institutionalised. They exist at all levels of governance but the municipal one: 'In order for every member to be able to attend, it also exists at the district level' (interview 5). At the AGMs, 'political aims are also being discussed' and delegates from all districts come and issue 'a sort of programme or statement which contains the most important tasks' (interview 6). It is at the federal level that the:

> very big issues are discussed, all the reforms, and where we coordinate the main directions with the members. And once the *Deutsche Bauernverband* has an official position, we bring it into the political process at the national level and we use it at the European level where we discuss it with our European organisation COPA (interview 3).

At the European level, there is the same process. COPA-COGECA also has its AGM, which brings together representatives from all the Member States to discuss the main directions of future policy positions and to 'officially adapt a programme, together with the election of the president' (interview 13). It is also at the AGM that the 'chairmen of the technical committees are elected, and together with them we develop a programme for their two years' chairmanship' (interview 13). In short, 'it's members who are members of the boards, and it's members who are members of the council, and it's members who are presidents, deputy presidents and vice-presidents' (interview 12).

Complementary to these institutionalised ways of finding a position, there are also more informal ways, such as organising an event. So, if 'certain processes get to a point where we think we need to discuss it, then we call in the technical committees … or we organise a larger event where we invite to debate a specific topic because we want to discuss with the farmers what their view is' (interview 6).

Sometimes, politics develop quickly and the democratic structures in place cannot be used fully. In such instances, it will normally be the steering committees of the concerned governance level – regional, federal, European – which will convene and decide what should be done, with its respective chairman or president as the ultimate authority: 'In *ad hoc* situations, it is the smaller managing board that will take the decision, that means the president and two vice-presidents, and if it has to go really fast, then the president has to take a decision on its own which he must get approved afterwards' (interview 2).

Similarly, the staffed offices, in particular those in Brussels and at the national level, obviously have a special role to play. They are likely to receive information first and have the resources to devote themselves to the development and drafting of positions and the search for compromises that involves. Therefore, in certain instances, 'one has to go ahead, at the top, and then say look, these are the things that may come up, and this could be a way to deal with it, go and discuss it. I think that happens in every organisation, but it is a democratic decision-making process' (interview 7). In particular with regard to EU issues, it is likely that 'it would be picked up first of all by the staff of the NFU, so you would either have the Brussels staff or the UK staff picking it up' (interview 11). Also, 'it will be mainly the staff that are feeding into EU policy' (interview 11). In between the moments of 'picking it up' and 'feeding into EU policy', the information is being fed 'back down through our committee system' (interview 10).

From the above, we learned that members are involved throughout the development of a policy position and that they are also the ones who authorise it, no matter at what governance level. Similarly, members are also the ones who hold their representatives to account. Members regularly receive information about the policy positions and their development, in particular, through monthly or even weekly newsletters or briefs. They can also keep themselves updated through related websites, which all the regional organisations have. If unhappy with a development, control can be achieved in more formal or more informal ways. Members may send letters to the chairman of their county or may call her/him or the staff of the regional organisation (interview 1). Or the chairman of a county gets in touch with the regional offices in case (s)he could not answer the question satisfactorily (interview 6). Furthermore, they can use the events mentioned above to voice discontent and bring their voices into the process. More formally, the technical committees and the steering committees as well as the AGMs are the institutionalised possibilities of exercising control: 'We have a structure of both geographical groups, central committees, our executive committee, we have country committees, we have our annual general meeting, so there's lots of channels for us to be held to account' (interview 10). And of course there are also yearly reports, which give account of what has been done and achieved. A policy officer of the German representation of the *Deutscher Bauernverband* in Brussels, however, points out that control would not function as in electoral representation here: 'That's not the way to think about it. ... You can only do little with control here. No, the members of our regional organisations need to be able to rely on us doing our best to represent their interests in the processes in Brussels' (interview 3).

3.3.2 How do CSOs mobilise support?

Mobilisation of the existing constituency

Given the highly democratic structures of farmers' organisations, one might expect that agricultural groups would also seek to mobilise their constituencies for the political representation of agricultural interests. Is that so? When asked directly whether they would mobilise their members for some of their lobbying activities, 57.1 per cent say that is regularly the case, 35.7 per cent irregularly, and 7.1 per cent rarely. However, whenever they did try to mobilise them, it seems to have been successful in so far as 100 per cent replied that members let themselves be mobilised.

The related activities are manifold. Some are rather regional and with a focus on debate, for example, when members are invited to meet politicians, amongst others:

We have divided our area into nine regions and we go to all the regions and invite representatives of the local groups to debates, exchange of views, with our steering committee. Every so often, the minister attends the meeting. ...

And then of course, there are also regular events in the winter, debates, where we also have representatives of the EU, both politicians and experts. Last week I attended an event on antibiotics, of our district organisation, where members were also invited. So we do inform and try to engage in will-formation and debate (interview 1; similarly interview 2).

Both at the regional and at the national levels, the interviewees also mention more confrontational activities: 'We inform the members and say now it's important to write cards, protest letters, send an e-mail to this address, or, as we have also done a couple of times, we organise a bus trip to Berlin or Brussels and protest directly' (interview 6). Such actions are organised in order to 'illustrate the consequences of certain political measures' (interview 4), for example, on 'the topic of milk, and also agricultural policy' (interview 5). Another example involves the mobilisation against land use, against which members were asked to sign a petition, the result of which was that '200,000 signatures were handed over to the petition committee [of the *Bundestag*]. Of course, this also includes supporters who are not farmers, but it went down directly to our members, through the district organisations' (interview 3). The demonstration, whilst still in use as a protest tactic, 'has lost in importance, it accomplishes ever less', even though 'large demonstrations as we know them from farmers, of course still exist', one example being 'the conference of agricultural ministers of the regions and the federal government in Konstanz. There we mobilised the farmers, our president was there, and we handed over a resolution' (interview 8). However, strongly confrontational means of protest seem to be in decline. These days, farmers only resort to strong protest:

> if it really hurts. That is not our permanent way of expressing ourselves, but perhaps every other year, sometimes possibly twice a year, when it's really urgent, we mobilise our members for actions of protest, for demonstrations. There are also other forms, e.g. we have distributed pieces of butter in front of Aldi [a discounter] in order to draw the attention to the situation of milk farmers. So there are different forms of protests. We also do campaigns every now and then. But it is not our main playground (interview 6).

Mobilisation of the wider public

Do groups mainly relate to their existing constituencies or do they also seek to reach out to the larger public, that is, do they try to maintain some relationship with the public and, if so, of what kind? Do groups merely pass on information to the public or do they seek to mobilise the public for activities or involve it in debate? In order to answer these questions, I shall look at whether CSOs inform the larger public about their policies and activities, particularly by making information available on their websites and entertaining relationships with the press; whether they try to mobilise a larger constituency, be it through more passive ways (becoming a member or donating money) or be it more actively, through online and street activities.

Informing the wider public about its activities is an important part of how a group maintains its relationship with them. Therefore, one question to address is how organisations provide the public with information and through what channels. These days, a major way of reaching a wider public is to have a website. So far as agricultural groups are concerned, all the regional, national and European organisations under scrutiny here have their own websites. In addition to a website, 50 per cent of the organisations also make use of social media such as Facebook and/or Twitter. On the websites, 78.6 per cent offer a regular newsletter and/or briefing notes in order to keep subscribers informed whilst 21.4 per cent do not. In 85.7 per cent of the cases, one can find statements from the organisations on the websites that explain the policy position farmers have on a given topic or policy process; in 14.3 per cent, this is not the case. In 83.3 per cent of the cases, the organisations explicitly address the press on their website, mostly by way of press releases and sometimes additionally with special information packages, whilst in 16.6 per cent of the organisations, this is not the case. Relating to the press and interacting with it therefore seems very much to be the rule. Indeed, as one actor put it 'media are of course also used to represent our interests. That is the channel through which our views are being spread' (interview 4). Another actor confirms that 'publicity of course also has its role to play, i.e. by working through the media' (interview 9).

The next thing we want to know is whether or not CSOs seek to involve the larger public in some of their activities. On their websites, 35.7 per cent of the agricultural groups offer membership to potential new members whilst 64.3 per cent do not. This comparatively low percentage may be explained by the very high level of organisation that exists already, by membership being limited to farmers and by the fact that recruitment is mostly done face-to-face, as several interviewees point out. Indeed, 57.1 per cent say they pursue active recruitment strategies whilst 42.9 per cent say they do not. These recruitment strategies may consist of 'doing publicity' (interview 1), of 'talking to farmers who are not members' (interview 2) and also of 'road shows and various agricultural shows' (interview 12). It is not exactly easy to attract new members, given the already very high degree of organisation and the decreasing number of farmers due to structural changes (interview 8); yet in many instances, there are concrete strategies to do so, mostly on a local level:

> We're always trying to join up people who don't belong, who aren't already in membership. So there's always a drive to increase membership of course. First of all you would need to identify who is not in membership. And then it's a question of going to talk to them to see why they are not in membership and to see if you can change their mind and show them the value of belonging to the organisation. Generally done face-to-face, on a very local level (interview 11).

Other actors suggest that there is not much of an explicit recruitment strategy (interview 9), that recruitment was 'not an active process' given that 'farmers' families generally are members of the *Deutsche Bauernverband* out of tradition' (interview 3) and given the restricted number of potential members (interview 4). Another, rather passive way of supporting an organisation is to donate money – however, this possibility is not offered by any of the organisations investigated.

Do agricultural groups seek to involve the larger public more actively in some of their activities? Overall, this does not really seem to be the case. In only two cases (14.3 per cent) are visitors of websites invited to join a campaign, sign a petition, send a mail to an MP or go to a demonstration; in 85.7 per cent of the organisations, this is not the case. However, this need not mean that farmers do not mobilise at all beyond their constituency. A national actor reports a signature list with around 200,000 signatures, not all of them members, that was handed over to the petition committee of parliament (interview 3). Also, demonstrations are reported, mostly as reactions to agricultural policy (interview 5; interview 8), even though actors point out that demonstrations had become less important in recent times (interview 8; interview 6). Is the larger public offered other means of interaction or participation? Not a single organisation offered the possibility of posting a blog on its website or to volunteer for the organisation. The only form of direct interaction that exists is public events – 78.6 per cent of the organisations advertise public events on their webpage whilst 21.4 per cent do not. Examples of such public events are an 'open farm day' (interview 1), or 'regular lectures in the winter, where every now and then representatives of the EU are present' (interview 1).

3.4 Interest representation strategies in EU policy making

Whilst the last section allowed us to see how representative CSOs are of their constituency, this section will show the activities of representation through which agricultural actors represent their constituency in EU policy making. To do so, I will first look at their degree of Europeanisation as defined in Chapter 2.4. The main part of this section concerns the addressees of agricultural-sector actors in EU policy making as well as the latter's strategies for addressing them. CSOs can use a multitude of channels for this. They may, first and foremost, try to lobby their relevant national ministries in the hope of thereby influencing Council decisions. They can lobby national MPs or MEPs, the latter in particular, since the EP is now involved in almost all European legislation by way of the co-decision procedure. They might address the European Commission directly and seek to influence legislative proposals in their very early stages. They might join forces and organise themselves under the head of a national and European umbrella organisation, in order to have a stronger voice vis-à-vis national and European institutions. Special attention will be given to this particular strategy so as to evaluate whether groups themselves see an added value in co-operating with other groups in order to influence EU policies and, specifically, whether groups co-operate both at the national *and* at the European level. Only if European-level co-operation happens could co-operation be taken as contributing to the emergence of a European *demos*, as is discussed in parts of the interested literature. If groups only co-operate with other groups from the same Member State, this would suggest that national differences between them, even within the same policy field, remain too great for stronger European co-ordination.

In a next step, I address whether being involved in EU policy making has an impact on agricultural organisations. This is relevant as it can give hints at why actors may be more or less engaged but also whether being involved in EU policy making distances the organisations from their constituencies in one way or another. Finally, some of the CSOs might consider going to the European Court of Justice if they felt a legal injustice that needed to be corrected had occurred. Or, indeed, they might use all these different channels in their efforts to influence policies. This section will explore the ways CSOs use these different channels, with a focus on the political (rather than the judicial) institutions and the lobby strategies actors associate with them and with special attention given to European umbrella organisations.

The chapter closes by looking at the incentive structure for agricultural actors to get engaged with the EU, as perceived by the actors themselves, thereby providing clues for the explanation of their engagement with the EU. This will involve exploring actors' perceptions of what are the positives and negatives coming from the EU; of differences in the work environments between the EU and their domestic environment; and of whether they find it easier or harder to be heard at the EU level than domestically. As regards the latter point, specific attention will be paid to the European Commission's consultation regime. It is relevant insofar as the Commission is not only the initiator of legislation in the EU and therefore a central actor. It has also developed a number of consultation and participation opportunities specifically for CSOs over the last 15 years or so. It is helpful to know how far these are accepted by CSOs because satisfaction with the Commission's consultation regime may be a strong incentive to become involved in EU policy making, whilst dissatisfaction with it may be a strong disincentive. I will end by addressing the degree to which, as a consequence, the agricultural constituency has been interested in EU affairs.

3.4.1 To whom are representing activities addressed and by what strategies?

In this sub-section, I will by and large draw on the qualitative data. Where informative, I will supplement it by quantitative data from the questionnaire in which I asked actors to qualify how important they thought it was to be in touch with specific actors in regard to EU affairs.

Degree of Europeanisation

When I asked, first, what importance dealing with EU processes had in their organisation, 83.3 per cent thought the importance was 'high' whilst 16.7 per cent thought it was 'medium'. Second, I asked whether the EU is an issue in their daily work. Unsurprisingly, 91.7 per cent say the EU is regularly an issue in their work, whilst only 8.3 per cent say this is rarely the case. Third, I asked how important it is to be present in Brussels in order to achieve the organisational goals: 92.9 per cent deem it 'very important' to be present in Brussels and 7.1 per cent think such a presence is 'rather important'. Finally, I have looked at the organisations' websites and checked whether or not they reported about EU policies, indicating that the organisation regards disseminating information about EU policies as important. Indeed, the high importance of the EU for agricultural groups is also mirrored on their websites: all the organisations report about EU policies on their websites (*see* graph 4 in the appendix).

The domestic level[2]

When seeking to influence policies, groups often form *alliances* with other groups in order to exert stronger pressure on those they are lobbying. Is this also the case for agricultural groups? In four instances (28.6 per cent), actors mention other business (sectoral) groups with which they have allied themselves. Environmental groups are also mentioned by several agricultural actors, though it is also pointed out that 'often we rather work in opposition to each other' (interview 5). Nonetheless, agricultural groups seek to consult with environmental groups, particularly before certain votes in EU committees, so as to avoid confrontation within those same committees.

So far as *intra-organisational lobbying strategies* are concerned, all regional agricultural groups are members of the same national umbrella organisations. When asked openly in interview, 75 per cent of the agricultural actors mention the national umbrella organisation as one channel they use in their EU-related work, whilst 25 per cent do not mention it. However, when asked explicitly in the questionnaire, all the actors reply they have strong links to their national umbrella organisation and use it to influence EU policy. Their satisfaction with the representation of the national umbrella organisation could not be higher. Actors agree that they are 'informed regularly and quickly, on a weekly basis, and if we need to discuss something, we get support immediately, contacts and meetings are being arranged, it's all to the best' (interview 1), not least because 'they have really good people there' (interview 6), a 'really, really well staffed office, with excellent experts' (interview 7). Similarly in the UK, farmers are highly satisfied and feel 'extremely well represented. Having held a couple of senior positions in other trade associations, the NFU is by far the best in representing its members' interests' (interview 11).

In regard to national institutions outside of their own organisation, 33.3 per cent say they are addressing *regional* ministries, whilst 66.7 per cent do not mention these when interviewed. This seems to be an exclusively German strategy, given the distribution of competences in the German federal political system. The reasoning

---

2. For the domestic and the European level, *see* graphs 5 and 6 in the appendix.

is to take issues to regional agricultural ministries because via the second chamber, the *Bundesrat*, actors can 'influence the federal government which in turn has an influence in Brussels' (interview 8).

All but one agricultural actor (91.7 per cent), in the interviews, said they address their *national* ministry when seeking to influence EU policies. Indeed, in the questionnaire, 71.4 per cent of the actors consider the national ministry to be a 'very important' and 28.6 per cent a 'rather important' addressee of lobbying activities in regard to EU affairs. Contacts exist either in bilateral meetings, in the context of ministerial working groups (interview 1), or when directly addressing the agricultural minister (interview 11). Finally, lobbying may be done both in Brussels to influence Council decisions and back home in the national capitals: 'We lobby our governments here in Brussels. But also nationally we lobby our government very heavily back in the UK – through the UK offices and the London office' (interview 12).

Interestingly, only 28.6 per cent (two national, two regional actors) in the interviews mention that they are in touch with national MPs to try to influence the CAP. This stands in sharp contrast with the data from the questionnaire, in which only 7.1 per cent say that MPs are 'very important' in EU affairs but 85.7 per cent nevertheless say MPs are 'rather important' whilst only 7.1 per cent find them 'rather unimportant'.

The European level

We can understand the Brussels office(s) of the national umbrella structures as the extension of this intra-organisational channel. They are used for the representatives to lobby on behalf of their national member organisations: 50 per cent of the actors say that they use the Brussels office against 50 per cent who do not mention it.

As at the domestic level, agricultural groups also sometimes form strategic alliances with other groups at the EU level. Again, this can be both sectoral groups and more value-driven CSOs:

> Sometimes we work together with other stakeholders. Sometimes it can be very useful to create alliances with other stakeholders. Sometimes we work together with the animal welfare NGOs, and sometimes we work together with other stakeholders from other parts of the food chain. So it really depends on the topic – we look at this on a case-by-case basis (interview 14).

Another way of 'going European' is to use the European umbrella organisation. At the EU level, this must be seen as a mixture of intra- and inter-organisational lobbying strategies. It is an intra-organisational strategy in so far as it is used to promote national interests; it is also an inter-organisational strategy since agricultural groups from all the Member States unite in an effort at the EU level and, typically, need to find a consensus in order to maximise their influence.

In the interviews, 66.7 per cent mention that they use the European umbrella structure – COPA-COGECA – whilst 33.3 per cent do not mention it. When asked in the questionnaire, however, 75 per cent said they entertained 'strong and regular' contacts with the European umbrella organisation; for 16.7 per cent the contact was 'rather strong if irregular' and for 8.3 per cent, there was no contact (*see* graph 7 in the appendix). The close links between the national organisations and their European umbrella organisation are complemented by a high degree of satisfaction of national actors with their European representation (*see* graph 8 in the appendix). The vast majority (91.7 per cent) of the actors say they are either satisfied (33.3 per cent) or rather satisfied (58.3 per cent) with the way COPA-COGECA represents them whilst only one (8.3 per cent) does not know. Those who are very happy with the representation say that the staff in Brussels are excellent (interview 7, interview 11) and that if they were unhappy with their representation, then 'we would change that. We finance it after all' (interview 3). The importance of the European umbrella organisation for agricultural actors is mirrored in this quote from a national German actor:

> For us, the most important organisation in Brussels is COPA-COGECA where we are one of the big members. If we have a strong common position in the European farmers' organisation, then the Commission and the EP cannot ignore it and put it aside easily. Here, it is not the national position which is decisive, though we try of course to have as much impact as possible. What matters here is to speak with one voice, the aggregation of the diversity of views. ... We always seek to make compromises with the European farmers. ... Then the MEPs can count on it being a strong position which corresponds with the political reality (interview 3).

Some actors, however, even if fairly satisfied with the European umbrella organisation, have a somewhat mixed evaluation of their representation by the European umbrella. This is generally linked to the issue of the 'lowest common denominator':

> In principle the representation is also good. The European umbrella has the problem that it assembles around sixty different organisations, from Cyprus to Northern Ireland, from Finland to Gran Canaria, and then you often have the lowest common denominator as a formulation that is generally acceptable as a result which is not really helpful when looking closer at things. It is rather unsatisfactory, but no one has come up with something better yet (interview 1; similarly interview 8).

Others are even clearer about the interests at stake which are 'always about the national position' (interview 4): 'Of course by now, it is very difficult to bring together twenty-seven Member States with different interests, and then more often than not you get compromises where the German interests cannot be enforced entirely' (interview 2). One consequence is that at times, national members will look for other lobby channels as this actor points out: 'Within that [organisation] then there are specific regional differences across the whole of Europe, and I think that's when we probably would not use the specific channels of COPA but would rather go directly ourselves' (interview 10).

In a difference from the two other groups under investigation in this study, agricultural groups do not use any other European umbrella organisation than COPA-COGECA.

The next European venue that actors may use to influence the CAP and other EU policies is the European Commission. In the interviews, 66.7 per cent say that they are in touch with the Commission directly to influence policies whilst 33.3 per cent do not mention the Commission. When asked directly in the questionnaire, 92.9 per cent deem it 'very important' and 7.1 per cent 'rather important' to be in touch with the Commission when seeking to influence EU policies. For *regional* actors, direct contacts with the Commission seem to exist mainly in three ways. The first is via participation in Commission advisory committees, which meet regularly to discuss the development of the CAP (interview 1; interview 2; interview 9). The second is that Commission officials are invited to meet the regional actors in the regions, to learn more about regional products and circumstances and discuss them with regional actors (interview 1; interview 2; interview 9):

> Last year there was a meeting with Commissioners Öttinger and Schöllnach in Baden-Württemberg which we initiated. This means the Commissioners are invited to the regions, in order to have a look at regional issues, to become aware of things – 'be careful when doing this or that, you need to take into account the diversity of the European regions' (interview 3).

Thirdly, it does not seem uncommon for regional actors to go to Brussels to meet Commission officials directly: 'We obviously would go and see the Commission official directly if we feel the issue is important enough. For instance, today we have a number of our staff out there on a range of meetings dealing directly with EU Commission officials' (interview 10; similarly interview 1). Another regional actor points out that he knows Commission officials 'who I call every now and then and simply say "Okay, I am coming to see you", and then I drive to Brussels in the evening and talk with them the next day' (interview 6). Where contacts are more irregular at the regional level, they still are very much the same as those described above.

At the national level, the contact is obviously even more straightforward and exists at all levels – both political and working level. As regards the former level, meetings with the Commissioners and chefs de cabinet are regularly arranged. As regards the latter, meetings often take place in the framework of COPA-COGECA, at which Commissioners also regularly show up:

> We would lobby Commission officials – the technical people, the desk officers. And then every level really. So we would lobby the department heads and then the Director-Generals of the various departments as well. The Commissioner himself and also his cabinet, his political advisors (interview 12; similarly interview 3).

An actor working on the representation of British farmers in Brussels explains the multitude of channels:

> We're in touch with them in the formation of policy – so years before any policy issue is actually on the table we would try to talk to them in advance to see what they are thinking about a given problem and what's coming up. We're in touch with them prior to them releasing proposals. We're in touch with them after they release proposals, to be clear on what the proposals mean. We call them up, we meet them face-to-face, we email them, we see them at events, all of that. We also have another means by which we are in touch with them, which is through the advisory groups. We're also in contact with them because they come out and speak to our groups – so, for example if we have a group of farmers over they will come and speak to them about a particular topic (interview 12).

At the EU level, contacts are the most intense. A COPA-COGECA official suggests that 'more or less 75 per cent, I would think, is focused on the European Commission because that's where legislation is initiated' (interview 14). Overall, agricultural representatives participate in a variety of consultation opportunities that the Commission offers – advisory groups, hearings, conferences, bilateral meetings or online consultations – in which they also regularly participate, no matter from which governance level they are.

Even more than with the Commission, national agricultural actors are in touch with MEPs. In fact, when asked openly in interview, 83.3 per cent of them say that they lobby MEPs directly; only 16.7 per cent do not mention this channel of influence. When asked in the questionnaire, 100 per cent of the actors say it is 'very important' to be in touch with MEPs to influence EU policies. Many actors stress the increased importance of the EP: 'The EP is very important. With the Treaty of Lisbon, the EP co-decides in all important matters, finances and agricultural policy included. The EP today has, if it wants, real room of manoeuvre. It is a really, really important interlocutor for us' (interview 3; similarly interview 8; interview 10).

More often than not, regional actors are in regular touch with their regional MEPs (interview 2; interview 7; interview 8; interview 9; interview 11). Only one regional actor indicated that the contact was rather irregular (interview 1). At the national level, the contact is obviously even more intense, so that actors will be in touch with all the national MEPs. This is done both via written statements (interview 4) and face-to-face. Meetings either take place in Brussels (interview 1; interview 6) and in the context of workshops or conferences, or, as all of those who are in touch with MEPs report, in the regions where MEPs have their constituencies: 'We do seek the exchange with MEPs which we invite time and again in order to inform them which positions we have just adopted, what impact it has on farms in their constituencies' (interview 1; similarly interview 2; interview 6). Sometimes, they will also be invited to attend hearings in parliamentary committees (interview 3; interview 12). Most likely, a mixture of all these different ways of lobbying MEPs will be used, as this actor suggests:

> We lobby the MEPs, we lobby them in Brussels and we also lobby them back in the UK. So our regional offices lobby them in their region and in their constituencies. And we lobby them here in Brussels and hopefully give them the same message (interview 12).

The same actor adds that they would additionally lobby 'MEP assistants and those working in the various committee secretariats' (interview 12). The increased importance of the EP is also reported by a European actor working for COPA-COGECA: 'Ever since the Lisbon Treaty has entered into force, our relations with the European Parliament have changed and in fact we have gotten much more active in that sense' (interview 14).

The Council, finally, is mentioned by four actors (28.6 per cent). However, actors stress that they mostly lobby their own government and respective minister 'back home'.

There is thus a multitude of channels that agricultural groups use in order to influence EU policy making, both domestically and at the EU level. Which strategy is chosen will depend on the concrete issue and 'at different stages of the process we target different people'. In principle, however, 'we'll basically lobby anybody who'll listen' (interview 12).

3.4.2 The impact of the involvement in EU policy making on CSOs

The last empirical question is whether or not the institutional environment of the EU affects the activities of CSOs and their interest representation strategies. It is not possible to dispute that the EU plays a major role for agricultural actors – indeed all actors agree that being involved in EU policy making affects the working of their organisation (*see* graph 10 in the appendix). The CAP obviously has a massive impact, by setting the legal and financial framework for farmers, and therefore also defines a good part of the daily agenda of agricultural interest groups:

> The CAP, and more broadly EU politics, defines to a very high degree our daily politics, our lobbying. Without it, not much is possible. The CAP is one of the rare policy areas where you have a truly integrated policy, where also a lot of money goes to, almost half of the EU budget. Therefore, to lobby for agricultural interests in a full sense without addressing and taking into account the EU does not work at all (interview 6; similarly interview 1; interview 2; interview 7).

While none of the agricultural organisations I investigated receive funding from the Commission for organisational purposes or projects, EU funding in the context of the CAP is obviously a massive incentive for farmers to engage with the EU and therefore is also very likely to have an impact on their work, in so far as they have to comply with EU regulation in order to receive EU funding.

A handful of (regional) actors (35.7 per cent) point out that their work is heavily influenced by the legal framework that the EU provides. Whereas some perceive the legal framework as over-regulation (interview 2), others, whilst sharing the perspective, also see the positive financial aspects for farmers if they comply with regulation (interview 1).

Finally, two actors (representing British and German farmers in their respective Brussels offices) point to another impact that being involved in EU affairs has had on agricultural organisations and farmers, over time, namely to help farmers to:

> understand that European agricultural policy is a bit more complex than national agricultural policy. That in itself is a high merit. That farmers understand that in exchange for what Europe gives us, we have to be ready to really compromise. That insight alone is worth its weight in gold. There simply is more appreciation, and that is a crucial aspect in my view. Our members get a broader understanding of European politics (interview 3; similarly interview 12).

3.4.3 The incentive structure for actors to engage with EU policy making

Positive and negative perceptions of the EU

Actors from agricultural groups overall tend to have a rather positive view of the EU: 50 per cent of them could only see advantages, 14.3 per cent only disadvantages and 35.7 per cent see both advantages and disadvantages. When looking at what actors mention as advantages and disadvantages, the former seem largely to outweigh the latter in substantive terms. In terms of positives, seven actors (50 per cent) mention the more general advantages that living in a common market has, economically:

> Farmers in Lower Saxony produce way too much for their population, so they are dependent on being able to export their products. And the huge part of their agricultural exports goes to other EU Member States. That's a huge advantage and much is accepted in exchange for that (interview 1).

Some of them are equally as appreciative of the EU's freedom of movement and the adjustment of living standards.

That the CAP exists is thought to be an advantage by 57.1 per cent: 'It's a blessing for farmers that Europe exists, that we have a CAP. ... It would be a catastrophe if instead we had national policies, an absolute catastrophe' (interview 6). For once, this positive assessment seems to be shared by British actors: 'We always felt that at a European level there was much more to be gained from an agricultural point of view of being involved in Europe' (interview 10). One EU-level actor puts it this way: 'It is our reason for existing. If the EU did not have advantages, then it would be difficult to justify our existence vis-à-vis our members' (interview 13).

Two actors additionally explicitly refer to legal aspects of a common framework:

It also means in terms of agriculture, from our perspective, on things like, as an example, animal health and welfare – if you have an integrated Europe, you know animal abuse doesn't recognise barriers or borders. So if you have a system that is more integrated and is working together, then you avoid problems maybe further down the line. And also if you think about it in terms of environmental stuff. If you look at water pollution issues, you know, whether it be rivers – for example – that might flow through numerous different countries, you're going to get a much better result in terms of improving water pollution by having an integrated approach through all of those countries than if each country has an individual approach (interview 12).

Nonetheless, the financial aspects of the CAP are obviously an important issue, even though not mentioned by many explicitly. One actor sees the financial advantages of the CAP in that 'the money from Brussels, once it's been decided, it's safe, safer than national funds, where governments may change or programmes may be cancelled because of cuts in the budget. So, from our perspective it's an advantage that once the EU has decided something, it's relatively safe, financially' (interview 8). Another actor mentions another beneficial financial aspect of the CAP: 'We certainly feel that being involved in Europe has actually benefited the agri-food industry in Northern Ireland on the basis that it's very much seen as a much more important industry at the European level than it was at the UK level' (interview 10).

Turning to the disadvantages coming from the EU, two general remarks were made. One relates to the lengthy policy process, which does not allow quick decisions (interview 14). The other focuses on the issue of the 'lowest common denominator' and the potential for domination:

Policy is a lot less focused because you have to take into account so many different views. I think that in some ways can isolate particular people or views or Member States, for example, who feel like their views are being dominated by other people, bigger people. I think it scares people – because people fear that they are going to lose their own nationality which they are generally very attached to. I think that it can be a cause for concern because people have different views on how things should be done and if they are sharing a common budget, for example, they feel like if things are not done their way the money is wasted (interview 12).

Two actors share similar concerns, yet focus less on issues of identity but on the nonsense that common solutions sometimes implies for farmers, given different regional climate conditions, products and markets (interview 1; interview 8). Other comments relating to legal aspects of the CAP focus on over-regulation and non-compliance respectively. As regards the former, one actor points out that in Europe 'we are over-regulated, and you can only ever get small successes in individual legislative proposals to try and push it back a bit' (interview 2). Two actors mention issues of non-compliance and, for once, British and German actors are united in complaining about the low level of compliance from French farmers:

> I think that we feel that sometimes the rules are not applied equally across the EU. For example, I think we feel that we comply with environmental regulation more, than say, the French do. If I drive down a French motorway I wonder: 'Where are their buffer strips? Where are their grass margins? Where are their hedgerows?' And so forth. All are things that we have to have – all sorts of regulations that we have to comply with that obviously aren't applied there. So I'm not sure that the laws are applied equally across Europe (interview 11; similarly interview 7 who notes that 'the French anyway don't do what the EU asks them to').

Differences in work environments

So far as differences in the work environment are concerned, three agricultural actors (two regional, one national, 21.4 per cent) find that it does not make any difference whether one is working at the regional, national or European level. Personal conversations and exchange are deemed important at no matter what level of governance (interview 6) and, in general, the working conditions and possibilities that are available are judged much the same (interview 9).

The large majority of agricultural actors, however, sees differences in the work environment, depending on the governance level. Of them, 35.7 per cent find that policy making gets more complex at the EU level. Mostly, this is perceived as being linked to national differences, both in mentality and culture, and in material interests. As a national actor based in Brussels points out: 'If you are working here in Brussels, you obviously need to understand different national mentalities' (interview 3). A regional actor explains:

> First, you have a multiplication of different interests throughout Europe. Then, second, there is the language. Linguistic (communication) difficulties are a huge problem. And then, third, you have cultural differences. If I only think of animal rights activists. In Germany, that is a huge topic. In other cultures, it's rather subordinate, e.g., bullfighting in Germany is almost impossible, whilst in Spain it is by and large accepted by the population. What we [Germans] have in terms of regulation in regard to animal rights, people in Greece or Southern Italy can only wonder at (interview 1; similarly interview 10; interview 12; interview 13).

One consequence of the described differences is that one has to:

> build partnerships, which is much more important. So that might be partnerships with other countries; it might be partnerships with other NGOs. So that's very important – I would say it's more important here than nationally. Because

otherwise you're seen as UK-centric, which is not necessarily a good place to be (interview 12).

Another difference in organising work, which results from the structural diversity between the EU Member States and the need to look for consensus, is that policy positions and formulations at the EU level are much more abstract, according to 35.7 per cent from across the different governance levels, than at the national, let alone regional, level: 'When we are in Munich, one can much more play the regional card. When one is in Brussels, everything of course is much more general, you have to put things in a broader way, because the affectedness is not as immediate' (interview 9). In consequence, it is deemed necessary to be 'much simpler in your communication' (interview 12).

Other remarks focus on other aspects which would make the two working environments different from one another: the strategic search for a majority in the EP (interview 1); EU policies being more reliable since they are not, as national policies, submitted to regular check by voters and therefore more stable (interview 3); and the difference between developing ideas and ultimately a policy at the EU level and implementing the policy – at a much later stage – at the domestic level (interview 11).

Is it easier or harder to be heard at the EU level than domestically?

As a result of the above-mentioned differences, a large majority of actors from agricultural organisations find it more difficult to have their voices heard at the EU level rather than domestically: 71.4 per cent think this is the case, 14.3 per cent say it's equally easy or difficult and another 14.3 per cent do not have an opinion on the issue (*see* graph 9 in the appendix). For half of them, and throughout levels of governance, what makes it more difficult is the multiplication of actors and interests, which renders lobbying more complex: 'There are so many interests represented here that sometimes in a meeting you have such a wide variety of stakeholders … it's sometimes a bit much' (interview 14). The multitude of actors calls for greater readiness to compromise: 'You have to compromise quite a bit and understand that you're not going to win on every topic' (interview 12). At the same time, knowledge of regional conditions and situations is often lacking at the EU level (interview 12). Indeed, two regional actors mention that the mere fact that Brussels is further away, which, in turn, means less regular contacts with officials and politicians, makes it more difficult to be heard there than domestically (interview 2).

An important way of being heard in Brussels is the European Commission's consultation regime. How do agricultural actors evaluate it? According to replies in the questionnaire, 35.7 per cent of the actors are either happy (14.3) or rather satisfied (21.4) with it. 57.2 per cent are rather unsatisfied (42.9) or unsatisfied (14.3) with it.[3] Those with a (rather) positive view find that 'it's fine the way it is. I would not know what to change. … We have every possibility of being involved' (interview 3;

---

3. The remaining 7.1 per cent do not know.

similarly interview 4). They are of the view that 'the European Commission itself is a much more accessible organisation than we would have with local government, for example. And generally they are ready to discuss things with you, have meetings with you, and hear your perspective' (interview 10). They also think that the Commission is offering real consultation (interview 10) and furthermore:

> believe this is working quite well for both sides. So I'm talking about the different kind of stakeholders on the one side that can hear what the Commission is working on and already express their views. And on the other side for the Commission, to test the waters – to see how is the reaction to a certain thing before you actually come out with the Communication (interview 14).

However, there also is some criticism of aspects of the Commission consultation regime and of online consultations in particular. Six actors (42.8 per cent, five regional, one national) criticise the lack of representativity of online consultations. On the one hand, this criticism relates to the different kinds of representativeness amongst the actors that participate in online consultations, for example, individual citizens, smaller and larger CSOs: 'In our view, it is a very questionable tool because the representativity is not assured and there is no weighting of the contributions, e.g., if we give our view, then we do it for 20,000 members, and if some NGO participates, then perhaps it speaks for twenty members. So we miss the weighting of contributions' (interview 2; similarly four other actors). On the other hand, the representativeness of the online consultations is questioned in a more general way:

> I'm asking myself whether these online consultations are representative. In one online consultation, I believe there were 6,000 participants. 6,000 – we have 500,000,000 citizens in the EU. So I am wondering whether this is not merely a pacifier, so that people have a playground, and afterwards it's being thrown in the bin and somehow roughly evaluated' (interview 8; similarly interview 2; interview 13; interview 14).

Another actor mentions similar as well as additional issues in regard to the online consultations:

> I think some of the consultation is just for the sake of it and they actually don't listen to the actual answers. I think sometimes it's just an exercise to tick a box rather than an exercise to get real benefits. It's an exercise to just say we've done it but they don't necessarily listen to what the results are in some cases. I also think that some of the consultations, particularly the online ones, ask the wrong questions. And it's difficult then to have the opportunity to ask the right questions and answer the right questions (interview 12).

Finally, three actors also point out that there are simply too many of these 'time-consuming' online consultations, and that it is therefore difficult to be involved in all of them (interview 1; interview 10; interview 13).

Constituency interest in the EU

It is not possible to dispute that the EU plays a major role for agricultural actors – indeed all interviewed actors agree that being involved in EU policy making affects the working of their organisation: 'It is very important for all farmers in Europe that they have a strong interest representation in Europe .... It would be bad if others would decide over our profession .... Then we would be externally driven, and that would be fatal' (interview 7). The CAP has a massive impact, by setting the legal and financial framework for farmers, and therefore also defines a good part of the daily agenda of agricultural interest groups:

> The CAP, and more broadly EU politics, defines to a very high degree our daily politics, our lobbying. Without it, not much is possible. The CAP is one of the rare policy areas where you have a truly integrated policy, where also a lot of money goes to, almost half of the EU budget. Therefore, to lobby for agricultural interests in a full sense without addressing and taking into account the EU does not work at all (interview 6).

Indeed, many actors point out that members regularly either bring up issues related to EU processes or participate in related discussions: 'That's permanently the case, daily business' (interview 2), and that EU policy processes are a regular topic at AGMs. In fact, five actors (35.7 per cent) note that the importance of the EU has increased over time: 'The EU has become more important, whether we like it or not' (interview 11). As a consequence, agricultural actors 'are probably putting more resources into Brussels now than we did and that's right and proper because there's more policy being decided. So you need more resource to keep on top of it' (interview 11).

In sum, it is clear that farmers have a lot to gain from being involved in EU policy making, and defending their material interests seems to be an important reason for their high degree of Europeanisation – an interpretation that is also mirrored in the fact that 100 per cent of them state that lobbying is a highly relevant aspect of their work at the EU level whilst only 28.6 per cent think that contributing to EU democracy is a highly relevant aspect of their work. The focus on representing their interests in the EU also became very clear in actors' perceptions of their role in the EU: two-thirds of them focus on lobbying and on making 'sure that farmers' voices and the voice of agricultural co-operatives are being heard in the European arena' (interview 14): 'It is very important for all farmers in Europe that they have a strong interest representation in Europe .... It would be very bad if others would decide over our profession .... Then we would be under alien control, and that would be fatal' (interview 7).

As we saw above, there are strong incentives for agricultural groups to be involved in EU affairs, given the legislative activity of the EU in the field and the CAP's budget (*see* graphs 11–16).Graph 3: Anti-poverty actors interviewed

Chapter Four

Representation by Environmental CSOs

At the start of this chapter, it seems useful to point out that in this chapter – as in the previous and the one that follows – it will mainly be the actors on the ground that will be given full attention. Whereas I have obviously structured the account and have added minimal information where this seemed necessary in order to understand what actors have said, I am not interpreting or analysing what actors say and do in this chapter, so as to keep their voices and my analysis clearly distinct. The analysis follows in Chapter Six.

4.1 The policy field and its main actors

Environmental policy comprises well over 500 directives, regulations and decisions adopted since the first directive on dangerous substances in 1967. It was not until the middle of the 1980s and the signing of the Single European Act in 1986 though, that economic and ecological objectives were put on a more equal footing within the Community.

EU environmental policy developed in response to international agreements, to increasing public attention and concern, to increasing awareness of the transnational nature of environmental challenges and to the Commission as a driving force. Initially, Community policy in this field concerned the harmonisation of product regulations to allow free movement of goods. However, the scope of EU action broadened to include water (e.g. water framework directive) and air pollution, noise, waste, the protection of natural habitats (e.g. habitats directive, birds directive) and amelioration of climate change. In addition to regulatory policies, the EU has also adopted a number of funding programmes for the environment. In 1997, the Treaty of Amsterdam furthermore recognised 'sustainable development' as a legal objective under the Treaties. The post-2008 economic crisis, however, has led to a marked decline in high-level policy interest in long-term policy objectives such as sustainable development.

EU environmental policy is shaped by a variety of actors including all of the main EU institutions – the European Commission, the Council and the European Parliament – as well as interest groups and sometimes academia. Member States shape EU environmental policy by working in the Council which co-legislates with the EP in the field of environmental policy. The EP is recognised to have become more important and so have MEPs: 'That counts for their reputation, their importance, in their constituency. That has fundamentally changed. Today, it is important who is in Brussels for a political party' (interview 25).

In the Commission, a full Directorate General for the environment has existed since 1981. Initially DG Environment was perceived as a relatively weak DG but it has gradually become more assertive through the development of technical and political expertise. As in the other two policy fields under study here, a wide range of participation and consultation instruments is in place in Directorate-General Environment of the European Commission. However, research indicates that while the Commission claims to be open towards the input of CSOs, it has a clear preference for expert and technical input (Hallstrom 2004; Pesendorfer 2006), so the level of participation by CSOs and citizens is relatively low (Persson 2007).

As early as 1974, environmental groups from all the Member States established a common representation in Brussels, founding the European Environmental Bureau (EEB). The EEB, some of the members of which have been interviewed for this study, is a federation of about 140 national environmental NGOs (which are often federations themselves). It gains a substantial amount of its income from EU subsidies. The EEB presents itself as a body that, besides campaigning, aims to generate knowledge, promote dialogue with EU institutions and, generally speaking, bargain and exchange information and knowledge in return for policy changes. Today, there are additionally a number of other large umbrella organisations with a representation in Brussels, such as Friends of the Earth, Bird Life International, Greenpeace, the World Wide Fund or the Climate Action Network. To some degree, they cooperate with each other under the head of a common umbrella structure – Green 10 – in order to influence EU policy.

This is the context of the policy field in which environmental groups today seek to defend their interests. Before we look at their understanding of representation and then their concrete practices of representation, let us briefly look at the actors I interviewed. In total, I interviewed nineteen environmental actors[1]. These comprise two actors from the European umbrella organisation; two representatives from two different English CSOs which are members of the European umbrella organisation; ten representatives from ten different German national peak organisations (including the one that is formally coordinating environmental CSOs' efforts in regard to the EU), all of which are members of the European umbrella organisation; and five regional representatives from organisations in five different regions in Germany.

Graph 2: Environmental actors interviewed

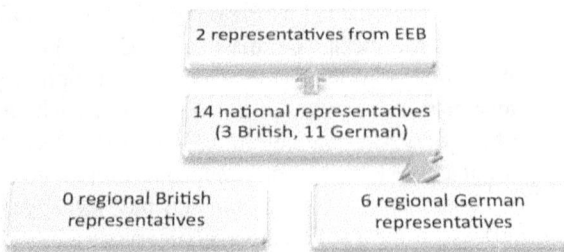

2 representatives from EEB

14 national representatives
(3 British, 11 German)

0 regional British representatives

6 regional German representatives

---

1.   These same nineteen interviewees plus an additional three actors accepted to fill the questionnaire.

4.2 Actors' understanding of representation

As in Chapter Three, I shall now address a number of issues that relate to environmental CSO actors' understanding of representation, such as: what is representation, in their view? Do they see themselves as representing a constituency or an issue? Do they perceive themselves as lobbyists or do they favour a more participatory approach that includes a perception of their role as more interactive? This question also relates to the issue of when actors think representation has been achieved – do groups seek the maximum output, which is influencing legislation or governmental policy programmes, or are they satisfied if they have influenced a discourse, or, less ambitious still, merely made their voices heard? Finally, how do actors conceive of the legitimacy of their activities – is it thought to be generated through input, by relevant constituencies, or through output, via expertise and/or achieved policies?

4.2.1 Representation of people or of an issue?

Actors in environmental groups mainly demonstrate two kinds of understanding of representation. One is that of representing *members*, the other that of representing a *public interest*, or, as some would put it, 'the environment'. Asked broadly about their understanding of representation, 40.9 per cent say they think of themselves as representing *members*. This response illustrates this perspective well: 'Our organisation is member-based, so our members are other environmental NGOs. ... So we are representing a collective view of what our NGO members want to work on collectively, to have a stronger voice, primarily in England, but also on particular issues in the EU' (interview 30). The proportion of those who say they are representing members increases to 63.6 per cent when interviewees are asked directly who or what it is that they are representing – rather than the broader question mentioned above. In total, members could mean organisations (9), individuals (9) or both (4), with individuals tending to be members of regional organisations, while national and European organisations tend to have organisations as members. At the European level, this can obviously amount to a rather high number of members: 'It represents its members. There are approximately 140 national or European or even – in smaller terms – local or regional organisations in the environmental field' (interview 32).

By contrast, 59.1 per cent of actors associate 'representation' with representing a *public interest*, with 31.8 per cent specifying this interest as the environment. This form of representation involves representing the 'interests of the general population to have a cleaner environment and the interests of future generations to have a sustainable economy and a sustainable way of living' (interview 17). To the extent this understanding is related to a constituency, it refers not merely to members but to the wider public: 'We see ourselves as representatives of the environment and of environmental interests, in the name of civil society, in particular our members, but also more generally' (interview 21; similarly interview 17). This is also illustrated by the fact that when asked who or what it is environmental actors represent, 45.5 per cent say 'the larger public' and 9.1 per cent 'the environment'. From such a perspective, interest representation is not as clear-cut as it is for agricultural groups, who exclusively focus on members. The claim that environmental groups may indeed (seek to) represent a quite diverse constituency that is much broader than their membership is well represented in this quote:

> I think we try to represent a broad range of interests. Particularly my organisation represents a broad range of stakeholders. On the one hand we are a typical NGO, we have members, we represent their views. But we're not particularly member-based. ... And then we have people who are not formal members of our organisation but are nevertheless very closely connected to it. So we are representing their views as well, but they're not paying members. But they might contribute to our organisation in other ways. And that's people from all walks of life. On the one hand, people you could refer to as the general public; on the other, quite a lot of academics are involved in our work – people from research institutes and think-tanks. We have people from ministries, from government involved, people from the Commission. And we are also trying to represent the views, I would certainly say, of some sectors of industry. ... And representing the views of other organisations as well that are affiliated with our organisation (interview 17).

Often, this kind of understanding of representation is associated with being the 'advocates' of nature or of the environment: 'In the end, we represent the interests of living areas and species' (interview 27). A couple of actors also mention representation as being in the interest of future generations: 'What we stand for is that biodiversity is also being secured for the coming generations' (interview 25). What is clear, then, is that *this* perspective conceives of representation as representing an issue rather than a constituency, even if organisations are member-based.

4.2.2 Achievement of representation

In regard to the perception of their role that the representatives of environmental groups have, the quotation above tells us that they do perceive themselves as being representatives – it is also rather difficult to engage in participatory processes with 'nature' or the environment. As the actors in agricultural groups, the representatives of environmental groups also primarily conceive of their activities as *lobbying*: 'Of course we also want to influence politics' (interview 12; similarly interview 24). One interviewee puts it like this:

> We have definitions of lobbying, which, I think, capture what we think of as representation. Presenting your arguments to somebody who is able to bring about an outcome that you desire. So representation is very much being able

to present your point of view to those people involved in the process of taking decisions that are relevant to your field of work (interview 31).

For 54.5 per cent, this role-perception implies that representation is achieved when legislation or a government programme has been influenced. Of course, sometimes this goal is 'achieved more and sometimes less, but it is our job to influence European legislation and to change it towards more protection of the environment and of nature' (interview 15). Successful representation, for many, is therefore only achieved if 'we've managed to get some kind of movement on a policy that we have been lobbying for. So if it was a bill, with certain amendments which we have lobbied for, for example' (interview 30). Others are even more outspoken: 'Representation is achieved when we advocate with the European institutions and then our positions are taken on board, and then what we say is incorporated' (interview 32). Indeed, influencing policy for many is the reason 'why we exist. I mean otherwise we would be an advertising agency or, I don't know, just put messages into the media' (interview 33).

However, 40.9 per cent of the environmental actors think that *influencing a discourse* equals having achieved representation. According to this view, representation is achieved 'when arguments are taken up' (interview 29). The EU co-ordinator of the German umbrella organisation reveals the lack of resources as the main reason why they cannot lobby in the same way as other groups: 'We are only a very few. We know of many member organisations which are really engaged in legislative work. We can't achieve that. We somehow work in a larger context. Try for specific Directives not to disappear from the Commission's agenda. Those are our main focuses' (interview 28). Therefore, the actors holding this perspective aim mainly at awareness-raising: 'One thing is, of course, if a position makes it into politics, or if, in discursive interaction with other actors with whom we network, there are co-productions and joint resolutions. If that is mirrored in legislative processes, that's good. But mainly it's about awareness-raising' (interview 18). Whilst ideally actors obviously wish to influence legislation, they still consider that this cannot always be achieved and therefore find that 'the minimum is an examination of the arguments which are being put forward by us' (interview 12). Even within legislative processes, it may sometimes 'mean you lose a vote. But if it's a lot tighter than it otherwise might have been then you have at least sent a signal' (interview 31). Thinking of representation as a discursive process seems to open the door to reflecting on the relationship with the wider public and wanting to interact with them and possibly persuade them. The ongoing, discursive nature of representation, interaction with the broader public and the desire to influence legislation come together well here:

If we have managed to be in the media and that so and so many recipients notice us, then we are present. Similarly, if we organise a demonstration, and we managed to get a certain number, not a hundred or a thousand, but at least ten thousand on the streets, then we have achieved that. The other thing is legislative processes, when we are being heard as experts, so when we have an official place in the debate, when our arguments are being listened to and find their way into the legislation. One cannot separate the one from the other. I think one's own position is more likely to be mirrored in legislation if one is perceived as being a strong player. So, if the BUND[2] manages to get 200,000 people on the streets, then it will be more likely to be invited to a hearing, and its argument will have a greater weight than if it was not as present in the public sphere. Therefore, I would not separate the two. Of course, our goal is always to change realities, and that is only done when the political goal is achieved. But in order to get there, in my view what is needed is representation on all levels (interview 26).

4.2.3 Legitimacy generation of representation

As we have seen above, 63.6 per cent say they are representing members when asked directly who they represent. It is therefore no surprise that a similar percentage – 59.1 per cent – states that the legitimacy of their representation derives from their members. As with the agricultural groups, this perception is based on a) the high level of organisation of interests in the field and b) the democratic mandate provided by the members; both can be found on all the different levels of governance. At the local/regional level,[3] an actor points out that they gain 'the legitimation through their numerous members – in Hamburg, we have almost 21,000 members' (interview 22). At the national level, one German organisation prides itself on having a large number of members: 'We are the largest member-based organisation in the field of the protection of nature in Germany, 500,000 members – that is a critical mass which legitimises us having our say in political processes (interview 21; similarly interview 25). Along the same lines, another national actor points out that their membership was much larger than that of the major political parties:

We have members that join – that pay to join the organisation. ... The number of members is over a million. That means we have more members than the top three political parties in the UK put together. So, your question was what makes you legitimate as an organisation? I think it's partly the membership (interview 31).

At the European – and even global – level as well, one can find a similar sort of reasoning:

We have a Friends of the Earth International, seventy-six member groups around the world. We have a kind of democratic decision-making process with

---

2. *Bund für Umwelt und Naturschutz in Deutschland* – one of the major environmental organisations in Germany.

3. Hamburg is both a city and a region.

all those groups, which gives us our legitimacy to speak on behalf of something between two and three million members around the world (interview 33).

The second element in this kind of legitimacy-generation is also frequently mentioned: actors point out that members are widely involved in the running of the organisation, that it was members who vote 'on new members and decide positions together' (interview 32). 'Well, the members – our members – are the ones that formulate policy and work on the lobbying. So we're a member-led organisation. So everything that we produce is signed off by the membership' (interview 30) – in fact so much that unanimity is required even at the European level:

> We do explain the EU processes and of course also recommend certain positions. But in principle, the last word is bottom-up. We are a translator between both levels … but our legitimation, our decision-making in the end comes from the bottom. In our Brussels office, nothing can be decided unless there is unanimity between all twenty-seven BirdLife partners, and we as NABU[4] also cannot do a thing if our regional members would be against it (interview 21).

As we have seen, there are actors who do not think of themselves primarily as representing a constituency but as representing an 'issue', the environment and the protection of nature, or the public interest more broadly. It therefore comes as no surprise that a significant number of actors – 40.9 per cent – think that their legitimacy derives a) from a public mandate or b) from the public feedback they receive. The first version of this interpretation is linked to the legal situation in Germany. A handful of actors point out that, by law, they had to be consulted and therefore were 'legally legitimated advocates of nature' (interview 27):

> We have in the discussion on the protection of nature and the environment the particularity in public law that it is recognised that the state alone is not the right advocate of the protection of nature and the environment. The state's recognition is, so to speak, an expression of the societal legitimation that environmental organisations can represent the interests of actors who cannot represent themselves, such as birds or types of habitat. And that is, as it were, the legitimation basis of the public interest. And we organise ourselves to represent these interests; that is, so to speak, the legitimation basis of the organisation (interview 22).

Some actors see their legitimacy as deriving from the more direct public feedback they receive, be it through the media, the internet, opinion polls or the mobilisation of large demonstrations:

---

4. Naturschutzbund Deutschland e.V. – one of the major environmental organisations in Germany – and German member of BirdLife International.

> We get our legitimation essentially from our activities receiving a certain feedback, mostly through the media, also directly via the internet, and that incites us to act in certain ways. Take the example of the 'environment zones'. Here we receive feedback that tells us that they are in the interest of a part of the public, and of that part which interests us (interview 23).

Other actors are slightly more tentative and reflective in their view on legitimacy-generation as deriving from public support:

> The broader public is more difficult – as an environmental organisation, we certainly lobby in the broader public interest. However, many do not perceive our activities in this way and would undoubtedly deny that we are representing their best interests. On the other hand, there is in the meantime a broader international and general consensus that Environmental Fiscal Reform is one vital policy instrument to make our society more sustainable and that without it, no economy can be 'greened' in the way experts and the international community are calling for. So our legitimacy could also be seen to come from this emerging consensus view (interview 17).

Finally, 45.4 per cent mention 'expertise' as that which confers legitimacy on their activities: 'I'd say because we have the competences we are doing it legitimately' (interview 18), whilst without the expertise 'we would get a legitimation problem' (interview 25). The expertise can have two sources. One is the expertise that actors gain through practical work in the context of projects (interview 27). Or the expertise can be scientific. Indeed, a number of environmental groups work closely with scientists so as to 'represent a scientific and academically correct approach' and use 'very strong academic arguments that have been developed to defend our position' (interview 17; similarly interview 31). In sum, 'science can be a source of legitimation' (interview 23) and can lead to a situation where 'we have huge influence solely because of our expertise' (interview 21). That the focus on scientific expertise can be in tension, to some degree, with legitimacy-generation through a democratic mandate given by the members is well acknowledged by this actor:

> It's a science-driven organisation, and so we base much of the advocacy on science. And of course what science tells us to do may be different from what our members are actively interested in, or particularly interested in. So there can be some – tension is the wrong word – but there can be some disparity between what our members would want us to do – or might even think we do – and what we actually do. I think that by-and-large, we're as clear as we can be with our members about what we do, and they buy into that on the basis of knowing what the organisation does (interview 31).

To be fair, it should be underlined that, in this case, the members of the organisation seem to be well aware that it is scientific expertise, and not a mandate from members, that drives the organisation's activities and still support the organisation nonetheless.

4.3 Organisational structures and processes of representation within CSOs

In this section, I am interested in the *practices* of representation within CSOs rather than, as in the previous section, in what actors *understand* by representation. Obviously, practices can be quite different from the more abstract understanding actors have of a certain issue, given there is a multitude of competing actors in the political arena and also a number of more structural, institutional and legal constraints on actors' behaviour and the realisation of their organisational goals. More concretely, I will be looking first at how the different groups involve their constituencies in the decision-making and internal governance of the organisation. This will involve addressing how issues get on to the agenda of organisations in the first place; how and where position-finding then occurs; how far members – or possibly constituencies which are not members – are involved in the authorisation and in the control of their representatives and what forms authorisation and control take; and how far existing constituencies are mobilised for activities beyond the internal governance of the organisation. Second, I will consider how far these organisations aim to mobilise a potential constituency, that is, the larger public, for their activities. Do environmental groups reach out to the public and seek to involve it in their activities? And do they seek to enlarge their constituency or do they mainly focus on their existing constituency?

4.3.1 Internal governance processes: agenda-setting, authorisation and control

How do issues get on to the agenda?

In regard to processes of agenda-setting, environmental actors also think that agenda-setting is mostly government- or environment-driven. When asked directly, only 13.6 per cent say that it is mostly members who define the agenda, whilst 77.3 per cent think that it is mostly defined by the government or environment and 4.5 per cent think that is entirely the case.[5] However, when looking at the qualitative data, the picture seems less clear and more actors suggest that members have a strong influence or that it is likely to be a mix of both external and internal inputs.

Those saying agenda-setting is government- or environment-driven tend to point to EU processes in particular. Along these lines, 'we first have to be informed, at all, that something is to be decided in Brussels, that something's coming up, and we have our umbrella organisations and our own offices in Brussels to let us know' (interview 21). At the EU level itself, staff are obviously concerned with EU processes, the timing of which is beyond their control:

> For example, debates on climate targets are very clearly driven by the EU
> agenda. Issues like CAP reform or EU budgets, discussion of the sustainability

---

5. One actor did not know (4.5 per cent).

of cohesion funds and structural funds, for example, are 100 per cent related to an EU agenda. And without the EU there would be no CAP to reform, we place that within a broader frame of food sovereignty – that's really the kind of legislative process that is driving our focus there (interview 33).

Actors who focus on agenda-setting as being driven by members repeatedly point out that it is the board that decides the agenda for the year: 'Issues emerge from the enlarged board, and sometimes are being proposed to the board by members' (interview 16; similarly interview 18). Others seem to have more of a mixture of ways for how agenda-setting occurs, even if it is, nonetheless, dominated by members:

It regularly happens that the individual member organisation says 'we would like you to organise this or that', so we try and take that into consideration. Second, we try to also take up issues that our umbrella organisation is working on, topics that are very much *en vogue*, in order to create synergies. And third, and very pragmatically, we also look at what worked well last year, e.g., an excursion which was already booked out 4–6 weeks in advance, so let's do it again because there is a real demand (interview 19).

At the EU level, information on this point is scarce but it is pointed out that it is the Annual General Meeting (AGM) of the organisation that adopts the work programme and, if something comes up in between AGMs, then that 'would be taken to the board' (interview 32), which consists of members, suggesting that members are pretty much in control of agenda-setting.

Half the actors suggest that agenda-setting is driven both by members and by factors outside the organisation. Many admit that the 'political agenda [of governments] dictates the issues to a certain degree' (interview 26, similarly interview 23).

Two actors point to different time horizons when talking about agenda-setting:

Both exist. … I have my long-term agenda, and break it down into mid-term and short-term goals. And the more the goals are short-term, the more they are of course defined by daily politics, which wants something, or does not want something, or does something that we don't want (interview 25; similarly interview 22).

Two other actors point out that whilst what is going on in politics – or in the EU in particular – sets the general framework of their activities, they themselves choose what to concern themselves with:

We decide as a group what we like to take positions on. We watch the news, we prepare, for example, every morning, a summary of what has happened in the press and political life. And then probably one of the more senior people in the organisation would take the lead to propose that we act on a particular development. And ... we would then discuss that with the steering committee (interview 17; similarly interview 15).

So, whilst it is the staffed office that proposes the issues that should be addressed, and issues are often government-driven, there is still some link to the organisation's members by means of having the proposition checked with the steering committee, which is drawn from the membership.

Structures and processes of developing policy positions, of authorisation and control

Let us now look at the processes of position-finding and of authorisation. Whether topics arrive on the agenda from outside the organisation or from within – as the urgency of the topic – can influence how the further position-finding process unfolds. Are there traces of both bottom-up and of top-down position-finding processes? Again, there are. Generally, the field of environmental groups is more diverse than that of agricultural groups. Many of them are not as systematically structured throughout the different governance levels and many of them are not organised under the same European umbrella structure, as there is more than one such.

All the organisations do have a democratic structure in place, in the sense that they have AGMs at which main policy positions are discussed and boards are elected:

> We decide everything democratically. Only a few days ago we had our AGM, it's called assembly of delegates. 300 delegates from Bavaria come together and define the political and substantial work, based on motions and drafts. And then it's voted, and the majority wins. This year almost everything was done by unanimity (interview 24).

Throughout the different governance levels, organisations have AGMs that have ultimate decision-making power and delegates from the respective governance levels are present. A national actor explains: 'Our members have the possibility to influence the policies of the BUND. We are a democratic organisation. Once a year we have an AGM where the regional organisations delegate members who can vote on the main lines of our work for the next year' (interview 26). As regards policy positions, actors consistently say that it is the federal or national level at which the main positions and guidelines are agreed – and where representatives in turn can be held to account. If something comes up in between the AGMs, then it is normally the staffed offices, sometimes in conjunction with the regional boards, that will take decisions. However, not all members want to contribute continuously to the organisation's activities or internal governance: 'I think part of that is what happens a lot in NGOs, that it is actually the elite that develops the position in any detail. I think it's often the case. Probably members would be welcome to provide input, but they don't. Simply because of time reasons – people are very busy' (interview 17).

How much of a democratic process there is beyond the basic AGM structure varies between organisations, even though the large majority seem not only to have additional democratic structures in place but also to use them regularly. In many instances, a bottom-up process is very much in place, across levels of governance, with 'a totally democratic structure where positions are being voted, committees elected, all by our local and district groups in principle. And therefore, our positions are defined by our members, not by other actors' (interview 21):

> It's like a Russian doll. So you have the federal level, in it you have, e.g. the *Land* of North-Rhine Westphalia, and in the *Land* you have fifty-four districts, and they themselves have their own organisations. And every level is responsible for itself, even though programmatically, what counts is what has been decided at the federal level, everyone below that is bound by that. ... And at each and every level, you have boards and AGMs, those are the committees where political decisions are made and where the boards are elected by the AGM (interview 25; similarly interview 22).

As with the agricultural groups, many of the environmental groups have specialised working groups that meet throughout the year and which gather experts who will do the main work on specific policy positions:

> So we have different working groups, and there are particular people within the organisation, so experts within the organisation on that particular policy area. There are seven working groups, and then we also have *ad hoc* working groups as well where we work on a particular issue for a short period of time (interview 30; similarly interview 22).

For two very large organisations in Germany, there are respectively up to nineteen or twenty such working groups, which meet regularly, often mirrored at the regional level. Once they have developed a position, that position must be legitimated by the board, on which, again, there are delegated members:

> Overall, our position-finding is accompanied by what we call a 'scientific advisory committee'. It's a committee that is made up of twenty working groups that deal with specific topics. And if we need a position ... then different working groups would develop a position and co-ordinate it between themselves. Then it would have to be co-ordinated with the federal headquarters and voted on by the federal board. ... These working groups consist of delegates from the regional associations. In each working group, there are at least sixteen people, who have been delegated from the different regional organisations. What matters is that they have the related expertise (interview 26; similarly interview 24).

The same working-group structure exists at the European level, where it consists of a policy officer from the staffed office and representatives from the member organisations:

> The policy officer would draft a paper, and in consultation with the members they would come to a position. There's one working group per work stream of the EEB. We have a working group on air quality, a working group on energy, a working group on chemical policy, a working group on waste policy (interview 32).

> …with the particularity that Member States send a delegate only to the working group(s) that are of interest to them, with the EEB paying for their attendance. The board of the EEB is similarly composed of members – one per country – and if something urgent needs to be decided outside the AGM, then it is the board that is consulted; otherwise, 'if it's not specific to the different policy areas, something comes up and it's not so radically different, then the working group would discuss things' (interview 32).

As for the agricultural groups, it is not always possible to use the democratic structures fully, for example, when decisions need to be taken urgently 'as was the case with the nuclear plant in Fukushima. All of a sudden there is something on the agenda which you could not have known a few months before. Here of course you have to be able to react *ad hoc*' (interview 26). In such instances, fewer actors are involved: 'If it's extremely *ad hoc* then only the federal organisation can react, and the federal board will take a decision. They can decide within days if necessary or even within hours. The federal level has the competence to take decisions, it can always react' (interview 25). In such instances, members cannot be consulted broadly but of course are involved through their delegates in the board. However, most organisations seem to have mechanisms in place to consult with their members, nonetheless: 'We have got mechanisms and the processes are in place so that we can get information out to the membership quickly to decide collectively whether they want to work on it' (interview 30).

Not all organisations follow entirely democratic processes throughout the year. Four organisations (18.2 per cent, one British, three German) stand out as not involving their members regularly between AGMs:

> In principle, members are not involved. There are exceptions, when a member organisation deals with a topic we are also dealing with. … Otherwise what we come up with is the position of the organisation, without us having to check it with everyone in the organisation (interview 15).

However, as the same actor points out, 'we do have a substantial basis for that which is discussed and adapted at the AGM and which tends to not change. We just don't discuss single positions in larger rounds in the organisation' (*ibid.*). So far as the British organisation is concerned, the actor says it is 'very uncommon' for members to be involved in the development of positions, in fact, it has 'never been raised': 'Generally it's done on the basis of science rather than on the basis of a sort of democratic procedure with our members' (interview 31; similarly interview 12).

Finally, it is again rather obvious that the headquarters of organisations always have a particular role to play; and not exclusively in emergency situations. For example, it is generally the staffed offices that will draft first proposals or motions, after consulting members and the managing director: 'The real expert work, the drafting of positions and the representation of the positions, that mainly and foremost happens in the headquarters' (interview 21; similarly interview 17; interview 23). However, that does not imply that members are not involved at all, as the staffed offices work in line with the main policy positions of the organisation and also need to get the legitimation of the board for their proposals:

> In principle, that's up to the staff of the headquarters. They know which positions the organisation holds on the big issues, so they decide in the framework of those defined positions what they say about a specific topic. And if it is important, then we also ask the board … so that there is an additional legitimation through the board (interview 21).

Therefore, if the main lines of positions are kept, the 'headquarters also has its own decision-making authority. Policy officers can decide jointly with the deputy director' (interview 26).

To control an organisation's activities, the same channels as for position-finding and authorisation are used. If members have questions or criticism, it is 'mainly at the AGM where they can voice it. But of course they can also get directly in touch with the board or the staffed offices of the district' (interview 23). At the AGM, there are delegates from all local groups 'which receive a yearly report of the president there, and where we report the most important developments of the year' (interview 27). AGMs are typically the opportunity for members to 'find out more about our departments and what's going on – that's their chance to hold the organisation to account' (interview 31).

Several actors suggest that control is likely not to function in traditional ways. Whilst their organisations also present a yearly report at their AGM, there is no belief 'that it ever happened that that was questioned' (interview 28). Another actor also points out that 'we don't usually experience, within our membership, a great deal of dispute. We don't produce positions that are very controversial. For people to be members of our organisation they believe in our general approach to the economy and environment' (interview 17). Two further actors say that the views of their supporters are not taken into consideration on a daily basis, but that 'we realise if we remove ourselves from them' (interview 23; interview 27). If there are issues coming up in between the AGMs, members could always send a letter or phone and:

> … we would always go out of our way to respond to that or take it into account. Or to then organise a discussion where they participated in a steering

group discussion about that issue and we discussed that all together – where we think we should be going and what we think the potential is to include the position. So I think we are very inclusive. It's just more that it doesn't happen much because members are quite happy to let us get on with it in a way (interview 17).

That control does not necessarily function exclusively or mainly as in electoral representation does not mean that it does not function: it may simply take other forms:

We try to be as responsive as possible to members in terms of giving them information about what we do. … We're always very conscious about trying to keep members informed and involved and try to respond to any questions they may have. Members can and do withdraw their membership if we do something that they disapprove of. RSPB just recently announced a partnership with a major supermarket chain in the UK – Tesco. And we were braced for losing many members and in the end we only lost a handful. So losing any member isn't brilliant but we go to great pains to make sure that what we do will not jar with what our members think (interview 31).

Furthermore, all of the organisations have websites and most of them produce newsletters or other publications, so that members can inform themselves about ongoing activities; it does 'happen every now and then that we are contacted directly by members "I read this and that and disagree". So, this possibility of direct intervention also exists' (interview 26). How far it leads to a reaction of the organisation 'very much depends on our assessment. It depends on what the substance of the criticism is. But in all cases will we look into it' (interview 26, similarly interview 15).

4.3.2 How do CSOs mobilise support?

Mobilisation of the existing constituency

Do the democratic structures that most of the environmental groups have in place correspond to a high degree of mobilisation of the constituencies, as we have seen for the agricultural groups? Not quite as much. 54 per cent state that they regularly mobilise their constituencies for their activities, 36.4 per cent say irregularly. For 9 per cent, this is rarely (4.5 per cent) or never (4.5 per cent) the case. The success at mobilising is very similar: 50 per cent say their constituencies let themselves be mobilised regularly, 36.4 per cent say this is irregularly the case, and in 13.6 per cent of the cases, it is rarely (9.1 per cent) or never (4.5 per cent) the case. What is the story behind these numbers?

Many actors mobilise their constituencies, not least because 'otherwise, we could not cope with things' (interview 16) and because 'that's our main work' (interview 19; similarly interview 22; interview 25). Mobilisation occurs across all levels of organisational governance, even though the focus of reaching out to members seems to be on the regional and local levels: 'It happens mostly at the municipal level, much less so at the regional, and still less at the federal level, because it's ever further away from the members' (interview 21).

Actors mention two kinds of mobilisation. One – likely to be the dominant form in reality though not mentioned often by interviewees – is the direct engagement with and for nature and the environment: 'We are concerned with the return of a certain animal to an area in which it used to live and does no longer. Here we need support, and they (the members, SK) get in touch with us about it. That's an example where it works' (interview 23). Another actor explains: 'It often starts with the "experience of nature", with bird-watching excursions, with presentations or some excursion, goes on with a practical assignment, practical protection of nature, all the way to political engagement. It first starts on the ground' (interview 21; similarly interview 22). One actor, referring to excursions, points out that the 'echo is so big, we can't really keep up … we simply can't cope. There's a really big demand' (interview 19).

The other kind of mobilisation is political mobilisation. Political mobilisation happens at all levels of governance and in different ways. Of course, not all local groups have a focus on lobbying or campaigning but most do get involved at least occasionally. One British actor says that 'at the moment we're actively trying to build up the involvement of members in political campaigning at the local level – trying to identify champions at the local level who will work with other local members to deliver activities in a more prolonged way' (interview 31). Some local actors are very active politically and indicate weekly pickets against nuclear power plants with between 30–150 people each throughout Germany (interview 24). Or they are lobbying parliament (interview 30). A third activity that seems quite common is to mobilise members for email campaigns. In fact, one actor says that most of the political mobilisation is 'online, petitions, where you sign in the net, for or against certain things' (interview 21). With RSPB, members can actually register:

> to be involved on the letter-writers list. So we have the campaigns team here who keep a list of members who have said they will write letters on issues of interest to the organisation. So once you are on that list you will receive letters saying: 'this issue is of concern to the RSPB. Please write a letter to your member of the European Parliament or member of parliament or local councillor to bring this issue to their attention.' So they can get involved that way (interview 31).

Other activities, mostly at the national level, include events with politicians and experts or larger demonstrations. One national actor mentions the preparations for the seventh EU environment framework programme as an example of member organisations being mobilised to participate in a workshop in order to develop a German position (interview 28). Another actor, referring to a European directive, says that 'jointly with the DNR and with a representative of the EP we have organised an event in order to see how members felt about it, what the tendency was, what the arguments were, whether it was worth developing another motion' (interview 16). Finally, if irregularly, there are demonstrations for which many of the organisations will try to mobilise their members: 'In January, there was this big demonstration in Berlin that was supported by many organisations, for the reform of the CAP. So we mobilised our members to go, and depending on the regional organisation, on the engagement in the local groups, they organised busses and went to Berlin' (interview 21). Another topic that mobilises members, as well as a larger public, in particular in Germany, are demonstrations against nuclear power plants (interview 26; interview 22).

At the EU level, mobilisation of members seems, foremost, to mean having them participate in the governance of the umbrella organisation, rather than regularly mobilising them politically: 'The EEB isn't principally a campaigning organisation, but we do run campaigns and we write letters or we have organisations sign up individually or use umbrella organisations as well. We sometimes use them, for example, for our press work' (interview 32).

Many representatives are quite positive about the success of their attempts to mobilise, particularly at the local and regional levels. A Bavarian actor points out that they are 'very, very well organised in that regard, and that within a very short period, and for a topic that really upsets – not all topics are easily transported – we can achieve quite some change in Bavaria' (interview 24). Referring to email campaigning, another actor says that 'we can count on several thousand letters going in to any response to a letter-writing campaign. And some of the bigger campaigns have had hundreds of thousands of signatures' (interview 31; similarly interview 19).

Others are a bit more hesitant and reflect social changes as well as barriers to the mobilisation of members. They notice that the engagement is not as great as it used to be (interview 23). Engagement more generally is observed to have changed over the years:

> You can't but notice that it has become more difficult to find people for more long-term, leading activities, who go into the board and who organise the organisation, that is more difficult now. The tendency to participate in activities, to help, however, is on the rise. So, the long-term liability decreases, but the spontaneous support increases (interview 25).

One actor suggests that people simply do not have enough time to become engaged:

> They are all too ... busy doing other things. They've got to work. They want to have some leisure time. They're all tired. They've got kids. And in the end this is why NGOs can still fulfil an important role, even though actually they're developing it all within an elite which is the staff and the board. But they aren't getting input from their members. But in a way, because their members as well are too busy to provide the input (interview 17).

A German local-level actor points out that they do try to mobilise their members but that 'possibly we are not as successful with it as others given the historical focus of our organisation has been the practical protection of the environment whilst lobbying and political intervention has been done by friendly organisations such as the BUND' (interview 22). Others mention the communication skills of local directors and the attractiveness of the programme as an incentive or disincentive to becoming engaged. Also, the age structure of local groups is an important factor: 'If you have a league of pensioners aged 60-plus, and you want to attract 20-year-olds, you've got some problems. So, it is also important to try and win young people who may need some action, and to include them as well in the activities' (interview 27). Finally, not all organisations are very large and, for some, the staffed office is simply too far away from members living in rural areas to be able to mobilise them regularly, particularly if members are living in a 'completely different world' to that of, for example, European Directives (interview 15). At the EU level, the mobilisation of members is said to have:

> ...varying success. I suppose not everybody is a member of the EEB for the same reason. Some are members because they want to get very involved in our work whereas some members want to receive information that we get here in Brussels. There are numerous different reasons. So not everybody would be responsive (interview 32).

Mobilisation of the wider public

I now address whether groups also seek to reach out to the larger public rather than merely to their existing constituency, that is, whether groups try to cultivate a relationship with the general public or not and, if they do, of what kind. Is it, for example, merely a matter of transmitting information or do groups seek to involve the wider public in debate or to mobilise it for activities? In order to answer these questions, I shall look at whether the groups inform the wider public about their positions and activities, particularly by making information available on their websites and entertaining relationships with the press; whether they try to mobilise a larger constituency, through more passive ways (becoming a member or donating money) or more actively, through online and street activities.

The necessity of engaging with a broader public is recognised at all levels of organisational governance. At the local/regional level, the need to acknowledge the wider public as well as other interests is recognised in a straightforward way: 'We are in a societal debate with others which of course we are trying to have. This means we do in part consider interests which are opposite but which we nonetheless hold to be legitimate' (interview 22).

At the European level, the need to enter a dialogue with the larger public is also acknowledged, yet the lack of a European demos seems to render the ambition more difficult: 'I don't think they matter less. But I think we have fewer ways of directly engaging the public' (interview 33).

Most of the environmental organisations seem to entertain an active relationship with the press. The vast majority, 86.3 per cent, explicitly address the press on their website whilst 13.6 per cent do not. Indeed, the press and other media work is intended to bring issues and positions to a larger public and also to exert a certain amount of political pressure: 'We use the public level in order to exert a certain public pressure, via media coverage' (interview 25), as it's 'important that we represent our cause in the street, in public activities as in the media' (interview 26), and it is claimed that also at the 'European level the media work that we do would certainly bring our issues to a quite broad European public' (interview 33).

How do environmental groups reach out to the public? To begin with, all 'cause' groups assessed here have a website. To have a website is today acknowledged as the main channel for reaching out both to members and the wider public: 'We have a quite well visited website and it's aimed mainly at EU decision-makers, but I think we reach quite a broad public actually with that. And that's probably the main way, both via the website and online communication, that's the way in which we directly would reach members of the European public' (interview 33).

Some 54.5 per cent of the organisations studied here additionally use social media to reach out to a larger public:

We try to use Facebook. But we don't have the capacity to do that in a big way as yet. We don't do enough on social media, I think it's safe to say. That's something that you need quite a lot of time for, and it would be nice to have a PR person working full-time for us, but we can't afford that at the moment (interview 17).

Others, namely 45.5 per cent of the investigated groups, are not doing social media (yet) as this regional actor points out: 'What we don't have yet is Facebook. Social networks, which are targeting more direct interaction with the members, that's still on our to-do list' (interview 22).

Newsletters and/or briefing notes for interested citizens are offered by 77.3 per cent of the groups whilst 22.7 per cent do not do this. We find exactly the same numbers for the availability of policy statements: 77.3 per cent have them on their websites, 22.7 per cent do not. Besides these means of reaching out to the public, there are additional ones: 'Through some of the materials we produce, I think that also reaches quite a significant number of people, whether that's directly through having a campaign leaflet or postcard in your hand or being a report' (interview 33).

Do CSOs also seek to involve the larger public in some of their activities? Of the organisations investigated, 81.8 per cent invite individuals, on their websites, to become a member of the organisation whilst 18.2 per cent do not. 54.5 per cent of the actors mention, in the interview, that their organisation deploys active recruitment strategies to get new members. This happens in a variety of ways, not least by speaking to people directly (interview 17; interview 19; interview 21; interview 24; interview 25; interview 26; interview 27). Another oft-reported strategy is to try to recruit new members at public events such as conferences, workshops, lecturers or stalls at markets (interview 19; interview 21; interview 24; interview 25; interview 26; interview 31). Some of the actors also mention their webpage as a means of recruiting new members (interview 21; interview 25; interview 16; interview 12). Finally, a number of organisations (22.7 per cent) engage in door-to-door, semi-professional recruitment, often done by (paid) students (interview 24; interview 25; interview 26; interview 31; interview 29). Slightly under half (45.5 per cent) of the 'cause' organisations say they are not pursuing active recruitment strategies. This seems to be particularly the case for national umbrella organisations, which typically have regional groups as their members, rather than individuals (interview 18; interview 23). Another, comparatively passive, way of supporting a group is donating money. This possibility of support is offered by 77.3 per cent on their websites.

What about more active forms of supporting the cause of an organisation? More than half (54.5 per cent) of the groups invite the public – as well as existing members of course – to participate in campaigns, sign petitions, write letters or emails or go on demonstrations; for 45.5 per cent, this is not the case. Examples that actors mention are demonstrations for reform of the Common Agricultural Policy (interview 21) or against nuclear energy (interview 22; interview 26; interview 24). Visitors to the website are invited to post a blog by 9.1 per cent of the organisations. Inviting the public to events such as workshops, conferences or public lectures is another way of interacting with it; 68.2 per cent of the organisations offer this form of interaction whilst 31.8 per cent do not. Such events may be more on the lobbying side of things, for example, when there is an event with MEPs and other politicians to discuss some European Directive (interview 16); or they may be more local in nature, such as when a group organises 'neighbours' water days', at which locals get engaged in improving the quality of river water (interview 22). Finally, a clear majority – 59.1 per cent of the groups investigated – offer the opportunity to volunteer in their organisation whilst 40.9 per cent of the cases do not.

4.4 Interest representation strategies in EU policy making

Whilst the last section allowed us to see how representative CSOs are of their constituency, this section will show the activities of representation through which environmental actors represent their constituency in EU policy making. To do so, I will first look at their degree of Europeanisation as defined in Chapter 2.4. The main part of this section concerns the addressees of environmental actors in EU policy making as well as the latter's strategies for addressing them. CSOs can use a multitude of channels for this. They may, first and foremost, try to lobby their relevant national ministries in the hope of thereby influencing Council decisions. They can lobby national MPs or MEPs, the latter in particular, since the EP is now involved in almost all European legislation by way of the co-decision procedure. They might address the European Commission directly and seek to influence legislative proposals in their very early stages. They might join forces and organise themselves under the head of a national and European umbrella organisation, in order to have a stronger voice vis-à-vis national and European institutions. Special attention will be given to this particular strategy so as to evaluate whether groups themselves see an added value in co-operating with other groups in order to influence EU policies and, specifically, whether groups co-operate both at the national *and* at the European level. Only if European-level co-operation happens could co-operation be taken as contributing to the emergence of a European *demos*, as is discussed in parts of the interested literature. If groups only co-operate with other groups from the same Member State, this would suggest that national differences between them, even within the same policy field, remain too great for stronger European co-ordination.

In a next step, I address whether being involved in EU policy making has an impact on environmental organisations. This is relevant as it can give hints at why actors may be more or less engaged but also whether being involved in EU policy making distances the organisations from their constituencies in one way or another. Finally, some of the CSOs might consider going to the European Court of Justice if they felt a legal injustice that needed to be corrected had occurred. Or, indeed, they might use all these different channels in their efforts to influence policies. This section will explore the ways CSOs use these different channels, with a focus on the political (rather than the judicial) institutions and the lobby strategies actors associate with them and with special attention given to European umbrella organisations.

The chapter closes by looking at the incentive structure for environmental actors to get engaged with the EU, as perceived by the actors themselves, thereby providing clues for the explanation of their engagement with the EU. This will involve exploring actors' perceptions of what are the positives and negatives coming from the EU; of differences in the work environments between the EU and their domestic environment; and of whether they find it easier or harder to be heard at the EU level than domestically. As regards the latter point, specific attention will be paid to the European Commission's consultation regime. It is relevant insofar as the Commission is not only the initiator of legislation in the EU and therefore a central actor. It has also developed a number of consultation and participation opportunities specifically for CSOs over the last fifteen years or so. It is helpful to know how far these are accepted by CSOs because satisfaction with the Commission's consultation regime may be a strong incentive to become involved in EU policy making, whilst dissatisfaction with it may be a strong disincentive. I will end by addressing the degree to which, as a consequence, the environmental constituency has been interested in EU affairs.

4.4.1 To whom are representing activities addressed and by what strategies?

Addressing the above questions, I will, by and large, draw on the qualitative data. Where informative, I will supplement that data by quantitative data from the questionnaire in which I asked actors to qualify how important they thought it was to be in touch with specific actors in regard to EU affairs.

Degree of Europeanisation

There are comparatively strong legal incentives for environmental groups to be involved in EU affairs. To a large degree, this is reflected in their degree of Europeanisation. When asked what importance dealing with EU processes had in their organisation, 35 per cent think it is high, 45 per cent medium and 20 per cent low. Second, when I asked whether the EU is an issue in their daily work, 50 per cent say the EU regularly is an issue in their own work, 20 per cent say irregularly and 30 per cent rarely. More concretely, 68.2 per cent of environmental actors think that lobbying is highly relevant in their EU-related work (against 90.9 per cent in the domestic context), 77.3 per cent consider networking highly relevant in that context (against 86.4 per cent in the national context) and 68.2 per cent find that exchange and information are highly relevant in the EU-context (77.3 per cent in the domestic context). Third, when I asked how important it is to be present in Brussels in order to achieve their organisational goals, 36.4 per cent think it is very important and 54.5 per cent rather important. Only 9 per cent think it is rather unimportant (4.5 per cent) or not important (4.5 per cent). Finally, I looked at the organisations' websites and checked whether or not they reported about EU policies. If they do, then that indicates that EU policies and informing about them are important to the organisation and *vice versa*. The result is that 68.2 per cent communicate about EU policies and related activities and 31.8 per cent do not (*see* graph 4 in the appendix).

The domestic level[6]

When seeking to influence policies, groups often form *alliances* with other groups in order to exert stronger pressure on those they are lobbying. Is this also the case for environmental groups? Most of the actors mention other, mainly environmental, groups as co-operation partners, with four of them using the term 'network':

> What we do very intensively is to work in networks. Networks with stakeholders, with citizen initiatives, but also with business. In part we do tough campaigns for or against something, but we also have different networks where we bring people together who normally don't talk with each other in order to find solutions (interview 23).

When asked directly, in the questionnaire, how important co-operating with other national NGOs is in influencing EU policies, 54.5 per cent say 'very important' and 29.6 per cent 'rather important'.

So far as *intra-organisational lobbying strategies* are concerned, the situation is more complicated than with agricultural groups. That is because there is no national umbrella organisation for British environmental groups (interview 30), as there is in Germany; but even in Germany, not all of the members of the EEB

---

6.   For the domestic and the European levels, *see* graphs 5 and 6 in the appendix.

are members of the national umbrella. As a result, only 25 per cent of all regional and national actors say, when asked openly, that they use the national umbrella to influence EU policies; whilst for 75 per cent, this possibility does not come to mind. When asked directly in the questionnaire, 43.8 per cent of the German actors say their contact with the national umbrella organisation is either 'strong and regular' (18.8 per cent) or 'rather strong if irregular' (25 per cent). However, 31.3 per cent say their contact is 'weak and rare' and 25 per cent have no contact at all.

Indeed, only for a very few actors does contact with the national umbrella seem to be very intense: 'NABU is very active in the DNR. So, e.g., when an EU Commissioner comes to Berlin, then it's mostly the DNR who will organise the meeting, and the top people of the different environment organisations will go there, and the DNR co-ordinates it' (interview 21). Another actor says that their 'Berlin office also works with DNR on European positions. We go to meetings together with the DNR in Europe sometimes' (interview 17).

For many actors, the link they have with the DNR seems to be rather weak or indeed non-existent. Interestingly, one actor thinks that the 'DNR does not do a lot, in Brussels', and so co-operation depends on the issue (interview 25). Another actor points out that for the issues that are of interest to his organisation, people from other organisations would be more active: 'If we want to achieve something at the EU level, then we get in touch with the NABU people, who in part work in the office of BirdLife International in Brussels. Activities of the DNR in this context we can hardly see' (interview 27).

Others do not seem to work with the DNR at all. One actor, when asked about the national umbrella organisation, does not link that to the DNR but to the headquarters of his own organisation (interview 19). Another one indicates that they are not using either the national (of whose existence he was not even aware) or the European umbrella structures but would be in touch directly with EU officials when the need arose (interview 12). A third says that 'the idea would not even come to mind to do something jointly with the DNR', when engaging with EU affairs (interview 22). Two actors, finally, point out that their organisations are not members of the DNR (interview 18, interview 23), with one of them having withdrawn because of 'political twists about the organisation and the relationship of the organisation with its different member organisations' (interview 23). As regards satisfaction with the work of the national umbrella, 18.2 per cent are happy with it and 27.3 per cent rather satisfied; 4.5 per cent are rather unsatisfied whilst 40.9 per cent do not know. This last number is so high because the British environmental groups are not organised under a national umbrella.

As regards national institutions, 25 per cent of the environmental actors mention that they are in touch with the regional ministries when seeking to influence EU policies. Again, this is exclusively the case for German actors: 'I have my regional government which is active in Brussels, and I try to influence the ministers in charge so that they become active along our positions in Brussels, in line with their competences' (interview 25). If not directly in Brussels, regional governments can also try to influence the national government through the second chamber, in Germany:

> Then there is the *Bundesrat* where the region of North-Rhine Westphalia started an initiative, with regard to the Life Plus programme, to reach a decision of the *Bundesrat*. That decision in fact was pretty much in line with our position, and North-Rhine Westphalia succeeded to pass it through the *Bundesrat* in a slightly milder version and thereby gave a mandate to the federal government to intervene in a specific way (*ibid.*).

Of the environmental actors, 60 per cent mention their respective national ministries as a venue for influencing EU policies when asked openly, whilst 40 per cent do not. Again, this stands in contrast to the replies in the questionnaires where, when asked directly, 50 per cent of the environmental actors reply that national ministries are 'very important' in influencing EU policies, and 40.9 per cent say they are 'rather important'. A national actor explains:

> Once the Commission has put forward its initiative …, and everything has been passed on to the Council and the European Parliament, then we are under even more pressure, at the national level. Then we have to develop a specific strategy for how to get the federal government to conduct the negotiations as we would like them to (interview 21).

Others pursue national channels because they believe their chances of lobbying successfully in Brussels are low:

> When compared with the well resourced lobbyists in Brussels, we are extremely small there. If taking the EEB, BirdLife and our two staff there together, then perhaps one ends up with two dozen people. As regards lobbying in Brussels, that is nothing. Therefore, one of course does not have the kind of influence others have on that level. So one has to compensate for that somehow by influencing the direction of national politics (interview 22).

The need to be present in the national capitals is also felt by a European actor:

> I think that interplay between Brussels and the capital is something where, in terms of strategic choice about where you put the weight of your involvement – you can't lose sight of the capitals, because so many decisions are made by the Council, which is obviously trying to follow national priorities which are quite hard to influence from Brussels (interview 33).

Surprisingly, none of the environmental actors mention MPs as addressees of their EU lobbying activities when asked openly. However, when asked directly in the questionnaire, 31.8 per cent say that MPs are 'very important' in that regard, 54.5 per cent 'rather important' and 13.6 per cent 'rather unimportant'.

The EU level

As regards European venues for influencing EU politics, reaching out to one's own office in Brussels is an option available for only a minority of the environmental actors – only 25 per cent say they do so when asked openly. This is likely linked to the fact that most of the organisations do not have their own representation in Brussels.

Another possibility for influencing EU politics is to be organised under the framework of a European umbrella organisation – all the contacted organisations are members of the European Environmental Bureau (EEB). When asked openly, 50 per cent of the environmental actors mention the EEB as of interest here, whilst 50 per cent do not. This is rather well reflected in the data of the questionnaire, in which 50 per cent say their contact with the EEB is 'strong and regular' (25 per cent) or 'rather strong if irregular' (25 per cent), whilst for 50 per cent, the contact is either 'weak and rare' (25 per cent) or there is 'no link' (25 per cent) (*see* graph 7 in the appendix).

Where the link is strong, therefore, actors point out 'that we work closely with the EEB on a lot of these topics – on the Energy Tax Directive, for example' (interview 17), that they work with them 'a great deal' (interview 31) and that 'amongst the European NGOs we are very strongly connected to the EEB' (interview 28). As the policy officer co-ordinating EU affairs in the German umbrella organisation points out, they also seek to involve their members in the work of the EEB:

> The EEB is the largest environmental umbrella organisation in Europe, it has members in almost all the Member States. … It is of absolutely great relevance, and we, e.g. do a learning and lobbying trip to Brussels once a year in order to show our German member organisations how important Brussels is, and to be in touch with people and develop networks (interview 28).

Other actors focus on the strategic relevance of being represented by a European umbrella organisation:

> There are lots of discussions on whether it is rational to try and be more present at the EU level, in order to be the 5001st lobby group, or whether it is not more rational to influence the German position in Brussels via lobbying in Berlin. I tend to opt for the latter. … We are more successful back home because we know the people here. Our networks are simply much more intense here than in Brussels, and we can't afford to be really good there. Therefore we are a member of the European umbrella, that is a middle way (interview 23).

Some actors mention their involvement in working groups of the EEB (interview 15; interview 17; interview 31), in which they meet 'twice a year, with other European NGOs, in order to develop common positions and joint publications' (interview 15).

For others, the contact with the European umbrella is weaker (25 per cent) or even non-existent (25 per cent). It is regional or smaller national organisations that are likely to have hardly any or no contact at all. At the regional level, actors tend to point out that they themselves have no contact with the EEB and that it is colleagues from their own federal organisation who entertain those contacts: 'Our expert in Brussels, he is really well connected there, and when it comes down to co-operating with the EEB which we do, e.g., on issues of transport, then it's the federal organisation who's in charge of it' (interview 22; similarly interview 25). Regional actors, in contrast, 'personally have nothing to do with them' (interview 27).

There are also two German federal actors (from smaller organisations) who say that they have no contact whatsoever with the EEB (interview 16; interview 18). Another federal actor points out that the connection is 'extremely loose' and varies from issue to issue. From time to time, the EEB gets in touch when it wants to develop a view on a particular topic but the relationship would not be very close and, in any case, the EEB would not say 'this is the goal we wish to achieve, and now let's find out whether members can support it and help to reach it' (interview 12).

However, even if there are some organisations for whom the link to the EEB is weak or non-existent this does not mean that they are not engaged in EU affairs at all. Indeed, 65 per cent point out that 'we are not active there [in the EEB], we are active in other organisations' (interview 18). More often than not, and both in Britain and Germany, actors are referring to BirdLife International as their primary European umbrella structure. This is not surprising, given that I interviewed several of the regional member organisations of the German organisation NABU, which has recently decided to be a member of BirdLife, rather than of the EEB. A German policy officer of NABU explains that BirdLife had greater capacity in their own primary field of interest: 'BirdLife has much more capacity in Brussels than the EEB so far as biodiversity and the protection of nature are concerned. The EEB also covers other issues which BirdLife does not cover. ... So depending on the issue, one would use different European umbrella structures' (interview 21; similarly interview 29). The same actor points out that there exists an important structural difference between the two umbrellas:

BirdLife has only one partner in every Member State, in Germany that's NABU. The EEB has many member organisations in every Member State. It is a huge network which is composed of many large and small organisations, it has many more members, and therefore is a much heavier structure. The EEB decides a lot more on its own, simply because it cannot easily consult its members all of the time, because there are so many of them, whilst BirdLife has exactly twenty-seven member organisations in twenty-seven Member States that you can consult rather quickly. So BirdLife is a bit more powerful in regard to its issues, I would say (interview 21).

European umbrella structures other than BirdLife International mentioned by the interviewees are Friends of the Earth Europe (mentioned twice) and Transport and Environment, Climate Action Network, Civilscape, Via Campesina, World Wildlife Fund and Greenpeace, each mentioned once respectively.

These mixed results in terms of links to the European level – either direct or through the national umbrella where it exists – are mirrored in the degree of satisfaction with representation by the EEB: 60 per cent are either happy (30 per cent) or rather satisfied (30 per cent), whilst 10 per cent are unsatisfied and another 30 per cent do not know because they had no contact with the European umbrella (*see* graph 8 in the appendix).

It is people who are in touch a lot with the EEB who tend to be (very) satisfied with the work the EEB does: 'I'm very happy with the way the EEB represents the interests of environmental NGOs generally, as well as our interests. For example on the Energy Efficiency Directive – they've done loads of good work on that' (interview 17). Quite rationally, one actor argues that they 'are paying member fees regularly. We would not do that, after all, if we thought that was lost money' (interview 23). He adds that it is really good 'to have people there who are knowledgeable about the EU, given its complexity' (*ibid.*). A British actor points out that the 'EEB does a very good job at circulating information on what's going on at the Brussels level and also getting people engaged in lobbying' (interview 31). A couple of actors reflect on the self-interest of national members in being represented: 'Absolutely. I am the German member of the board of EEB, so it's my job to make sure that the EEB represents the German organisations and me' (interview 28). Or, from another perspective, 'what the EEB then does for us, in that sense, is that we gain a higher profile as well because we work with them together' (interview 17).

Others are more critical in their evaluation of the EEB. However, it should be pointed out that the following criticism comes from an actor who is not personally in touch with EEB, at all: 'Sometimes, of late, we get the feeling that things have not been handled the way they should have been. This is also linked to the EEB receiving lots of money from the Commission and not being as pugnacious as we'd like them to be' (interview 24), a consequence being that 'things that are important to us are not being dealt with as intensively as we would like them to be'. Another actor points out that they had not been very successful in co-operating with the EEB, because of 'how the EEB is run', and therefore would now prefer other lobbying via channels:

Their communication back to their members is not very … it's quite hard to input into the EEB process because of the way that they are set up. So it's easier for us, even though we would be more successful if we went through a known voice like EEB, it's easier for us to go directly to the person that we are trying to lobby, or the organisation that we are trying to lobby. … I think that for national organisations in the UK that are members of the EEB that's probably quite a common position, that people don't use them that much because of …

Well, I don't think their communication is very good – it's very hard to know what they're doing and what's going on. So we do a lot of work on CAP but I don't know what the EEB is doing on CAP reform because I don't get any information about it. So it's more a communication problem I think. Without them communicating to their members what they are doing, it's hard to then be able to input into what they are doing (interview 30).

Three regional actors, finally, cannot tell how well they are or feel represented by the EEB – they simply do not know, because there is no contact: 'I could not tell you because I am not following it. It does not have any importance for me' (interview 25; similarly interview 22; interview 27).

As regards the European Commission, 65 per cent say that they address it directly to try to influence EU policies, whilst 35 per cent do not mention it when asked openly. When asked directly in the questionnaire, 45.5 per cent deem the contact with the Commission 'very important', whilst 27.3 per cent think of it as 'rather important' and 27.3 per cent as 'rather unimportant'.

Where contacts are irregular or rare, they tend to be very much related to concrete policies or policy proposals rather than environmental actors being part of a systematic kind of exchange as, for example, in advisory committees, hearings or consultations. In such cases, actors report that Commission officials have come to their region to get information or participate in debates or that they have met them at events in Brussels (interview 15; interview 22; interview 27; interview 30). Some actors, however, have no contacts with the Commission, at all (interview 16; interview 19).

Where there is regular contact, at the regional level, two actors report regular contacts with Commission officials and four venues are mentioned by them. The first is contacts on a working level (interview 24). The second is participation in online consultations that the Commission organises (interview 24). The third venue is proceedings for failure to fulfil an obligation, when actors mobilise for the Commission to sue a Member State and therefore have bilateral contacts with Commission officials. And the fourth is events in the official representations of German *Länder* in Brussels, which tend to be attended by regional ministers and high-ranked Commission officials (interview 25).

At the national level, actors make use of the full range of possible contacts with Commission officials. Firstly, most actors have direct bilateral contacts, both on the working and the political level (interview 12; interview 23; interview 26; interview 28; interview 17; interview 31). Sometimes, this will actually be initiated by the Commission, which receives complaints from citizens but does not have the resources to assess the issue on the spot. In such cases, it might ask environmental organisations, which will then ask their regional organisations, which will then report back (interview 21; similarly interview 23). Secondly, national actors participate in or themselves organise events such as workshops or conferences (interview 12; interview 23; interview 17; interview 31). Third, some actors mention direct and/or online consultations that the Commission organises for stakeholders: 'If you only start being in touch once the Commission has started an online consultation, then it's more often than not too late. You have to be more active than that' (interview 21; interview 26; interview 23; interview 31). Fourth, one national actor mentions advisory committees to which the Commission invites stakeholders (interview 21). Finally, many of those who want to protect the environment 'see the EU and the Commission as an ally, often against their own government', when envisaging whether to call on the Court of Justice of the European Union (interview 21). So if 'certain deadlines are not met, then you have, as a consequence, a proceeding for failure to fulfil an obligation. And if those are not initiated by the Commission, then we potentially get in touch with the Commission and ask them about it' (interview 23). Therefore, there is 'this sort of ping-pong game between Brussels and Berlin, which, in part, is mastered quite well' (interview 28).

At the European level, the contacts are, of course, very intensive and exist at all the different working and political levels as well as throughout the different venues described above:

> Probably at all levels. From Barroso down to where there's an internal desk officer. So the higher level staff right the way down to going for a coffee with some junior member of whichever unit you're trying to get information out of or get positions into. And everywhere in-between, heads of units – quite extensive. And across several DGs as well (interview 33; similarly interview 32).

So far as contacts with MEPs are concerned, when asked openly in interview, 40 per cent of the environmental actors mention MEPs as one channel of their EU-lobbying activities whilst 60 per cent do not. These figures stand in contrast to actors' evaluation of the importance of lobbying MEPs: 54.5 per cent, in the questionnaire, reply that it is 'very important' to lobby MEPs, with 22.7 per cent finding this channel 'rather important'. In contrast, 22.7 per cent think it is 'rather unimportant' to lobby MEPs in EU affairs.

Those actors who do have regular contacts, both regional and national, are mainly in touch with their regional MEPs, and meet them in their constituencies, but also simply send them information about their policy positions (interview 24; interview 25; interview 30). The EU co-ordinator of the German umbrella organisation points out that they organise 'learning and lobbying' trips to the EP, which the EP partly subsidises (interview 28). Another national actor says their organisation participates in a range of EP committees (interview 31). This is clearly also the case at the European level, as this actor working for the European umbrella testifies:

> So the EEB would have contact with MEPs, their assistants, the secretariats of the different groups, the secretariats of the different committees, in some cases the officers of the different vice-presidents, the vice-presidents relevant to the different areas that we work on. So numerous contacts, and they are contacts that we use often (interview 32).

For others, contacts with MEPs are more rare (interview 21; interview 27). Still, there seems to be an increasing awareness of the increased importance of MEPs, leading actors to develop multi-level strategies to pursue their aims:

> As regards the MEPs, we try and mobilise our local and regional groups increasingly. We seek to address MEPs in two ways. On the one hand, our colleagues in Brussels meet them. On the other hand, and at the same time, we try to get our regional groups to meet the MEPs in their constituency, on the same issues, because perhaps they are more open-minded there than in Brussels. So it's always a rather complex strategy, but we always try and harmonise our position across levels of governance and to be coherent (interview 21; similarly interview 24; interview 25; interview 30).

The Council, finally, is mentioned by 18.2 per cent. As pointed out above, actors stress that they mostly lobby their own government and minister 'back home'.

There is thus a multitude of channels that environmental groups use in order to influence EU policy making, both domestically and at the EU level. Precisely which strategy is chosen will depend on the concrete issue. In the end, as one actor puts it very clearly,

> Everybody is lobbying everybody, that's how you have to think about it. Even while the Commission is formulating proposals; even if it's not formulating a proposal, it's being lobbied by the European Parliament – either to make it in their interests or to do something when they're not. ... Everybody's constantly lobbying everybody – including NGOs lobbying other NGOs and the industry lobbying other NGOs to support them, or industry lobbying the institutions (interview 32).

4.4.2 The impact of the involvement in EU policy making on CSOs

The last empirical question is whether or not the institutional environment of the EU affects the activities of CSOs and therefore their interest representation strategies. In the questionnaire, 81.8 per cent of the environmental actors reply that being involved in EU policy making affects the workings of their organisation whilst 18.2 per cent think this is not the case (*see* graph 10 in the appendix).

One way the EU can potentially affect CSOs is through EU funding: 40.9 per cent of the environmental organisations that I investigated were receiving EU funding at that time and another 4.5 per cent had done so in the past. In turn, 54.5 per cent of all the organisations did not receive EU funding when interviewed nor had they done in the past. Reflecting these figures, equally, 40.9 per cent of the actors say that funding is highly relevant in their dealings with the EU, 36.4 per cent say it has a medium relevance and, for 22.7 per cent, it has no relevance. Of the ten organisations that received EU funding at the moment of the interview or in the past, two are regional organisations, six national and two European. More often than not, funding occurs in the context of project funding. However, at the EU level, structural funding is also possible under an operating grant and, indeed, both the umbrella organisations that were interviewed – the EEB and Friends of the Earth Europe – receive such structural funding. In fact, the EU is their 'biggest donor' (interview 32; similarly interview 33).

Three environmental actors – two national and one European (13.6 per cent) – do not think that receiving funding from the EU makes an impact on their work (interview 32; interview 33). What is more, the idea that EU funding 'has made us any more reluctant to criticise the Commission for things they have or have not done' (interview 31) is rejected.

Other actors – three regional and four national (31.8 per cent) – notice that EU funding does have an impact on their organisation. One impact noted by three actors is that EU funding 'has made some projects possible that otherwise would not have been possible. So it's enabled things to have happened that otherwise might not have' (interview 31; similarly interview 23). Two actors say their work had become more international as a response to the demands of EU funding (interview 12; interview 27). Whilst EU funding does not change the substance and the direction of the organisation's work, one national actor reflects that in order to increase the likelihood of receiving EU funding for its goals, the organisation does try to take into account specific priorities of the Commission, such as the 'activation of citizens' (interview 26). Other effects of EU funding that actors note are a professionalisation of staff due to the high bureaucratic demands of EU funding ('Wherever these projects are implemented, the work has become much more professional', interview 25); that the reputation of one's work increased because of EU funding (interview 27); and that there had been an increase in information (interview 18). The majority of environmental actors, 54.5 per cent, however, could not tell whether or not receiving EU funding changed their organisation in some way, which should not surprise, given the high level of environmental organisations that had never received EU funding.

A bit surprisingly, given the degree of integration in environmental policy, only 13.6 per cent (all regional actors) mention that the legal framework the EU sets has an impact on their work:

> Locally, our work of course is heavily influenced given the EU sets much of the framework in terms of environmental law. That is very far-reaching. The Habitat directive, the CAP, that heavily influences our work these days. When we win trials, it most of the times has a lot to do with EU law (interview 25; similarly interview 22; interview 27).

Five national and one European actor (27.3 per cent) mention that awareness of the importance of the EU in their policy field has increased over the years as a reaction to involvement with EU affairs. They all indicate that they used to work 'much more at a national level and the international was something we didn't do nearly as much' (interview 17). Whilst the Brussels world still remains alien to many members, most, by now, 'have understood that the protection of the environment is mostly decided in Brussels, for the better and the worse' (interview 21; similarly interview 26; interview 31; interview 33). Actually, two (national) actors mention the possibility, in the case of non-compliance, of taking legal action against a Member State in order to achieve environmental protection as one reason why their members had become more aware of the EU (interview 23; interview 21). Furthermore, three (national) actors mention that being involved with EU affairs had broadened their horizons and increased the number of issues they were looking at (interview 17; interview 29; interview 18). Finally, actors note that the level of transnational co-operation has increased, not least because of related efforts by the European Commission:

> It is often the case that this (co-operation) starts at the EU level and that it's in the interest of the Commission to moderate such processes of dialogue. And then you try to break it down from the EU level to the national, and then the regional level, so it's a top-down approach to co-operation (interview 21).

4.4.3 The incentive structure for actors to engage with EU policy making

Positive and negative perceptions of the EU

Actors from environmental groups share with agricultural groups a rather positive appreciation of the EU: 40.9 per cent of them only see advantages, 4.5 per cent only disadvantages and 50.0 per cent see both advantages and disadvantages.[7] A general positive that is acknowledged by 27.3 per cent of actors is that the EU sets a common legal framework that is crucial for the protection of the environment:

> Without Europe and the European protection of nature our work would have certainly developed in an entirely different way here. I myself was the German representative in different conferences on the Habitat Directive, and I have to say it's been one of my professional highlights how we went from 2 per cent of protected surface to over 11 per cent in Germany. We never would have reached that without Europe, never (interview 27; similarly interview 22; interview 26; interview 32; interview 31; interview 33).

As two actors point out, EU legislation helps them to hold their government to account in case the latter do not abide by the laws they had previously signed at the EU level (interview 30; similarly interview 23). Even in Germany, which used to be a front runner in environmental policy, actors now turn towards the EU in the hope of finding support for environment-friendly policies there (interview 23; similarly interview 21).

Exchange and networking with other organisations is mentioned as a positive by 22.7 per cent. Exchanges are generally thought to be very 'fruitful' (interview 18) and only exist thanks to the EU (interview 19). Involvement in networks in which ideas are exchanged with other environmental groups is an additional

---

7.   The missing 4.5 per cent is accounted for by one actor for whom the information is missing.

motivation (interview 15). Additional benefits include groups learning from one another; seeing what has worked elsewhere and why it did not work back home; forming strategic alliances (interview 21); and that the group is stronger when united under a common structure or umbrella (interview 26; similarly interview 16).

Three actors (13.6 per cent) mention EU funding as an advantage. In a nutshell: 'The EU certainly is an important employer of us' (interview 20). Others pride themselves on being the organisation in Bavaria that has completed the most EU-funded projects under a specific programme, namely eight (interview 27). At the EU level, one actor justifies the existence of the umbrella he is working for in part by what it was doing for its members in terms of fund-raising:

> In terms of fundraising, we probably do quite a good job of helping our groups access EU budget lines by having joint fundraising with them. And I think that's one of the benefits, one of the real and tangible benefits that a lot of our groups feel from being Friends of the Earth Europe (interview 33).

Equally 13.6 per cent mention that being involved in EU affairs has had a positive impact on their reputation and standing. This actor focuses more on political influence: 'I think launching our European work has meant that generally we've gained at the national level as well in terms of reputation and standing. My opinion is that that's something that we've definitely gained from by also trying to influence international processes more' (interview 17). Two other actors also have the larger public in mind:

> When implementing such projects, we obviously have to show the EU-logo and the Natura 2000-logo. And for the local implementation this suggests a certain level where people then say 'Wow! Even Europe is interested in what you are doing here locally'. Generally, that significantly increases the importance of the project (interview 27).

> … since it means that one is doing important projects, as otherwise, the EU would not finance them. So it is an up-valuation of our work when it's co-financed by the EU (interview 27; similarly interview 18).

Above, I have cited several actors who think that environmental policies in Germany have actually benefited from the EU of late. However, there are also those with opposite views, who find that those same policies in Germany are suffering under the lowest common denominator policies of the EU:

> The disadvantage is that the standard which is being agreed upon at the EU level is not always what we would like to see happening. You have to be considerate of the slower states, and therefore the standards sometimes are lower than what one could achieve for Germany alone (interview 22; similarly interview 26).

A related point one actor makes is that legislative changes take very long to happen at the EU level (interview 25).

Two regional and three national actors (22.7 per cent) point out difficulties with EU funding. A main difficulty, felt both by regional and by smaller national organisations, is the necessity of co-funding and of generally having to advance money ahead of its being refunded by the European Commission. For example, one regional actor points out that his organisation would have needed to raise some €150,000 in advance in order to get an EU-funded project started. Since the organisation did not have such resources, the consequence was that for three months straight, he and his colleague did not receive any salary. He concludes:

> So far as content is concerned, support by the EU is sufficient. The financial support, however, is more than insufficient. It can kill a small organisation such as ours. ... Therefore, I don't know whether we can have a second project. It is propagated that NGOs should participate, but it is not supported, not by the EU, and not by the region either' (interview 19; similarly interview 23, interview 17, interview 28).

Another regional actor confirms that getting the co-financing from the region is not necessarily easy, because regional and local authorities are afraid of the high bureaucratic demands that EU co-funding puts on them (interview 25). In fact, some smaller organisations cannot even apply for EU funding because this involves first getting an audit that many groups are not able to afford:

> We've made a strategic decision not to apply for Life Plus because to do that we have to have audited accounts by a professional auditor. We have people who come in and look at our accounts and pass them for the German system. But they're not professionally audited by a chartered accountant. So we can't apply for Life Plus funding and it's a conscious decision because it costs between six and ten thousand euros to get the audit. ... It's a strategic decision not to try because we need to spend a lot of money before we know if we'll get any return (interview 17).

Another disadvantage that 13.6 per cent mention is more substantial: the negative effects of the CAP:

> The threats, for example, posed by the Common Agricultural Policy in terms of subsidies for very harmful farming practices either in terms of biodiversity within Europe or social and environmental impacts on the rest of the world through massive imports of soya, for example. That's a really huge danger (interview 33; similarly interview 21; interview 30).

Differences in work environments

Out of all the environmental actors, only two (national actors) think that it does not matter, in terms of work organisation, at which governance level one acts. Most actors, however, identify differences. To begin with, 18.2 per cent (three national, one regional actor) state that policies are much more abstract at the EU level than domestically. At the EU level, one is concerned with agreeing framework conditions and regulations whilst at the regional or local levels, one is dealing with very concrete measures:

> At a national level it's easier to make very concrete proposals. You may be very specific at the national level, you can make a specific proposal as to how something should be different. When we work at the European level, more often the proposal that you make might be less precise. … At the national level, you can very specifically produce a proposal with very, very concrete ideas of how things could be reformed. At an EU level it's more difficult to do that (interview 17; similarly interview 21; interview 22; interview 30).

The reason for positions being more abstract at the EU level is of course the multitude of actors, interests and regional differences: 'Our strategy for representation would be different on a national and on an EU level I think. Because there's a much more complex mixture of actors, if you are looking at the EU level, the Brussels networks and so on, than there is at the national level' (interview 17).

Also, 18.2 per cent mention the absence of a government and an opposition at the EU level, which would have an impact on how politics functions:

> Domestically, you have a straightforward and clear situation. You have a government and an opposition. At the EU level, you have a parliament, in the end an administration with the European Commission, and a sort of government which you cannot really grasp. Because it is Councils which come and go (interview 23).

The consequence of not having a government and an opposition is that in the EP, you:

> … much more have substantial discussions in which you find very different, also broad alliances. That of course is different with governments and the parties forming the governments in Germany. Debates with MPs can be more difficult given they are bound by coalition agreements and therefore have their hands tied (interview 25).

Two British actors point out that the institutional differences in the political system also make for a different political culture: 'The style of politics in the European Parliament – looking for consensus solutions in coalition and within groups and then everyone making compromises – is obviously very different to the British system, which is quite partisan and oppositional' (interview 32). As a consequence, 'the relationship we have with decision-makers is different. So I find many of the MEPs that I work with are very open, very relaxed. My perception is that it's more relaxed at the EU level' (interview 31).

Equally 18.2 per cent – three national, one European actor – furthermore point out that national actors have fewer direct contacts with people working at the EU level than with domestic actors – 'here we know the people' (interview 29; similarly interview 33; interview 18) whereas we 'certainly have fewer direct contact persons in the Commission than in the federal environmental agency' (interview 26).

Finally, some actors note differences that relate to their own work in Brussels and to how they relate to similar organisations or the larger public. A first point, mentioned by two national actors, is that there is greater co-operation between environmental organisations in Brussels, in order to form coalitions:

> The co-operation, in Brussels, between the environmental organisations, is very objective and good whilst at the national level there is quite some competition. That's only logical because in Germany, one competes for members, for donations, for attention by the media and politicians, whilst the umbrella organisations in Brussels don't have these problems (interview 21; similarly interview 26)

Another point that is mentioned by a European and a regional actor is that the work in Brussels is quite different from the work of member organisations in the Member States:

> because we don't have the direct contact with individual members of the public. ... To engage individual members takes a different skill-set I think, and also different technologies, and maybe a different way of designing your campaigns. ... I think that shapes the way in which we work as an office really (interview 33, similarly interview 25).

Is it easier or harder to be heard at the EU level than domestically?

Mirroring the above, 18.2 per cent find it easier to make their voices heard at the EU level whilst 63.6 per cent find it harder and 9.1 per cent say that it is equally easy or difficult no matter at what level of governance or that they do not know (*see* graph 9 in the appendix). Those who find it easier to be heard at the EU level relate this mainly to a different political culture but also, in part, to the institutional setting of the EU. They point out that the Commission would be much more willing than national ministries to listen to the expertise of environmental organisations, not least because the Commission itself does not have sufficient experts of its own (interview 21, interview 28) but also because it has fewer hierarchies than, for example, the German federal environment ministry (interview 21). Another point that two actors mention is that compared with MPs, MEPs are more free to form coalitions on a case-by-case basis rather than being in a permanent coalition (interview 28; interview 25). One actor, finally, suggests that it is currently easier to influence policies at the EU level because the European political context was more favourable than in the UK:

'I would say it's difficult to influence national policy on nature conservation because the government is also very hostile to nature conservation at the moment' (interview 31).

More numerous are those who find that it is easier to make their voices heard at the national level. Four national and one regional actor (22.7 per cent) find that just the (higher) number of lobbyists, actors and therefore of interests makes it more difficult to influence policies in Brussels (interview 15; interview 22; interview 23; interview 26; interview 17). Two national and one regional actor (13.6 per cent) say that they simply had fewer contacts at the EU level and that this makes it more difficult to influence policies (interview 26; interview 27; interview 29). Equally, 13.6 per cent (three national actors) mention the complexity of the EU political system and policy processes, which make EU politics more time-intensive to follow than domestic politics (interview 16; interview 18; interview 12). Another 13.6 per cent, all from the national level, see a lack of resources as being a major hindrance to lobbying at the EU level (interview 23; interview 29; interview 30). Finally, two national actors mention linguistic problems as a factor that makes it more difficult to be heard at the EU level (interview 15; interview 18).

An important way of being heard in Brussels is through the European Commission's consultation regime. How do environmental actors evaluate it? Their evaluation is quite mixed. In quantitative terms, 50 per cent are either happy (13.6) or rather satisfied (36.4) with the online consultations. In contrast, 36.3 per cent are either rather unsatisfied (31.8) or unsatisfied (4.5) with them; 13.6 per cent say they could not tell because they had never participated in such consultations. It is acknowledged that the Commission tries to balance different views and bring all the interests to the table, particularly by means of increased internet consultations: 'My impression is that if you have the resources, access to the Commission is not too bad. They try and propose ever more participation possibilities via the internet. My impression is that the possibilities to participate via the internet have improved' (interview 23; similarly interview 27; interview 28).

Most of the environmental actors enjoy some experience – some more, some less – with the online consultations of the Commission – only three do not. In the interviews, not many actors spoke positively of the consultations. Only two actors think that 'it's good to be able to have the opportunity to put your views across' (interview 30) and that the Commission looks at the inputs very scrupulously (interview 28).

More actors make critical comments about the online consultations. Mostly, and across levels of governance, they wonder about the impact on policies and legislation the consultations have (31.8 per cent):

Sometimes it's difficult to see how a legislative proposal relates to all of that which was contributed in the context of a consultation process. There is not really a logic behind it. Of course, there are also other forces in such a process, and everyone tries to influence it in their direction. However, sometimes it is striking indeed how little is being taken up in a legislative proposal as against to which inputs had been made (interview 15; similarly interview 18; interview 24; interview 25; interview 31).

A number of actors also find that the results of the consultations can be skewed in favour of economic interests or:

> ... often heavily skewed to get the answer that they want. ... I think on a few of the dossiers we've seen the debates between DGs or between Commissioners really overshadowing any external input. So between Oettinger and Hedegaard on climate targets, for example. I think we could have shouted as loud as we wanted, through whatever consultation process (interview 33; similarly interview 31; interview 32).

Indeed, another actor, somewhat similarly to an agricultural one, confirms that the online consultations seem biased from the way the questionnaires are constructed: 'I think it's very much multiple choice and you know what they want you to say really, and they are quite tailored to going in a particular direction and it's less of a proper consultation process that they ask, but more of a kind of statistical exercise' (interview 17).

As a result of the critical evaluation of the online consultations, three actors conclude that 'the consultations are useful but it's more effective to be in direct contact with Commission officials' (interview 31; similarly interview 17) whilst it would be 'naïve' to be 'confident that our views will be listened to as fully and in as much detail as they deserve ... So we have to do more than just take part in these consultation processes' (interview 33).

Constituency interest in the EU

In environmental groups, awareness that the EU is becoming ever-more-important for the policy field about which they are concerned, has clearly increased – mainly at the European and national levels of organisational governance, however: 'I think by now almost everyone has realised that the protection of the environment is in large parts decided in Brussels, for the better as for the worse. And therefore our members expect our organisation to be involved in Brussels' (interview 21; similarly interview 26; interview 31). The result is multiplying contacts with other organisations in the same field and European issues being pushed up the organisation's agenda (interview 18), or the employment of a co-ordinator of EU policies, be it in Berlin (interview 28) or in Brussels (interview 21). Similarly, an actor based in Brussels indicates that:

> ... probably the clearest change has been the growth in the size of the European office, which is partly a reaction to member groups telling us we need to do more work at the European level. That we need to follow more dossiers, that they are not able to do that work at the national level because decisions are being made in Brussels' (interview 33).

At the regional level, there are obviously fewer staff available for EU affairs. Nonetheless, one actor says that the EU is regularly an issue at AGMs (interview 27).

However, a considerable number of actors also suggest that the individual members of environmental organisations are not all that interested in EU affairs; and this is felt throughout all levels of organisational governance. For a number of actors, the EU simply seems to be too far away, too abstract, to interest people who are concerned with local issues of environmental protection: 'EU issues effectively are only of interest to higher levels of governance, so far as interest representation is concerned. People on the grassroots only have a, let's say, formal interest in that' (interview 27; similarly interview 19). People engaged in local environmental protection are happy to leave the task of interest representation to the higher organisational levels, such as regional or even national (*ibid.*; similarly interview 22). As a consequence, it is difficult to get regional, let alone local, members involved in EU affairs because, for them, the EU is 'simply another world' (interview 15), which is 'too far away for members to want to consult about it' (*ibid.*). One national actor points out that he invites regional member organisations time and again to participate in specific EU processes and they, in turn, invite their members to do so. However, 'in reality, both the interest and the knowledge are not of such a kind that everyone would want to contribute to EU affairs. Most of the times, these are so complex that they stay within headquarters' (interview 21), not least because the early stages of EU legislative processes are not reported in the national media (*ibid.*). In the UK, the additional factor of Euroscepticism enters the picture:

> European issues get discussed, but the EU doesn't come up as a topic on its own. I don't know how long you've been in the UK, but you may have picked up quite a lot of Euroscepticism. I find it a challenge within the organisation to bring up EU issues. EU stuff does make it on to the members' events. And at those events we do presentations on international work. But only rarely would we present information on EU policy because it's actually quite a dry subject – it's difficult to get people enthused and interested about it. As soon as you say 'EU' people switch off and say: 'Oh God, gravy train, we should pull out of it.' And if you're trying to present the benefits of EU membership, it starts to become a bit of an uphill struggle (interview 31).

Finally, also at the EU level, it is felt that the individual members of member organisations are often not involved in EU affairs. Asked whether or not they received sufficient input and feedback from their individual members at the EU level, one Brussels-based actor replies:

> No, I think, would probably be the consensus answer to that. … I think it's sort of a disappointment that the EU is working on – to get more of a direct link with our members' members. The problems are probably multi-faceted and to

do with how people feel connected to the EU, how they feel it's connected to them, anything from that to linguistics potentially (interview 32).

Another internal reason why environmental actors are likely to be less engaged with EU policy making than agricultural groups is that many of them simply lack the resources to be more engaged, let alone to be present in Brussels. Indeed, 27.3 per cent of all the environmental actors, from both the regional and the national levels, commented on their financial capacities, generally indicating that these are too limited.

In sum, the evidence shows many environmental actors have ambivalent views of the EU. If they are willing to handle the more negative aspects for the sake of EU involvement, then this is certainly because of their preferences and the desire to influence legislation – 68.2 per cent of the environmental actors say that lobbying is a highly relevant part of their work at the EU level whereas contributing to democracy was perceived as highly relevant by only 27.3 per cent (*see* graphs 11–16). The focus on lobbying also becomes clear when actors reflect the role they have in the EU: almost half of them thinks that 'it would be lobbying' (interview 30) whilst just above a fifth of them state that they saw themselves as 'transmission belts, from the people on the grassroots to the higher levels of governance' (interview 19) and with a 'very important role to play in feeding the opinion of civil society' to the European level (interview 31).

Chapter Five

Representation by Anti-Poverty CSOs

At the start of this chapter, it seems useful to point out that in this chapter – as in the two previous empirical chapters – it will mainly be the actors on the ground that will be given full attention. Whereas I have obviously structured the account and have added minimal information where this seemed necessary in order to understand what actors have said, I am not interpreting or analysing what actors say and do in this chapter, so as to keep their voices and my analysis clearly distinct. The analysis follows in Chapter Six.

5.1 The policy field and its main actors

Social policy is a policy field characterised by a low level of legal integration within the EU (Daly 2006). Still, there have been a few relevant directives, such as the directive on occupational pensions. Because social policy is not strongly integrated, the focus is very much on soft governance processes, not least the Open Method of Coordination (OMC), in order to foster processes of mutual learning and socialisation (Natali 2005; Kröger 2008b, 2009; Zeitlin 2005). The social policy OMCs were mainly developed by the Commission and the administrations of Member States, which send national delegates into EU committees, originally with considerable support from CSOs, particularly in the social inclusion process (Kröger 2006); however, this involvement later ceased when the processes became less ambitious. Political parties and social partners were now absent from the processes altogether (Kröger 2007a), even though an explicit aim of the early OMC was to mobilise 'all relevant stakeholders'. Beyond the social OMCs which have now been streamlined, there are also online consultations in social policy. Actors in these online consultations and soft governance processes are the Commission, Member States, the EP, CSOs, national administrations and academia, with the Commission and CSOs as the central actors while other actors play a minor role.

Turning more specifically to EU anti-poverty policies, the first steps towards introducing anti-poverty programmes were taken by the Commission in the mid-1970s (Bauer 2002; Kröger 2007b). While these programmes only engaged a limited number of CSOs and researchers who developed networks and a common anti-poverty discourse, they nonetheless contributed to creating an awareness amongst CSOs that there is a European dimension to poverty; that the EU may have a role to play in anti-poverty policy and should therefore be lobbied; and, not least, that Brussels may be an important *locus* of funding. Starting in the mid-1980s, the

EU expanded its activities in the field of social policy. The Commission set up the Social Dialogue, which engages social partners at the EU level. Since then, however, the dialogue is perceived to have deteriorated:

> before, the Commissioners for employment and social affairs used to try much more and find alliances between the important actors of the social dialogue or civil society, and that has decreased over time. Instead, we have a much more formalised participation process, which, however are not real participation processes, but rather some sort of participation machinery in which you have to participate, but where you don't have the impression it's a real dialogue. The results of it are not picked up, so it increasingly has an alibi character. So there is more mass than class (interview 34).

In fact, the change in culture from 'true' consultation and participation to 'alibi' or 'façade' kinds of participation is also noted in the domestic sphere (interview 48). Other factors that render engagement with public authorities increasingly difficult would be an increased resistance against (expert) advice (interview 49); less interest 'in the views of NGOs like ourselves and I think also less interested in the views of people experiencing poverty' (interview 54; similarly interview 57); overall less influence of anti-poverty groups on governmental policies (interview 50; interview 47; interview 54); and cuts in public funding (interview 57).

The Commission also looked for partners in other areas than employment. This proved more difficult since groups such as 'homeless people', 'poor people', 'disabled people', 'women's groups' or different 'ethnic groups' lacked representation at the EU level and were organised in very different ways in the different Member States. In this situation, the Commission became an entrepreneur and created the representation of these groups in Brussels. It started bringing together national organisations in the fields of homelessness, anti-poverty, anti-discrimination, gender issues and so on and encouraged them to form a European network. Examples of such networks are – the European Anti-Poverty Network (EAPN, established in 1990); European Federation of National Organisations working with the Homeless (FEANTSA, established in 1989); the European Women's lobby (established in 1990); the European Disability Forum (EDF, established 1996); and the European Network Against Racism (ENAR, established in 1997). These and other European umbrella organisations have since joined forces and united under the head of the Social Platform, a European umbrella of European umbrella organisations.

In this study, I am interested in EAPN and its national members. It is one of the oldest and also one of the most thematically encompassing European umbrellas today; and one that almost entirely relies on structural funding by the European Commission. At the constituting meeting in 1990, EAPN accepted ten national networks as members. It took until 1994 for 'Germany' to enter EAPN, which was due to a mixture of factors. There was limited acknowledgement, in Germany, from key organisational leaders of the benefits of having a European network and little political recognition of the need to have a European anti-poverty policy. Today, EAPN consists of twenty-nine national networks. These twenty-nine national networks constitute the cornerstone of EAPN's membership basis. However, the network also has a large number of other Brussels-based CSOs as members, for example, ATD Fourth World, Caritas Europa, EMMAÜS International, Eurochild, EURODIACONIA, the Salvation Army, the Red Cross, and so on. EAPN's internal documentation points to a total of almost 1600 national, regional and local CSOs as members of national networks and hence indirect members of EAPN. Some national networks have as many as several hundred member organisations (Portugal, the UK and Ireland), while other national networks have 20–30 member organisations (Germany, France, Italy). The president of EAPN suggests that the willingness to co-operate and form alliances between members has increased of late:

> I would say even in the last five years that the emphasis on alliances or the work on co-operation between social movements and social NGOs and between trade unions and social NGOS – that that has grown a lot in the last five years and particularly as a response to the crisis where the need for social forces to unite becomes more obvious (interview 60).

Formal membership criteria are defined in a fairly broad manner, as long as the organisations in question are directly involved in the fight against poverty. In contrast to many voluntary organisations or NGOs, their main membership basis is other organisations, rarely individuals. EAPN has an annual turnover of approximately €1.3 million. It has expanded its secretariat and nowadays employs ten to twelve people.

This is the background of the policy field and actor constellation in which anti-poverty groups today seek to defend their interests. Before we look at their understanding of representation and then into their concrete practices of representation, let us briefly look at the actors I interviewed. In total, I interviewed twenty-eight actors. These comprise two representatives of the European umbrella organisation; seven representatives of seven different British members of the European umbrella organisation; one representative from a local English organisation that is a member of a British member of the European umbrella organisation; ten representatives of ten different German umbrella organisations which are all members of the European umbrella organisation; one representative of the representation of a German welfare organisation in Brussels; four representatives of four different regional organisations which are members of German peak organisations which are members of the European umbrella organisation; three representatives of three different local organisations which are members of the German peak organisations which are members of the European umbrella organisation.

Graph 3: Anti-poverty actors interviewed

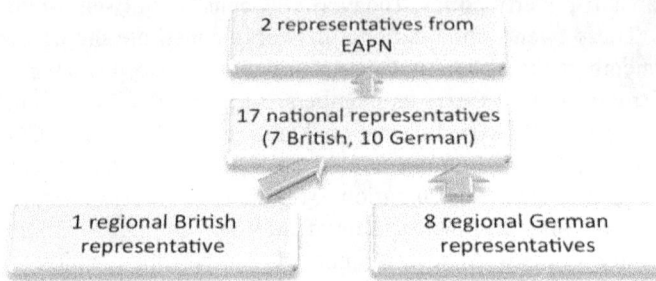

```
                    ┌─────────────────────────┐
                    │ 2 representatives from   │
                    │          EAPN            │
                    └─────────────────────────┘
                              ↑
                    ┌─────────────────────────┐
                    │ 17 national representatives │
                    │  (7 British, 10 German)  │
                    └─────────────────────────┘
                       ↗              ↖
   ┌─────────────────────┐      ┌─────────────────────┐
   │ 1 regional British  │      │ 8 regional German   │
   │   representative     │      │  representatives     │
   └─────────────────────┘      └─────────────────────┘
```

5.2 Actors' understanding of representation

As in the previous two chapters, I shall now address a number of issues that relate to the understanding of representation by the actors involved, such as: what is representation, in their view? Do they see themselves as representing a constituency or an issue? Do they perceive themselves as lobbyists or do they favour a more participatory approach that includes a perception of their role as more interactive? This question also relates to the issue of when actors think representation has been achieved – do groups seek the maximum output, which is influencing legislation or governmental policy programmes, or are they satisfied if they have influenced a discourse, or, less ambitious still, merely made their voices heard? Finally, how do actors conceive of the legitimacy of their activities – is it thought to be generated through input by relevant constituencies or through output, via expertise and/or achieved policies?

5.2.1 Representation of people or of an issue?

Unsurprisingly, many actors from anti-poverty groups associate advocacy for the weak with 'representation'. When asked about their understanding of representation, 74.1 per cent reply it is advocacy for the weak, whilst for 22.2 per cent representation relates to 'members' and for 3.7 per cent to a 'public interest'. It is in fact remarkable how often and almost naturally the words 'advocacy' or 'advocates' appears in this context: 'Of course we think of ourselves as an advocate of disadvantaged people who need support' (interview 37), be it 'because they are ill, because they are unemployed, because they need special care, because of whatever problems they may have in their lives. For them we are advocates and try to change politics by bringing their causes into the debate' (interview 39). These are 'generally people who do not enjoy any or at least little political representation of their interests, and we try to give them a voice, also on the European level' (interview 43).

Similarly, when asked who it is they are representing, 74.1 per cent reply 'the weak', meaning 'poor people and disadvantaged people' (interview 36, similarly interview 39; interview 40; interview 54; interview 59; interview 61), 'people who need support in all kinds of living situations' (interview 37; similarly interview 50), 'the most vulnerable' (interview 38; similarly interview 43; interview 46; interview 60), 'people who are unemployed or have difficulties staying in the job market' (interview 42), 'families whose incomes are below the poverty line or just around it' (interview 56) or 'first and foremost members of ethnic minority communities' (interview 57). These findings suggest that the large majority thinks of itself as representing a constituency rather than an issue.

That things are not necessarily as clear-cut becomes evident when looking closer at the replies to the question of who or what it is they are representing. While only 22.2 per cent from anti-poverty groups think of representation as representing members when asked broadly about their understanding of representation, when asked more directly who it is they are representing, 55.6 per cent say they are representing members, 33.3 per cent say they are representing their own organisation and 74 per cent 'poor people'.[1]

In some of the organisations, particularly in the UK, 'members' are individuals, whereas in others, they are organisations that are members of regional or federal umbrella organisations. Particularly in Germany, 'member' often refers to a regional or local 'branch' of the federal welfare organisation, for example, the Diakonie or Caritas. Therefore, when referring to 'members', actors do not point to organisations or individuals outside of the federal organisation but to their 'own' institutions, on lower levels of governance, which are members. These institutions (members) are either administrative and political units (on the regional and sometimes local level) or those service providers who work directly with the poor and disadvantaged:

> Representation means, because we are a regional organisation, to represent our organisation and the interests of its member facilities at the regional level, here in Württemberg. More concretely, representation in my work very much focuses on the representation of our member institutions, those facilities which are direct service providers for our target groups, the disadvantaged (interview 37; similarly interview 36; interview 48).

Conceiving of themselves as representing 'members' or as being advocates of 'the weak' seems to imply that anti-poverty groups do not really take interests of other than their own immediate constituency into account when developing positions and designing policies. Two actors refer to donors as influencing their work in some indirect way – not least by deciding for which activities they were donating money (interview 38; similarly interview 49). Another two actors refer to politics and the respective governments: 'What we of course have to take into consideration – which does not always mean that we share the policy – is the position of the respective government and the related design of certain social programmes' (interview 50; similarly interview 47). Mostly, however, actors are influenced by those touched directly by poverty and inequalities: 'We feel we are an organisation

---

1. Interviewees could give two responses.

that builds with some of the poorest people that exist and so they are the most kind of extreme. They are an example of the impact of policies on particular poor people. And that does influence our policy work, probably more than our general membership' (interview 55; similarly interview 49; interview 51; interview 53).

Do actors from anti-poverty groups perceive themselves as representatives engaged in lobbying, or do they favour a more participatory approach? Differently from the agricultural and environmental groups, actors seeking to represent 'weak interests' seem to be more divided between a traditional role perception as lobbyist *versus* that of someone who, ideally, seeks to involve those affected by poverty and disadvantage so that they can directly speak for themselves.

Some actors focus on the lobbying aspect: 'We think of ourselves as lobbyists for people who are socially disadvantaged in our society, for people touched by poverty' (interview 49; similarly interview 42). This means, that 'we will bring forward our positions *vis-à-vis* the region, the government, the Commission, the Council. And of course we are currently very active in the Council as regards the next budget period' (interview 42; similarly interview 46). Others point out that they are 'a network of urban areas projects and of regional networks and see it as our task, with regard to representation, to take issues that these networks and projects bring to us to the political level' (interview 51). A role perception as lobbyist also exists *vis-à-vis* the European institutions. Several actors see it as their role to 'transfer the interests of our organisation, a member organisation, to all European institutions, and linked to that, the concrete lobbying, i.e. the concrete influencing of political processes' (interview 44; similarly interview 43).

Many anti-poverty actors emphasise that involving the poor themselves in lobbying is very important to them, thereby reflecting a more participatory approach to the issue of representation:

> I think it's taking issues that affect people experiencing poverty to the appropriate level, where we can best influence the policies that impact on those individuals and communities. And, as far as possible we aim to do that through participatory approaches, so it's people that are directly affected who are making representations for themselves (interview 54).

More than a quarter (25.9 per cent) of the anti-poverty actors say they regularly involve the poor in their lobbying activities whilst 55.6 per cent say this happens irregularly. Only 18.5 per cent say they never involve the poor in related activities. Seeking to involve poor people in lobbying activities is important to and practised by anti-poverty groups across all levels of organisational governance. At the local level, several actors point to their attachment to the idea of self-representation:

> I am someone who argues that people should, ideally, represent their interests themselves. So we have set up a citizen's representation, which I support in defending its concerns itself. I think that those who have their flats here, who live here, know best what's good. So first I always check whether those who have interests can represent themselves (interview 40).

A local English actor states that 'part of my philosophy would be to draw people that we are campaigning for, into, to be involved in the campaign and we try to do that in Church Action Poverty and in our asylum group' (interview 57). Particularly in the UK, there is a strong tradition of involving the poor themselves in the lobbying:

> I wouldn't call it representation. As an organisation, we are very into participation. So we see it as very important that people who are affected by poverty have a voice not only through the policy work that we do. We carry out something called participatory research. So, for instance, we are doing research at the moment on the experience of single parents moving from income support, off jobseeker's allowance, and we trained up single parents to interview those single parents. And they have been carrying out that research. We are going to fully involve them in drawing the conclusions back together and taking them to parliament. And they will be speaking to parliamentarians. We also train them up in research skills, so they are getting training and accreditation from the University of the South-West. So that is an intrinsic part of how the charity operates. ... We're an organisation that prides itself on giving voice to single parents rather than finding out their voice. As much as possible we want them to participate in influencing policy and we have a history of doing that (interview 55; similarly interview 53; interview 59).

Finally, also at the European level, EAPN also seeks to involve those affected by poverty more: 'More and more, EAPN have become the network of people experiencing poverty, not working for, but *of* people experiencing poverty. More and more are people experiencing poverty and social exclusion in our governance structures' (interview 61).

5.2.2 Achievement of representation

Let me now turn to the question of when anti-poverty actors think representation is achieved. Respondents are mainly divided between seeing the influence on legislation or on governmental policy programmes as that point (48.1 per cent) and influencing a discourse as having achieved representation (37 per cent). Furthermore, 11.1 per cent say it is sufficient to have managed to get one's voice heard in order to have achieved representation while one thinks of representation as an ongoing activity (3.7 per cent).

The view that representation is achieved when legislation or programmes have been influenced exists across all levels of organisational governance. From such a perspective, representation is:

> ... more than just consultation, so we don't spend much time just responding to consultations that we think may impact. Our aim is always to achieve actual policy change. So, the issues that we pick, that we go to work on, are ones

where we think we can have some actual impact on how policy is implemented (interview 54; similarly interview 49).

At the regional level, and in regard to the EU, actors focus in particular on European funding schemes: 'For example, if funding programmes are such that disadvantaged people are also taken into consideration. If our demands have influenced the provisions of the Commission or the guidelines of programmes, the provisions for single funding programmes, then we have achieved our lobby work' (interview 36; similarly interview 37). Similarly, at the national level, actors see representation as achieved 'when you are able to effect the changes that you want to change' (interview 57). In other words, 'unless we are able to effect change with politicians and policy-makers then we're missing a really important step there' (interview 53; similarly interview 43). Some actors, whilst also seeing political, legislative influence as the main goal of representation, are a bit more tentative in their response: 'It is, of course, very clear that we will hardly ever achieve our own interests 100 per cent. It is always a compromise between the different actors, and sometimes we will have a greater, sometimes a lesser influence, depending on the issues, that really depends' (interview 38). At the European level, then, 'it could be considered that's achieved when people experiencing poverty will be really associated with decisions' (interview 61), which we can assume would have a major impact on those decisions.

As mentioned above, 37 per cent think of representation as being achieved when they manage to *influence* a discourse. This view is most often found at the regional level. Often, this is associated with the occurrence of dialogue and exchange. Accordingly, one actor points out that he would measure the achievement of representation not 'in terms of categories of influence, but whether or not there has been a reasonable weighting of different positions' (interview 41; similarly interview 59), whilst another says that 'it's not only about the articulation [of their view]. Of course, ideally it will be reflected in the political debate and in the positions of the political parties' (interview 51).

Finally, 11.1 per cent, from both the regional and national levels, say that representation has been achieved when they have made their voices heard: 'The representation, in my view, is already achieved when one has been invited and has been listened to' (interview 39). An even more minimalist view is expressed by another national actor, who states that 'representation is achieved, when one has formulated one's own position and made it available to third parties' (interview 44). There also is an awareness that representation is possibly never fully achieved (interview 53) but is realised in different steps and always ongoing:

Of course, when you bring interests into a process, then that is in part a success … There are also process goals. Possibly when you've got an MP to come to our town hall. Those are things where people say 'we have achieved something, we have been listened to'. It's not as immediate as a concrete improvement of a policy, but you can bring concerns into such debates if it goes well. Just to be listened to, to be acknowledged, for me that is an important result in terms of process (interview 40).

5.2.3 Legitimacy generation of representation

As discussed before, there are two possibilities for how actors understand the legitimacy of their interest representation. Either they see legitimacy as primarily deriving from the input of their group's constituency. Or they think of legitimacy as stemming from the output generated just by their involvement in policy making. This could be achieved by 'doing the right thing', either because of their expertise or their faith, or by the outcomes of the political process (policies). In the case of anti-poverty actors, 44.4 per cent think it is the democratic mandate of their members that provides their activities with legitimacy; 22.2 per cent that it comes from a mandate and thereby is democratic. For 44.4 per cent, legitimacy is generated via expertise, for 25.9 per cent it comes from involving the poor whilst for 14.8 per cent, it is faith that generates legitimacy.[2]

The view that legitimacy is created through democratic processes of will-formation can be found throughout the different levels of organisational governance. From this perspective, legitimacy derives from a democratic mandate: 'As a member organisation, we have corporate members, and people who are touched by poverty, and they of course give us a mandate' (interview 46; similarly interview 43). One national actor explains:

> Our representation is legitimate because we organise long-term processes of will-formation which are public. For the will-formation, we use a professional journal that everyone can access. We use the instrument of workshops and every two years have a big federal general meeting. There are at least 4–5 further expert workshops per year which are open to everyone and where we begin processes of discussion and debate. We have a system of expert committees. Not unlike trade unions or political parties, they are organised along topics. Our different members delegate experts in these committees who, in conjunction with the staffed office, work on policy positions. Finally the representatives attend the steering committees which are elected by the membership. And the steering committee decides, in the last instance, about the policy position (interview 47).

As for the other two groups, actors do point to the democratic structures they have in place and how they were 'merely' the organ of their members when trying to influence policies: 'We as a steering committee are democratically elected. So the representation is on the basis of our elected function' (interview 45). Similarly, it is pointed out at the European level that there is a broad membership basis, which feeds into policy positions and thereby provides EAPN with legitimacy: 'By and large we have a very wide membership base. It's not true in every country but in most countries we have a very wide and active membership base with a clear

---

2. Actors could chose two answers.

governance process' (interview 60). In other words, 'the way EAPN is formed ... it's a structure that's going through all the levels – I mean from the local to the EU level. At each level there are structures and representations of all the aspects of poverty and people's concerns' (interview 61).

Some actors also point to their degree of mobilisation as providing them with legitimacy, which to them shows that 'people see us as legitimate and effective interest representation' (interview 47):

> I think our growing membership is actually key. I think we started about eighteen months ago with 300 or so members. So we saw a huge rise in the people wanting to join and be part of the AgeScotland coalition and recognising the power which we have. We actually have incredible influence and access to government and we do often recognise that when we try and push things, and speak with the voice of the people behind us, governments and politicians do react and do listen to us (interview 53).

Still on the input side, 22.2 per cent of the anti-poverty actors think of legitimacy more broadly as being generated by a societal mandate. This is particularly the case in Germany, where the law prescribes that the state organises the welfare of its citizens in partnership with the free social services, making of them 'an important partner in social policy overall' (interview 37) who have a 'public mandate' (interview 41). Traditionally, it has been the two largest churches (Catholic and Protestant) in particular, as well as organisations inspired by socialism, that have implemented this role for welfare in Germany:

> An entirely different form of legitimacy comes from the social services organisations enjoying a specific role for the welfare state in Germany. And part of that role is the further development of the welfare state, and to influence that. To that extent the social services organisations, because of their role for the welfare state, enjoy a political legitimacy (interview 50; similarly interview 40).

Involving the poor themselves and being in close contact with them is a source of legitimacy according to 25.9 per cent. This perspective could imply either an input or an output view of legitimacy: the input deriving from (poor) people speaking directly for themselves; the output deriving from the expertise poor people have about their own situation and from working with them. Indeed, we find both aspects in the data. For one actor, it's 'an ethos of participation and valuing the views of the parents that we work with' (interview 55) that provides legitimacy; for another, 'it's because we have programmes that work directly with people in poverty and the whole purpose of those programmes is to enable the party to identify the changes they want to see made and then to accept for themselves how to make those changes' (interview 54; similarly interview 59). Both elements – the close contact with the poor and the attempt to involve them – are well reflected in this statement:

It's the close contact with the poor. That we are active on the ground. That we have structures which allow the poor to participate. That we are in constant dialogue with the poor. That we try to involve them. There exist both at the regional and at the federal levels institutionalised events, every year, where there is a direct exchange with the poor. And jointly with the poor, we try to pass on the results to the politicians. So it is not one for the others, but acting together with the poor (interview 49).

What we do not find here on the input side of legitimacy-narratives are any actors pointing to the high degree to which groups are organised as one way of legitimising their activities.

Throughout the different levels of organisational governance, 44.4 per cent of the anti-poverty actors see legitimacy located on the output side, particularly generated through expertise. In a nutshell, from this perspective, 'it's technical expertise. … We hold this hub of incredibly specialised knowledge, and we are able to stretch it forward and challenge things that we need to. And in terms of policy work, I think that flows over into our policy expertise, it's really an expert-led approach' (interview 56; similarly interview 42; interview 57). In other words, 'interests can only ever be represented legitimately if the agent has expertise in the topic in question. Also, one does not get noticed otherwise in politics … I would say that expertise here plays a crucial role, because one can only engage in representation if one can bring in technically sound contributions. Otherwise one is not taken seriously' (interview 38).

Finally, for 14.8 per cent, the legitimacy of their representation activities is rooted in their faith and the mandate that faith gives them (and their employer). This is not surprising, given many of the social services in Germany are provided by the two main denominations. Because of their faith, as one actor points out, 'we have something like a partiality for the poor and disadvantaged. For us, that is a source of legitimacy' (interview 50). In this reasoning, it is not the democratic, but clearly the divine mandate that matters:

Of course, we have not been elected by these target groups to represent their interests. We take the mandate of our Christian idea of man, which we want to spread in Europe. We take it from the mandate which, for us Catholics, comes from the Bible. We are committed to the Catholic Church, and our mandate is simply to create a social Europe and to be there for people, and to lobby for people who, for different reasons, cannot represent their interests on their own (interview 36; similarly interview 37).

5.3 Organisational structures and practices of representation within CSOs

In this section, I am interested in the *practices* of representation within CSOs rather than, as in the previous section, in what actors *understand* by representation. Obviously, practices can be quite different from the more abstract understanding actors have, given that there is a multitude of competing actors in the political arena and also a number of more structural, institutional and legal constraints on actors' behaviour and the realisation of their organisational goals. More concretely, I will be looking, first, at how the different groups involve their constituencies in the decision-making and internal governance of the organisation. This will involve addressing how issues get on to the agenda of organisations in the first place; how and where position-finding then occurs; how far members – or possibly constituencies which are not members – are involved in the authorisation and control of their respective representatives and what forms authorisation and control take; and how far existing constituencies are mobilised for activities beyond the internal governance of the organisation. Second, I will consider how far these groups mobilise a bigger potential constituency, that is the public at large, for some of their activities. Do groups reach out to a larger public and involve it in some of their activities? Do they seek to enlarge their constituency or do they mainly focus on their existing constituency? Overall, this section should allow us to see how representative CSOs are of their constituencies.

5.3.1 Internal governance: agenda-setting, authorisation and control

How do issues get on to the agenda?

According to 40.7 per cent of the anti-poverty actors, agenda-setting is mostly driven by members but 51.9 per cent think it is mostly government- and environment-driven. The remaining 7.4 per cent suggest it is exclusively government- and environment-driven. When agenda-setting is driven mostly by members, this seems to come in four versions, mentioned by both regional and national actors. First, actors mention members as the source of agenda-setting: 'It's only engagement with member groups that actually has any impact on the actions we take' (interview 53). Sometimes, members' views will be identified via consultation processes: 'Last year we did a consultation with our supporters as to which issues they wanted us to work on and through that process identified the strategic issues for us to work on for the next year' (interview 54). Sometimes, they will be identified at AGMs:

> We have an annual meeting every year where members are invited to attend. We have speakers on different issues and then participants can prioritise areas that they think are particularly important – we are very interested in their views influencing our priorities. For instance, eighteen months ago we did a manifesto which drew together the main themes that the single parents had brought to us at our annual meeting. And then that became our document for our priorities (interview 55).

A second way by which members can mostly drive the agenda is via the steering or advisory committees, which are generally made up of delegated members:

'We have a steering committee of three people, and that committee has the political and legal responsibility and, in principle, defines our strategies' (interview 42). Third, members may drive agenda-setting by what their organisation's statutes say: 'It's help for the young, the old, etc., it's laid down in our statutes and thereby fixed. We work under political conditions which are sometimes more, sometimes less favourable, but we've been doing it for the past 120 years. So we don't change our goals daily' (interview 48). Finally, agenda-setting happens via working with the poor and seeing and learning from them what the priorities should be: 'It simply is the living situation of the poor. Their problems become clear when directly working with them. And that is exactly what we then try to put on our agenda. We don't want to do that in a theoretical way that is not connected to the reality of people' (interview 49; similarly interview 52).

Only two actors, one regional, one national, say that the agenda of their respective organisation is mainly driven by the government and/or the environment: 'I would say that the large majority of what we do is determined by external circumstances, and that we react to that' (interview 50). With regret, another actor notes that 'at the moment, we are incredibly reactive, so we react to what the government does' (interview 56).

More often than not, however, agenda-setting is a result of a mixture of internal and external factors and processes. For example, a starting point for a local project was 'citizens who were consulted. Then it passed on to the institutions which had to evaluate it, and so the communal inspection which provides the money has a role to play. If they don't give us any money, then we can voice as many wishes as we wish, but no project will be implemented' (interview 40). Indeed, funding often plays an important role; precisely what groups will do will, to a certain degree, depend on available funding: 'In the current climate with the funding being how it is, what we work on is to some extent dictated by the funding that is available. So the issues that we work on might be the ones that there is funding available for' (interview 57; similarly interview 36). Other actors focus on more directly political developments that will have a significant impact on their agenda:

We are legally and politically independent as an organisation. So it is us who define our work priorities. However, we are not alone in the universe, which means that we are very much influenced by political developments and societal issues and challenges. There is no directive coming from politics as to what our priorities should be, but of course there exists a close relationship with societal developments (interview 37; similarly interview 34; interview 52; interview 39; interview 43; interview 44).

In particular, those organisations that do not have a very close bond to their members seem to be quite influenced by the government agenda:

If we have an issue we want to explore and a funder in mind, then sometimes it just comes down to a member of the team having a good idea. And that idea won't have come out of nowhere, that will be responding to what is going on in the environment and policies in the area so I guess one of the influences is obviously government policy in the area. So because we are a policy research organisation we will be thinking to tie it quite closely with the policy agenda of the UK government, so that would be a major factor (interview 57).

The mixture of agenda-setting between members and the external environment also exists at the European level:

We have two approaches. One, we're very committed to engaging and shaping the official processes. So of course what we do is also very shaped by what processes exist for the social issues. ... On the other hand, we have a process of saying we want our own agenda, which is about a type of development model that can really deliver on poverty and social exclusion. ... But these two things get linked as well (interview 60).

However, not all anti-poverty organisations have a formal agenda, as this national actor points out:

There's not a sort of formal agenda in the respect that we have a meeting every week where we raise issues from older people. But we have a number of the older workers who work with the older people's groups and they have a daily engagement with these groups and they'll take back feedback from them about issues and where relevant they'll pass that back to the appropriate teams to see if they can actually do anything about them (interview 53; similarly interview 52; interview 57).

Structures and processes of developing policy positions, of authorisation and control

Let me now look at the further process of position-finding and means of authorisation and control. Whether topics arrive on the agenda from outside the organisation or from within – as with the urgency of the topic, of course – can influence how the further position-finding process unfolds. Are there traces of both bottom-up and of top-down position-finding processes as the evidence previously presented in this chapter would have us expect? There certainly are.

Many German actors stress that they have democratic structures in place, which are set up according to the federal structure of the German political system: 'The DGB has its democratic structures to organise will-finding processes with its eight members. We have them at the level of the steering committee, then there are committees, working groups, written co-ordination, the normal programme' (interview 34). Positions are developed bottom-up 'since at all levels there exists the possibility to pass on positions, from the communal level to the district, from the district to the regional organisation, and from the regional organisation to the federal organisation' (interview 38); and 'at each level, every member can voice its concerns, there are respective committees for that where the interests of members can be aggregated' (interview 44; similarly interview 54; interview 49). Receiving input from members which work at those levels where poverty operates is more important the higher the level of governance. In Brussels, this is particularly felt:

> We are dependent, in the end, on getting assessments of how policy processes impact living conditions from our members, since we are a bit far away, here in Brussels, from the work that Caritas is doing locally. Whilst we can be the bridge to the institutions, we lack the technical expertise to write such positions on our own. So there is a very broad consultation process going on in the organisation (interview 43).

Only three actors, all from the national level of governance, point to AGMs as the place where will-formation, decision-making and authorisation take place: 'The core obviously is the yearly AGM. It is the highest institution which can take all the decisions and decide about general directions' (interview 45; similarly interview 49; interview 53).[3]

The common way of organising position-finding is, as for the two other kinds of CSOs, to meet in expert committees, which exist at the regional, federal and European levels:

> We have a system of expert committees. Similar to trade unions or political parties, they are sorted along major policy areas. In these committees sit experts that the organisations are delegating and who develop, jointly with headquarters, a policy position. The position will then be passed on to the elected steering committee which ultimately decides about the policy position (interview 47; similarly interview 34; interview 37; interview 38; interview 42; interview 48; interview 50; interview 52; interview 60).

Two actors, one regional, one national, actually mention expert groups that deal with EU issues in particular: 'There are regular meetings for Europe organised by the federal organisation where the respective policy officers of the regional organisations come together' (interview 37; similarly interview 39). At the EU level, expert committees have 'one member per every national network and a number of members from other European organisations' (interview 60). And this group, he continues, is 'designated with the responsibility and the decision-making around it' (interview 60), the delegation either coming from the respective national network or through the European umbrella. Once a year, these groups report back to the executive committee, so that there exists a 'clear democratic accountability structure, possibly a little heavy, but that's the reality' (interview 60).

---

3. At the EU level, the number of delegates national networks can send to the AGMs of EAPN largely depends on the size of the population of the respective Member State. Today, the United Kingdom, Germany, Spain, France and Italy have eight delegates; Greece, Ireland and Portugal have six, while Belgium, Denmark and the Netherlands can send four delegates. The smallest country – Luxembourg – was allowed to send two delegates to the meetings.

In general, who and which group precisely will be dealing with a specific process or position depends on how long-term and important the process is and whether the organisation has already developed a position on a given topic in the past. If the latter is the case, then 'every policy officer can handle it on its own. If it is not the case, then we need the respective decisions of the committees, which take their time'. In many instances, it would:

> ... suffice for the respective expert committee – to which organisations of the lower governance levels delegate representatives – to develop a position on a given process. For more serious decisions it needs to go into the conference of managing directors in which sit the managing directors of the regional organisation and of the federal organisation. And for even more serious issues, the steering committee of the federal organisation needs to convene (interview 44; similarly interview 59).

Important decisions or policy positions in general need to be made or adapted by the steering committee, which is the body with the ultimate political and legal responsibility. Steering committees are almost always exclusively composed of members who have been delegated to it, in an attempt to assure the balanced representation of all the different member constituencies of the federal organisation: 'We try and organise, in the steering committee, a representation of the different regional organisations and networks, so that we have the entire federal system represented in the steering committee and therefore also in our decisions' (interview 51; similarly interview 52; interview 54).

In some organisations, position-finding and decision-making is more top-down. In such instances, the steering committee has a stronger role to play whilst members beyond those in the steering committee are not necessarily involved or consulted (interview 35; interview 57), or involved to a lesser degree anyway: 'Since I am in the steering committee, these things would be discussed there and would then move to the directing conference where the members would not be directly involved' (interview 46). Some organisations seem to operate in a more decentralised manner and therefore do not always consult all the members:

> Our board of trustees has an influence. ... But we don't have a group which we have to consult, as a whole. I think on a project-by-project basis, even if it's a short-term project, we would normally have a steering committee or an advisory project of experts in that area that would seek to guide the project. But it wouldn't operate for the whole organisation (interview 57).

It is, of course, common that the members of the different organisations will also be in touch with each other, and with staff, in more informal ways, in order for will-formation and decision-making to take place. This may happen through getting in touch directly with members of the steering committee (interview 51) or through consultations, magazines or events (interview 53; similarly interview 59).

On actor, in fact, points out that 'as far as EU issues are concerned, there really are no formalised procedures. Of course we have to speak with the relevant member of the steering committee. In this case, that is the general secretary of the German Caritas who has the final word and needs to sign a given position. AGMs in general do not deal with such policy processes' (interview 43).

Finally, the staff normally plays an important role in processes of will-formation and decision-making and, in particular, the headquarters staff of the organisation (interview 46; interview 51; interview 56; interview 59). In a nutshell, 'in reality a lot of the strategic thinking is done by the staff and then presented to the trustees' (interview 54). A national actor explains:

We are the administering headquarters after all. Of course we also have many possibilities to launch an initiative. We also have the right to launch an initiative. If we are of the view that we need an initiative on a given topic, then we draft a paper and pass it on to the steering committee, without any of the members having contributed to it (interview 47).

So far as control of groups' activities is concerned, half of the actors mention yearly reports and, more particularly, AGMs: 'Absolutely, it's an organisation. The AGM is the highest body, and the steering committee, in principle, is only managing the daily business in between the AGMs. Through the reporting, the steering committee's actions are formally approved, and it needs to engage in related debates' (interview 51; similarly interview 35; interview 36; interview 39; interview 42; interview 43; interview 45; interview 47; interview 48; interview 49; interview 53; interview 54; interview 56; interview 60). However, 18.5 per cent point out that this would not really correspond to 'control', given that people would sometimes not read the relevant passages or not question them if they did read them; that the reports would not be voted; or that AGMs may be poorly attended (interview 36; interview 42; interview 56; interview 48; interview 45). Instead, some of them point out that 'control' would happen more informally: 'The other means are probably more informal. It's a case of actually continuing to impress enough to make sure they get the response that they want from the charity' (interview 53; similarly interview 43). One actor explains:

The people concerned with EU affairs regularly spread information, which, ideally, members will get. They can read that and see what's been going on. So it's different from the members of a political party or the like. It really is entirely different. They are supporting members of the DRK and, of course, follow what's happening to the donations they are giving us, and that's fine and the way it should be. But the involvement with social policy issues in general and EU social affairs in particular is absolutely low (interview 38; similarly interview 45).

So, members and supporters are invited to follow homepages and read newsletters and 'if we notice they cannot relate to it, then we know we've done a bad job. And they would tell us pretty directly "that's bad, there's an error in that paper, it's wrong legally". But that hardly ever happens' (interview 47). Another form of informal control that actors mention occurs in meetings and by members and staff when developing positions (interview 49; interview 60).

5.3.2 How do CSOs mobilise support?

Mobilisation of the existing constituency

Do the democratic structures that most of the anti-poverty groups have in place correspond to a high degree of mobilisation of the constituencies? By and large, they do. Of all the actors interviewed, 81.5 per cent say that they mobilise their constituency either regularly (63 per cent) or irregularly (18.5 per cent); 14.8 per cent mobilise their constituency rarely whilst 3.7 per cent do not mobilise their constituency at all.

In those cases where the mobilisation of constituencies does not or only rarely occurs, actors point out that the political mobilisation of members either is not required 'because the direct co-operation with the official sites makes it possible for us to place our positions directly' (interview 38); because members 'are people who want books' (interview 56); or because, 'if they are a member of CPHE, they've pretty much already agreed that poor families need more money' (*ibid.*).

What form does mobilisation take, when it occurs? A first means of mobilising members is to consult them about the activities of the organisation, to try to find out what their assessment is and what should be the organisation's priorities or positions in certain political processes. This is mentioned by 11.1 per cent (all from the national level):

> We do a lot of consultation, going out to visit local groups and asking their views on policies and traditions. We engage a lot through our website and through Facebook and Twitter, and get the views and opinions of all the people and we have a quarterly magazine that goes out to all our member-groups as well; again, telling what the charity is doing but also making sure that we're not going too far and that they support all of the work we are doing on their behalf (interview 53; similarly interview 45; interview 52).

Indeed, the internet seems to be ever more used for the mobilisation of the constituencies: 'People can put their views to us through a website called OneSpace, where single parents can bring an issue. So we had a very big issue around the government work programme, and real concerns about it. Actually single parents were the ones to really draw that up as an issue' (interview 55).

Another way to mobilise already existing members is to organise training and workshops – indeed our work 'can only be implemented in close co-operation with our members. This means that our thematic days are normally not only conceptualised in the regional headquarters, but are planned and implemented with our members' (interview 37; similarly interview 36; interview 40; interview 42; interview 48;

interview 50). Whilst these sorts of trainings and workshops are rather directed at the membership, organisations also more or less regularly organise events: smaller or larger conferences or meetings to which the larger public is also invited and for which they try to mobilise their constituencies (interview 51; interview 43; interview 50).

Then, there are forms of mobilisation that target both members and supporters as well as a potentially larger constituency; and these are forms which tend to be explicitly political. They occur via lobbying MPs and organising days of action or campaigns, throughout the different levels of governance. As regards more traditional kinds of lobbying, this may include everything from 'writing to an MP or possibly to a minister' (interview 57); organising 'parliamentary evenings', at which MPs and MEPs are invited to discuss issues of concern (interview 36; similarly interview 53); taking people to parliament and either having people affected by poverty bear witness to MPs of their experiences (interview 55) or having an MP give a talk: 'In practice, we hold them in parliament. So to encourage people to come we always provide a controversial MP to give a talk about something controversial. … We get about all of the staff to go, and our policy advisory committee goes and a lot of people who we work with very closely come. And we spend the time talking to the politician that we are talking to' (interview 56).

The success at mobilising is rather mixed: 37 per cent of the actors say that the constituencies let themselves be mobilised regularly and for 51.9 per cent, this is irregularly the case. In 7.4 per cent of the cases, mobilisation only occurs rarely whilst for 3.7 per cent, no mobilisation occurs.

In some cases, and again throughout levels of organisational governance, mobilisation does not seem to be a problem; in fact, members are expecting to be mobilised and become active themselves: 'I would not like to phrase it in a passive way. Members actually are really interested in a high degree of activity. Often, it is rather the case that members tell us "there is something to do here or we should be more active here, let us get engaged here". I perceive them as being very active' (interview 37; similarly interview 36; interview 39; interview 42; interview 44; interview 48; interview 53; interview 59). At the EU level, one actor points out that all the activities of EAPN are member-based:

All of our activity is membership-based, so there's nothing that we do which isn't rooted in inputs from our members. … In terms of our activities, they are always rooted in inputs from the members. Members are the primary givers of input and usually the event is designed with input from our members as well (interview 60).

Other actors have a more mixed evaluation of the mobilisation of their constituency. A number of actors point out that whether or not mobilisation is successful very much depends on the topic and, more precisely, whether people are themselves touched by the issue at stake: 'It depends on the issue. If it is placeable and close to everyday life's problems, then it works. But with EU policies, there are many issues which seem very far away to our members, and then it's more difficult to mobilise' (interview 34). Similar responses were given by actors from the local, regional and European level: 'It depends. So soon as members see an added value for themselves, then it definitely works' (interview 46; similarly interview 40; similarly interview 47; interview 50). A factor that seems to hinder the mobilisation is the lack of time individuals have at their disposal. Indeed, in '90 per cent of the cases, the issue is to find someone who will draft an article or get a project started. We do wish for it to happen, but the time of members is simply limited' (interview 45), which is why 'it's a struggle, actually, mobilising people, it's not easy or straightforward' (interview 57). Therefore, the:

> reality is that it can be a limited number of individuals, no matter how big our national network might be. So in some cases it can be several hundred organisations. But very often the work is carried out by a limited number of individuals. It's hard to mobilise large numbers within the countries to follow some of the detailed policies that we follow. And I know from my own experience when I was a member, when I was working for a member organisation within Ireland. You're very happy that somebody is taking on this work, you give some support to it. But often within the daily challenges that local organisations are facing, it's often hard to devote time to look at policies like the European Employment Strategy, to reflect on and look at the national reform programmes under the Europe 2020 strategy (interview 60).

For the legitimacy of anti-poverty groups, it matters whether or not they seek to involve those affected by poverty. Is this the case? Of all the actors, 25.9 per cent indicate that they regularly involve the poor themselves whilst 55.6 per cent say that they involve them irregularly and 18.5 per cent of the actors say their organisation does not involve people affected by poverty. Involvement, where it occurs, takes four forms: committees; projects; events; and lobbying.

Two actors from each level of governance (22.2 per cent) mention that they either currently have poor people on their governance committees or have had them in committees in the past: 'We have one who is personally poverty-stricken who would be in the office on average once or twice a week, and who would then be part of the broader team' (interview 59; similarly interview 57; interview 50). In another case, those affected by poverty have set up their own governance committee and working groups (interview 44). Particularly at the EU level and within EAPN, there is a real effort to have poor people involved, also in the governance of the organisation, which 'wasn't the case at the beginning. It changed, it gave EAPN legitimacy and it also changed our work because we can have more in-depth analysis, closer to reality, it's quite different than studies or surveys' (interview 61). These days, people affected by poverty are also represented in the different working groups of EAPN and co-decide policy positions (*ibid.*).

A second way of involving poor people is to include them in concrete projects: 18.5 per cent mention this possibility, mainly from the regional level: 'Ideally, we aim to mobilise them all, in different ways. So a lot of our programme work is around mobilising people in poverty – training them, providing local groups with skills to do their own representation' (interview 54). This sort of involvement seems rather common in the British context:

> We might, for example, have a project where the aim is for young people to gain skills in film-making. And that would be a direct benefit to the community members. Or we might try and run an event which is not just about raising awareness but also kind of like a training event – getting people to realise how they can get their voices heard (interview 57).

In other instances, more likely in the German context, it will depend on 'whether the projects allow for poor people to be involved. If so, we do it on a very small scale' (interview 41; similarly interview 48). One actor gives a concrete example of a project where the idea was:

> to let the people speak for themselves who live in poverty in Hamburg, to let them give their perspective on their lives. It was a small research project and a public event, and then also an exhibition came out of it. There we had the possibility to bring these perspectives into the public sphere. Normally, it's always other people speaking for the poor. This was an opportunity for the poor to speak for themselves and articulate themselves (interview 50).

A third way of involving poor people is events and, again, examples of this are provided by actors from all organisational governance levels. Events relating to issues of poverty are organised every now and then by 25.9 per cent, one of the goals being a 'direct exchange with the affected, and to try and pass the messages to politics together' (interview 49). Therefore, 'we always try, when we have panels, to also have representatives of the groups of unemployed on them' (interview 50; similarly interview 36; interview 43; interview 46; interview 57; interview 60).

Finally, one actor mentions a more traditional kind of lobbying in which poor people would also be involved:

> In terms of parliamentary work we have a real ethos that we want to involve single parents. If we do, or if we are doing any parliamentary events or events where we are asked to speak, we will bring along single parents to talk about their own experience or where they've researched on other single parents, to talk about that (interview 55).

There are obviously a number of difficulties when seeking to involve poor people in an organisation's activities and governance; and the higher the level of governance, the greater these are likely to be. Indeed, at the EU level, 'there can be a gap between the theory of that and the reality of that. There are many barriers, like language. Also, even if we are able to reimburse the costs of attending meetings you always have additional costs associated. You may have to wait for reimbursements' (interview 60). His colleague adds that 'for people experiencing poverty, the time is not the same as for decision-makers. People living in a situation of social exclusion, they are always living in a kind of emergency. The time is really short for them and they would like to have changes, visible too. ... And that's one of the biggest difficulties, the difference of time...the difference of emergency' (interview 61).

Other difficulties with involving the poor may be located on the side of the organisation. Indeed, in particular, a number of the German organisations may not be quite ready, so far as their organisational culture is concerned, to truly involve poor people. At least, it seems that a discussion about it has been initiated: 'Yes, we do discuss it in our unit because we do see it as a shortcoming. The Diakonie, in its mission statement, has the slogan "Strong for others". One could develop the mission statement further in the direction of "Strong with others". But all of this is still very tentative, I would say' (interview 50; similarly interview 37).

Mobilisation of the wider public

Do groups also seek to reach out to the larger public, that is, do they try to maintain some relationship with it or not and, if they do, of what kind? Or do they mainly relate to their existing constituency? Do groups merely pass on information to the public or do they seek to reach out to the larger public in order to involve it in debate or mobilise it for activities? In order to answer these questions, I shall look at whether CSOs inform the larger public about their policies and activities, particularly by making information available on their websites and by maintaining relationships with the press; I will also see whether they try to mobilise a larger constituency, either through passive means (becoming a member or donating money) or more actively, through online and street activities.

Informing the larger public about one's activities is a part of maintaining a relationship with it. Therefore, one question to address is how organisations are providing the public with information, and through which channels. These days, a major way of informing a larger public of one's activities is to have a website. All the anti-poverty organisations investigated have a website. Social media, in contrast, is only used by approximately half of the groups: 51.9 per cent use them, 48.1 per cent do not. What sort of information can we find on the websites? Regular newsletters or briefings to which one can subscribe are mentioned by 77.8 per cent whilst 22.2 per cent do not have these: 'We issue an electronic newsletter to our members as well as to political lobbyists and relevant people such MPs and others, where we inform about EU policies, new EU programmes or certain aspects of labour-market policy. Every fortnight this goes out to a list of approximately 500 organisations' (interview 36). Publishing statements online is a way for 66.7 per cent to inform the public about their positions on specific policy processes whilst 33.3 per cent do not do this. As with the other two CSO groups, most of the anti-poverty groups also maintain active relationships with the press, though considerably less than 'members' and 'cause' groups – 65.4 per cent offer press releases and/or special information packages for the press on their websites whilst 34.6 per cent do not. Press and media work is considered 'important' (interview 45), 'primarily to attract attention to an issue and sensitise people about it' (interview 49), but also to 'advertise for the organisation' (interview 44). By some actors, the importance of media work is acknowledged: 'We have the impression that something can only be changed sustainably if the public pressure increases. This means that our work with the media has gained ever more in importance. If I am present there, if something is being reported in the press or on television, then the political representatives are ready to think about it more intensively' (interview 49).

Do anti-poverty groups also seek to involve the larger public in some of their activities, in passive or more active ways? Not to a great extent, it seems: 44.4 per cent of them invite individuals to become members whilst 55.6 per cent do not. When asked explicitly about it, 70.4 per cent of the actors say their organisation has no active recruitment strategy whilst 29.6 per cent say it has such a strategy. Where there are active efforts to recruit new members, this mostly seems to happen via the internet and media work (interview 38; interview 44; interview 46; interview 49; interview 59). Where there are no active efforts to recruit new members, the question about an explicit recruitment strategy seemed to take interviewees somewhat by surprise and a rather common answer is 'I am not sure, really'. For a range of actors, having an active recruitment strategy is not an issue because their constituency is structurally limited to begin with. This is the case for all the service-providers and lobbyists who work within either the Protestant or the Catholic Church in Germany, as the majority of German actors do. In these cases, only organisations which share the principles and aims, if not the faith, of the Church can become members or are 'natural' members by their origin (interview 37; interview 39; interview 42; interview 48; interview 50). Finally, in 66.7 per cent of the organisations, the possibility of donating money is offered on their website, against 33.3 per cent of the cases where this is not the case.

The findings for more active forms of interaction and involvement are similarly mixed. The large majority of the organisations do not invite the larger public to participate in campaigns, petitions, mailings or demonstrations. However, 33.3 per cent of them do, across all levels of organisational governance. A number of anti-poverty actors mention campaigns as a form of broader mobilisation. These will more often than not have MPs as their addressees and, obviously, relate to ongoing welfare reforms or the potential impact of these on poor people (interview 44; interview 46; interview 47; interview 60). Often, these campaigns are organised online 'where we would encourage them to email a minister or their member of parliament or somebody else and we've invested quite a lot of time and resources into that over the past few years' (interview 54; similarly interview 57). One actor explains:

We're running a campaign at the moment. So it's a public-facing campaign about child benefit. And we're trying to discourage the government from doing a couple of things which they have announced they are going to do to child benefit. And we did online mobilisation for that. And so we worked with 38 Degrees to get a letter to MPs out, and we sent that around to some mums we contacted and, more importantly, the other organisations we work with in End Child Poverty, who then forwarded it to their networks of supporters to get people to email their MPs. So we do that sort of stuff (interview 56).

Another actor points to a demonstration that is related to a campaign his organisation is engaged in: 'We're doing a demonstration outside the front of the Scottish Parliament towards the end of March. That's an event where we are trying to gather and get as much support and older people as possible to come along and lend their support and lend their voice to the campaign' (interview 53). Demonstrations are also organised in Brussels: 'In 2010 we mobilised people to make a human ring around the EU institutions in Brussels. This year, for the eleventh EU meeting of people experiencing poverty, there was a protest during the meeting, I mean participants showed a red card to the EU institutions. During the same meeting, some of the participants went to the Council to demonstrate' (interview 61; similarly interview 34; interview 53).

Other mobilising activities, such as workshops, conferences or public lectures, are less contestatory in nature and these provide forums for discussion and interaction. According to their websites, 66.7 per cent of the anti-poverty groups organise such events whilst 33.3 per cent do not. Mostly, this seems to relate to workshops and lectures (interview 43; interview 48): 'There is a discussion series, "Just City of Hamburg", which takes place six times a year. A third of the public are unemployed and poor people, the rest are experts or interested citizens' (interview 50). Alternatively, these sorts of activities include inviting prominent people to speak about important reform packages so as to make the larger public more aware of their potential effects (interview 57) or organising press conferences to get the media interested in policy positions and mobilising both members and people affected by poverty for that (interview 39). Finally, one local actor points to a number of activities he is organising locally, such a street party for kids, a cooking course and a yoga class (interview 40).

Only 18.5 per cent provide the opportunity to post a blog on the website whilst 81.5 per cent do not – even though this figure is higher than for the other two kinds of groups. Finally, about half of the groups offer the opportunity to volunteer in the organisation and thereby get to know it better and also support it – for 55.6 per cent of these organisations, this is the case, for 44.4 per cent not.

5.4 Interest representation strategies in EU policy making

Whilst the last section allowed us to see how representative CSOs are of their constituency, this section will show the activities of representation through which anti-poverty actors represent their constituency in EU policy making. To do so, I will first look at their degree of Europeanisation as defined in Chapter 2.4. The main part of this section concerns the addressees of anti-poverty actors in EU policy making as well as the latter's strategies for addressing them. CSOs can use a multitude of channels for this. They may, first and foremost, try to lobby their relevant national ministries in the hope of thereby influencing Council decisions. They can lobby national MPs or MEPs, the latter in particular, since the EP is now involved in almost all European legislation by way of the co-decision procedure. They might address the European Commission directly and seek to influence legislative proposals in their very early stages. They might join forces and organise themselves under the head of a national and European umbrella organisation, in order to have a stronger voice vis-à-vis national and European institutions. Special attention will be given to this particular strategy so as to evaluate whether groups themselves see an added value in co-operating with other groups in order to influence EU policies and, specifically, whether groups co-operate both at the national *and* at the European level. Only if European-level co-operation happens could co-operation be taken as contributing to the emergence of a European *demos*, as is discussed in parts of the interested literature. If groups only co-operate with other groups from the same Member State, this would suggest that national differences between them, even within the same policy field, remain too great for stronger European co-ordination.

In a next step, I address whether being involved in EU policy making has an impact on anti-poverty organisations. This is relevant as it can give hints at why actors may be more or less engaged but also whether being involved in EU policy making distances the organisations from their constituencies in one way or another. Finally, some of the CSOs might consider going to the European Court of Justice if they felt a legal injustice that needed to be corrected had occurred. Or, indeed, they might use all these different channels in their efforts to influence policies. This section will explore the ways CSOs use these different channels, with a focus on the political (rather than the judicial) institutions and the lobby strategies actors associate with them and with special attention given to European umbrella organisations.

The chapter closes by looking at the incentive structure for agricultural actors to get engaged with the EU, as perceived by the actors themselves, thereby providing clues for the explanation of their engagement with the EU. This will involve exploring actors' perceptions of what are the positives and negatives coming from the EU; of differences in the work environments between the EU and their domestic environment; and of whether they find it easier or harder to be heard at the EU level than domestically. As regards the latter point, specific attention will be paid to the European Commission's consultation regime. It is relevant insofar as the Commission is not only the initiator of legislation in the EU and therefore a central actor. It has also developed a number of consultation and participation opportunities specifically for CSOs over the last fifteen years or so. It is helpful to know how far these are accepted by CSOs because satisfaction with the Commission's consultation regime may be a strong incentive to become involved in EU policy making, whilst dissatisfaction with it may be a strong disincentive. I will end by addressing the degree to which, as a consequence, the anti-poverty constituency has been interested in EU affairs.

5.4.1 *To whom are representing activities addressed and by what strategies?*

In this sub-section, I will, by and large, draw on the qualitative data. Where informative, I will supplement it by quantitative data from the questionnaire, in which I asked actors to qualify how important they thought it was to be in touch with specific actors in regard to EU affairs.

The degree of Europeanisation

There are neither strong legal nor strong financial incentives for anti-poverty groups to Europeanise themselves. However, as we've seen above, there might be more ideational reasons for them to get involved in EU affairs. How does the incentive structure play out in practice? To this question, 19.2 per cent say dealing with EU processes in their organisation has an 'important' role, 30.8 per cent evaluate its importance as 'medium', 34.6 per cent say its importance is 'rather low' and 15.4 per cent think it is 'not important at all'. Second, I asked whether the EU was an issue in daily work: 30.8 per cent say the EU is 'regularly' an issue in their work, for 15.4 per cent this is the case 'irregularly', for 34.6 per cent 'rarely' and for 19.2 per cent 'never'. More concretely, 59.3 per cent of the anti-poverty actors think that lobbying is highly relevant in their EU-related activities, against 88.9 per cent in the domestic context. Other activities also enjoy considerably less importance at the EU level when compared with the domestic context: this is the case for funding, which 51.9 per cent consider highly important at the EU level against 85.2 per cent at the domestic level; for networking (59.3 per cent against 100 per cent); and for exchange and information (74.1 per cent against 92.6 per cent). Third, I asked how important it is to be present in Brussels in order to achieve organisational goals. In reply, 40.7 per cent think it is 'very important' and 33.3 per cent find it 'rather important'. However, there are also 18.5 per cent who think it's 'rather unimportant' to be present in Brussels or 'not important at all' (another 7.4 per cent). Finally, I have looked at the organisations' websites and checked whether or not they report on EU policies. If they do, that indicates that EU policies and informing about them are considered to be important in the organisation and *vice versa*. The comparatively low salience of the EU is mirrored in communication the anti-poverty organisations have with the larger public – 77.8 per cent have no information on the EU and related activities on their website while 22.2 per cent do have some information (*see* graph 4 in the appendix).

The domestic level[4]

When seeking to influence policies, groups often form *alliances* with other groups in order to exert stronger pressure on those they are lobbying. Is this also the case for anti-poverty groups? In the domestic arena, six actors see themselves as being part of networks (interview 34; similarly interview 45; interview 47; interview 37; interview 51; interview 57): 'It probably would be other NGOs seeking to influence the same policy agenda. So we do quite a lot of work in partnership with other organisations' (interview 57). Some actors stress that there are changing coalitions over time: 'There's a broader range of NGOs that we do work with from time to time and occasionally come together as a coalition to lobby central government' (interview 54). Exactly who would co-operate with whom depends on, amongst other factors, 'where the common interests are greatest, and also

---

4.   For the domestic and the European levels, *see* graphs 5 and 6 in the appendix.

who is the counterpart on the political level' (interview 43). Indeed, forming such coalitions with national CSOs when seeking to influence EU policies is deemed 'very important' by 37 per cent of all the anti-poverty actors and 'rather important' by 29.6 per cent, whilst 33.3 per cent think that such coalitions are 'rather unimportant'.

In terms of inter-organisational strategies, many actors mention being in touch with a national umbrella structure. By 'national umbrella structure' here, I mean that umbrella organisation that is the official member of EAPN in a Member State. In Germany, this is the *Nationale Armutskonferenz* (NAK). In the UK, whilst there is a national umbrella structure, it hardly seems to be known amongst the anti-poverty actors, thereby slightly distorting the answers. When asked openly, 53.8 per cent mention the NAK as one channel of lobbying whilst 46.2 per cent do not mention it. This contrasts, to some degree, with the data of the questionnaire, in which I asked the actors directly how strong their links to the national umbrella organisation are. Here, 38.5 per cent say they have strong and regular links with the national umbrella and 3.8 per cent rather strong if irregular links. However, 38.5 per cent say their link to the national umbrella is weak and contact is rare and some 19.2 per cent say they do not have any link at all.[5]

Those who have strong and regular links with the NAK tend to come from the federal level. One actor explains that the NAK 'has a very important role to play in the context of anti-poverty policy because it opens the door to EAPN. And since we are also active in the field of anti-poverty policy, of course we contribute to and participate in the work of the NAK. ... This means that we participate in the decision-making and contribute our own topics' (interview 44; similarly interview 38). For some, the national umbrella organisation seems to be the only channel of collective lobbying in EU affairs: 'We would exclusively do that via the NAK. The NAK organises meetings with MPs, also with MEPs, and this is how we may be in touch with them. And if we really try to bring an issue on the agenda, such as health, then we would do that via the NAK' (interview 49). Others also point out that there exists 'very close links' with the NAK (interview 42), not least when people happen to be on the board of the NAK (interview 42).

Others say that the NAK is not so important for them as an umbrella structure. A number of reasons why that is so are mentioned by the different actors. For one actor, the NAK is not so important as it 'is limited to the issue of poverty' whilst on the European level, there are also issues coming up, by way of directives, that the NAK 'simply does not cover' (interview 39). A second reason that appears repeatedly – both at the regional and the national level – is the lack of resources for becoming involved in the NAK:

We simply can't afford to satisfy these structures. It's a question of capacities. I have only just withdrawn from the next delegates' conference because I

---

5. For the German actors, only, 38.9 per cent say they have strong and regular contacts; for 5.5 per cent it is rather strong if irregular; for 50 per cent the contact is weak and rare; and for 5.5 per cent, there is no contact at all.

simply can't make it. If you're busy locally, talking with the citizens about small things, you almost can't balance the act between the local and the national level, because we don't have the capacities for it (interview 40; similarly interview 45; interview 51).

Therefore, for regional or even more so local actors, the NAK 'does not play an important role, and it's rather indirectly via the federal level that the contact is organised' (interview 37).

Despite not always actively using it for their lobbying, many actors across levels of governance seem to be rather pleased with the way they are represented by the NAK in EU affairs: 'I think they represent us well' (interview 40; similarly interview 36, interview 46), because 'the positions of the NAK are to 98 per cent positions that we also defend' (interview 50); 'because they have very competent and engaged colleagues there and the communication works very well, it's a process that has worked' (interview 44), and because 'whenever we did contribute something, it got picked up and was integrated in respective resolutions' (interview 45).

Five German actors, four of which are regional, could not tell how well they were being represented by the NAK: 'I could not tell you whether or not these actors represent us well. That's a question one would have to address to the federal organisation' (interview 37). 'I would assume that they represent us well, I could not tell you in any detail, because I don't follow up on how they do it' (interview 42), says another actor. A third one indicates that he was particularly following the issues that were of relevance domestically and less (or not at all) the European aspects of the work of the NAK (interview 51).

As regards the German anti-poverty organisations, many of them are, in fact, organised under a different umbrella structure from the NAK. Historically, the six large welfare organisations in Germany have united to form a platform called *Bundesarbeitsgemeinschaft der Freien Wohlfahrtspflege* (BAG FW). The goal of the association is to co-ordinate the activities of the six organisations and to co-operate in influencing social legislation and welfare policies. The co-operation exists both at the federal level and in all of the sixteen *Länder*. So, historically, the BAG FW predates the NAK. But also, its organisations are dealing with all sorts of issues related to poverty, disadvantages and social policy more broadly whereas the NAK is, more or less, a one-issue organisation that focuses on poverty. Finally, the six organisations that form the BAG FW are all large organisations that tend to operate in similar ways and therefore have similar institutional backgrounds and concerns. The NAK, in contrast, brings together a multitude of organisations with quite dissimilar degrees of institutionalisation and of political activism. Interests are therefore much more heterogeneous than in the BAG FW. Therefore, for many actors, the BAG FW 'is simply closer to our interests' (interview 38) than the NAK: 'I think the most important coalition in this context is the BAG FW. ... There is a committee on the EU which convenes four times a year, and we try to co-ordinate our views there and develop a joint position. ... The cooperation within the BAG FW is much closer than that with the NAK' (interview 43).

Indeed, this structure is mentioned by all those (German) actors who work for one of the six large organisations that established the BAG FW. Furthermore, co-operation between the large welfare organisations also seems to be desired by the relevant federal ministry, rather than the ministry being lobbied by the welfare organisations individually (interview 38). Finally, the BAG FW entertains an office in Brussels whilst the NAK does not, to the point that one actor asked 'why should I use the NAK?' (interview 35)

In the UK, the range of potential CSO partners seems to be more varied and adopted on a case-to-case basis: 'We work quite extensively with other organisations and we certainly get them to help out in our lobbying and campaigning. So, for example, the welfare reform stuff we are doing at the moment, it's the Welfare Reform Consortium. All of the charities getting together and speaking. So we work with a whole bunch of other organisations in terms of lobbying and campaigning' (interview 56; similarly interview 54).

In regard to national institutions outside welfare organisations, 28 per cent mention regional ministries as institutions they seek to lobby when trying to influence EU policies. As for the two other CSO groups, this strategy is only used by German actors, given the federal political system in Germany, in which regional actors can hope to influence federal policies by way of the second chamber (interview 37). Also along those lines, regional MPs are mentioned by 14.8 per cent of all actors.

When asked openly, only 38.5 per cent mention national ministries as a venue for influencing EU policies whilst 61.5 per cent do not. However, when asked directly in the questionnaire, 44.4 per cent say that national ministries are 'very important' when seeking to influence EU policies, 22.2 per cent find this channel 'rather important' and 25.9 per cent find it 'rather unimportant'.[6] Actors may send ministries their positions in written form, have in bilateral meetings with them, participate in stakeholder consultations or organise workshops and other events to which they invite officials from the ministries (interview 34; interview 38; interview 39; interview 42; interview 44; interview 46; interview 54; interview 57):

> As regards EU affairs, we in particular try to address the national ministries and to influence them with our positions. That seems to be the only way to give weight to our position and, in fact, it pays back twice, as we can manage the national and the European levels in one go. Of course in the end it's the Commission who is the addressee. But given we are one out of six peak welfare organisations in one out of twenty-seven Member States, our influence is accordingly marginal and so we focus on the national level. From our perspective, that has paid off' (interview 44).

When asked openly, 25.9 per cent – six national, one regional actor – mention that they address MPs when trying to influence EU policies (interview 34; interview

---

6. Two answers are missing.

38; interview 39; interview 46; interview 54; interview 56; interview 57). Once again, the picture changes significantly when asked directly in the questionnaire. Here, 14.8 per cent of all the actors think MPs are a 'very important', 48.1 per cent a 'rather important' and 33.3 per cent consider them a 'rather unimportant' channel of influence as regards EU policies.[7]

Finally, the municipality, political parties, national agencies and media are each mentioned by 7 per cent respectively.

The European level

With regard to lobbying channels in Brussels, some of the larger organisations, in particular, the Diakonie and the Caritas in Germany, are entertaining their own office in Brussels and seek to also lobby through that. Indeed, 42.3 per cent of the actors, both regional and national, mention this venue as one strategy to influence EU policies:

> In terms of lobbying, our Brussels office is doing a really good job, and if you have parallel lobbying structures, that does not always lead to greater success. So we co-ordinate our positions and strategy well, but do not get in the way of our colleagues who have the direct contacts to the Commission and the European Parliament (interview 36; similarly interview 37; interview 39; interview 42; interview 46; interview 48).

Sometimes, lobbying individually through the Brussels office is preferred to forming alliances: 'There are issues where we have a high degree of common interests and where we leave it up to the BAG FW to develop a position and contribute to it in that framework. However, there are also some relevant issues where it is important to us to have our own position, in addition to that of the BAG FW' (interview 44). This is confirmed by another actor who indicates that 'it's absolutely possible that, in addition, we also develop our own position, as an organisation. There is no recipe, and we decide from case to case how to proceed' (interview 43).

Next to maintaining one's own office in Brussels and using that for lobbying purposes, anti-poverty organisations are also members of European umbrella organisations. Indeed, being part of networks is deemed particularly important in Brussels, where individual national organisations are not as well known as at the domestic level and therefore, perhaps, listened to less (interview 43). All the organisations studied here are members of the EAPN. When asked openly, only 23.1 per cent mention EAPN as a channel through which they try to influence EU policies. This stands in contrast with the data from the questionnaire, in which, when asked directly, 7.7 per cent say the link is strong and regular; 26.9 per cent evaluate it as rather strong if irregular; 30.8 per cent find the link weak and rare; and 34.6 per cent have no link at all (*see* graph 7 in the appendix).

---

7.   One answer is missing.

Some of the actors indicate that they are involved in EAPN's work either themselves or by means of a colleague who is a delegate to the EAPN and therefore they 'participate in the discussions' in that way (interview 34; similarly interview 36): 'I am on the board of EAPN and of course bring the German views and positions into the network. … There we are, of course, a member of a network which is a member of a huge network. … It's simply another structure, which has its advantages and disadvantages, as everything. But EAPN definitely plays an important role so far as the issue of poverty is concerned' (interview 38). Other active members interpret their role differently: 'I am also a delegate of the NAK to the EAPN. … A part of our delegates regularly participate in task forces, workshops and in the working groups who meet approximately twice a year. And one of our delegates is on the board. … I am more someone who attends the AGMs. My time simply does not allow for me to be engaged more with them' (interview 49).

Many actors, however, have only very loose contacts with EAPN. This can be for various reasons. For some, EAPN does not work in their primary areas of interest:

> I don't work much with the results and information from EAPN. In the areas in which the EU with its policies really can influence German policies, that's not social policy, which tends to be the topic of EAPN, but rather labour-market policy. When you look at the service directive, that is not the focus of EAPN if I am rightly informed. Then you have other channels which are important (interview 39).

Others mention that contact with EAPN had only been established very recently but was promising (interview 57); that the work of EAPN was only of very limited relevance to their work: 'It's incredibly far away. What is being discussed in the EAPN and what happens here locally, it's very difficult to bring it together' (interview 40; similarly interview 45); that contact existed at a higher level of governance, mostly at the federal level (interview 48; interview 46; interview 37); or that contact was indirect, by means of the NAK (interview 39; interview 44; interview 50; interview 45): 'The information all passes through the NAK which also has the role to sum it up a bit. We then receive the information by the mailing list of the NAK' (interview 44).

Other actors don't have any contact to or information from EAPN whatsoever (interview 56). This is the case for most of the British organisations. One reason can be that resources are too limited:

> It's not something that we tend to … we don't get involved in European issues at that level at all. … We don't really have the resources to examine EU policy and look at lobbying at a European level. So while I think we may be members I think that may be more of a symbolic state rather than having a practical application (interview 53; similarly interview 52; interview 57).

How satisfied are anti-poverty actors with the way EAPN represents them? Despite the often rather weak or even non-existent link with EAPN, 42.3 per cent say they are happy (23.1 per cent) or rather satisfied (19.2 per cent) with the way the European umbrella represents them, whilst 11.5 per cent are rather unsatisfied. Not surprisingly, 46.2 per cent say they do not know how well EAPN represents them (*see* graph 8 in the appendix).

Those with a positive evaluation of the representation by EAPN come from both the national and the regional levels of governance: 'We think that EAPN is a very experienced partner which networks very well and which therefore can very well bring certain interests into the policy process' (interview 44). Another actor adds that 'so far, I have not had anything to criticise and have repeatedly thought that there is a strong overlap with our interests indeed' (interview 45). One actor reflects the difficulties of dealing with anti-poverty issues at the EU level, given the related policy-competence is not really there: 'Not everyone agrees, but I believe that when you reflect what can be done, at all, given how little competence there is at the EU level, then you have to change your benchmark, and I believe they are doing good work' (interview 47).

Other actors have a more mixed evaluation. Particularly from a German perspective, the fact that the German welfare state is much more developed than, for example, Eastern Member States does seem to pose a problem for some, though positive aspects are also acknowledged:

It's difficult. It really is a very big organisation, with a lot of member organisations. I attended the last three AGMs, and the problem is that there exist absolutely different interests. Of course, the representatives from Romania, Bulgaria, etc. are at a completely different point from where we are. … That's really difficult. Sometimes I think it's yet another big machine. Still, I think it's good that this organisation exists. I think it's good that it assembles as many member organisations. I always think it's interesting to get to know the perspectives of the representatives of other states. And we can mutually learn from each other. But of course it's very heterogeneous, that's likely to be the problem (interview 49).

Another German actor refers to differences between Member States in the organisation of welfare-provision, which make it difficult to go beyond lowest-common-denominator positions:

I could not generalise – sometimes we are satisfied, sometimes less. As the German Caritas organisation, we have the special situation that we have over 25,000 service providers and institutions and thereby a certain power on the market which other organisations in other Member States do not have. The result is that we face problems that others possibly don't have. This often makes it difficult to agree on positions which are more than the lowest common denominator in European networks. … The lowest common denominator is often so small that it does not really make sense for us any more (interview 43).

Finally, there are some actors who could not tell whether they are well represented by EAPN or not, simply because they are not involved or, at least, not in any direct way: 'I could not tell you for sure. I could not say anything negative but I also would not have a concrete example at hand where I could say that they have explicitly represented our interest' (interview 37; similarly interview 51, interview 34; interview 52; interview 57).

Besides this structure, however, it is fairly normal for larger organisations also to work through other networks when lobbying in Brussels. As shown above, the larger German organisations mainly work through another common structure, the BAG FW, which they also use at the EU level:

> Of course it is very difficult for EAPN to take on board German interests, interests of the German Red Cross. EAPN is a European network, and the social standards and policies in Germany are of course far more developed than in Romania. And accordingly, we in Germany have very high standards, which still need to be created in other EU Member States. And so of course it's clear that German positions and demands do not always play the greatest role. ... One has to see that. So often, representation via the BAG FW is simply closer to our interests, in the end (interview 38; similarly interview 43).

When asked openly, 26.9 per cent indicate that they go through another European umbrella than EAPN to pursue their EU-related goals:

> We are members of other networks. For example, at the European level, there is Caritas Europe, our European network. Between the European networks and the German Caritas, there generally is Caritas Europe. So Caritas Europe is a member of other European networks, whilst we generally work with Caritas Europe (interview 43).

Other actors have similar umbrella structures that they privilege over EAPN, be it Euro-Diakonia for the Protestant Church (interview 48), the European Roma Information Office and the European Roma Rights Centre for the Irish Travellers (interview 52), FEANTSA for issues of homelessness (interview 48), or a 'structure called ENAR, which is the European Network Against Racism. So most of our work in there, on European issues, is done through that umbrella network, ENAR' (interview 57).

When asked openly, 59.3 per cent of the anti-poverty actors say that they directly lobby the European Commission when seeking to influence EU policies, against 40.7 per cent for whom this channel does not come to mind. This corresponds rather neatly with the replies in the questionnaire, in which 44.4 per cent find it 'very important' to address the Commission in order to influence EU policies and 18.5 per cent 'rather important', whilst 33.3 per cent think it is 'rather unimportant'.[8]

---

8.   One reply is missing.

Those with regular contact with the Commission use different venues for staying in touch. First, 14.8 per cent (two regional, two national actors), mention that they participate in online consultations (interview 37; interview 46; interview 44; interview 43). Second, and similarly, 14.8 per cent mention bilateral contacts, either more informally or in the context of meetings to which they invite Commission officials (interview 37; interview 34; interview 44; interview 43). Third, they attend workshops and other events that the Commission organises (interview 46; similarly interview 43). Finally, some actors will be in touch with Commission officials because of their participation in EU structural funds, which is accompanied and assessed by Commission officials, who attend the relevant supervisory committees (interview 37; interview 44).

For a number of anti-poverty actors, four of them regional and four national (29.6 per cent), contact with the Commission is either irregular or rare. In such cases, regional actors are in touch with Commission officials in the context of yearly events such as a conference they organise themselves (interview 42); when questions arise in the context of the implementation of an EU co-funded project (interview 41) or again in the context of advisory committees for EU structural-fund-related projects (interview 42; interview 50). Similar opportunities seem to exist for national actors, who mainly indicate direct bilateral contacts and contacts in the context of events (interview 35; interview 57; interview 38; interview 52).

Finally, 40.7 per cent of the anti-poverty actors (six regional, five national) say that they have no contact at all with Commission officials: 'We don't have a relationship with any European institutions at any stage or level that I'm aware of' (interview 53).

When asked openly in the interview, 30.8 per cent of the anti-poverty actors, half regional, half national, say they lobby MEPs directly to try to influence EU policies, whilst 69.2 per cent do not mention this possibility. These figures are not mirrored in the data of the questionnaire, in which 33.3 per cent say it is 'very important' to lobby MEPs directly in order to influence EU policies, 22.2 per cent say it is 'rather important' whilst only 37 per cent find it 'rather unimportant'.[9]

Regular contact with MEPs seems hardly to exist at the regional level. For many actors, the contact with MEPs is rare, if it happens at all. They might have once invited an MEP to an event they organised or they might have met an MEP in Strasbourg or Brussels, but this would be the exception rather than the rule (interview 36, interview 37, interview 42, interview 48, interview 50, interview 57). Only one regional actor talks of being regularly in touch with MEPs, both via mail and face-to-face, both in the region and in Brussels (interview 46). Similar opportunities exist for national actors: 'We organise a major events series. We contact MEPs and invite them to what we call 'parliamentary breakfast' in order to have them meet members of our executive committee. We also send letters to MEPs or go and see some of them individually' (interview 34; similarly interview 44). That there may not be a huge incentive for MEPs to be in touch with anti-poverty actors, given the limited EU police-competence in the field of anti-poverty policies, is illustrated by this quotation:

---

9.   Two replies are missing.

We've tried to work with the Parliament now and with the rapporteur to try and have a more timely mechanism for the Parliament. And in a way, they can do that a little bit by giving a little bit more visibility to the messages of the social NGOs because we are able to work a bit faster around these sorts of issues (interview 60).

Finally, 30.8 per cent of the anti-poverty actors say they are not in touch with anyone about EU policies, whilst for 69.2 per cent this is not the case.

In regard to their lobbying strategies, several actors point out that they sometimes use EU policies to 'remind' or to try to force their national governments to comply with EU law:

What I think is politically interesting is that often you get further with your demands in Brussels than with the federal government. Politically, it is exciting how one can link these different possibilities to one another, for example, how one reminds the federal government of the European goals and commitments they have made in Brussels. If those are in line with our demands, then it's more difficult for the federal government to escape. We call it the constructive pincers (interview 48; similarly interview 44; interview 57; interview 52).

A European actor also indicates how they try to lobby the relevant people from different sides, both national and European:

It's a double effort. Once we finalise the positions, our members will go directly to their national parliaments, go directly to their European parliamentarians, go directly to the relevant ministries. In our work the Social Protection Committee and the Employment Committee and the national members of that are a key target. So they would try to speak directly with those people. ... And then at the European level, we will directly work with the rapporteur in the Parliament, Marije Corneilissen, who is the MEP writing the report on the follow-up to the annual growth survey and the national reform, and try and influence the Parliament's positioning around it. Of course the Commission, we will aim at the Commissioner, but also to the Director-General, the Secretary-General, because so much of the Europe 2020 and national reform programme process is driven from secretary-general level (interview 60).

5.4.2 The impact of involvement in EU policy making on CSOs

Does being involved in EU policy making have an impact on the way anti-poverty organisations work, either on their strategies or the substance of their work? In the questionnaires, 50 per cent of the anti-poverty actors reply that being involved in EU policy making affects their organisation whilst 3.8 per cent think it does not; 46.2 per cent do not know (*see* graph 10 in the appendix).[10]

---

10. One actor did not respond.

A key way that the EU can potentially have an effect on CSOs is through EU funding. Of the anti-poverty organisations that I have contacted, 44.4 per cent benefited from EU funding at the time I contacted them, 18.5 per cent had done so in the past while 37 per cent of them had never received EU funding. Both regional and national organisations benefit from project co-funding. At the EU level, anti-poverty umbrellas benefit from operating grants, that is, structural funding from the Commission (interview 60; interview 39).

When asked openly, 22.2 per cent (three regional, three national actors) suggest that receiving EU funding does not affect their work and activities in a substantial way (interview 38; interview 45; interview 47). EU funding would only be used if it was meaningful to the organisation and related to what it was doing anyway (interview 42; interview 46; interview 50). This stands in contrast with the data from the questionnaire, in which 48.1 per cent say they do notice ways in which EU funding does impact on their work whilst only 3.7 per cent say this would not be the case and 44.4 per cent do not know.[11]

What are the ways in which EU funding affects anti-poverty groups? First, three actors (two regional, one national) point out that the demands of European funding have had an effect on the way they work. The EU-related work had become more target-driven and organisations had adopted a different 'quality standard' in terms of the evaluation of projects (interview 52). Another effect was a different understanding of administration (interview 46): 'We never used to have to define such targets before we started getting involved with the EU. Also the billing standards are very high. ... For me personally, these standards are entirely new, I did not know them before and had never done it this way. They are new standards, high demands, sometimes excessive demands for someone who is working locally' (interview 40).

Second, EU funding can affect organisations' work, according to 25.9 per cent (two regional, four national, one European actor), in that organisations need to adapt, to some degree, to the programmatic agenda of the EU and, in particular, of the Commission. Projects are expected to have a European added value, to have a European orientation – not least by including a minimum number of project partners that have to participate in any given project (interview 43): 'If you are an organisation which does seek to do some European work, obviously you are going to apply for European funding and that would mean that the issues that you would focus on might be dictated more by the sort of European agenda than the national one' (interview 57; similarly interview 38; interview 44). Indeed, two (regional) actors point out that they now have a focus on labour-market integration of migrants that they would not have had without the EU (interview 36; interview 40).

Third, 33.3 per cent (six regional, three national actors) mention that as a consequence of EU funding, their organisations had benefited from internationalisation and, more particularly, from mutual learning processes and exchange of expertise (interview 35; interview 36; interview 48):

---

11. One reply is missing.

It has effects. Indeed, new aspects are introduced into our work, by means of exchanging with international or transnational project partners who bring new stimuli for our work. New challenges to our work also arise by being confronted with other approaches to similar questions. This has immediate effects on our work as we ask ourselves how could this be implemented, does it need to be questioned, and how does it function here? (interview 37; similarly interview 49).

By all these actors, this kind of impact is warmly welcomed. It is perceived as an 'ideational development, an increase in competences, a broadening of one's horizon' (interview 45), a potential for innovation (interview 42; interview 43). By some it is, even so, appreciated that they have made a strategic organisational decision to invest more time and organisational resources into drafting related proposals and making the exchange of expertise and knowledge one of the core elements of their work (interview 41).

Fourthly, three actors say that EU funding was also a means of generating a positive image of the EU (interview 40; interview 36) and of the funded organisation itself:

The effect is such that our organisation, with these projects, is present in the public sphere. It's an example of how the organiser of the project which we implement here really supports the project, represents the project publically, rather than simply acknowledging it. We have thereby gained in strength as an interest group. With these projects and this kind of work, we are in the newspapers at least once a month. Whereas before, there was a little report once a year (interview 40).

Fifthly and finally, three actors note that as a result of the involvement in EU policy making, their organisation had decided to invest more resources in EU staff so as to be able to engage more fully both with lobbying activities at the EU-level and with EU funding possibilities: 'It was a deliberate reflection process how to organise the lobbying at the EU level more effectively, to have more fine-tuned instruments for that' (interview 44; similarly interview 37), because we 'want to motivate our members to get more involved. We are in the middle of a process the aim of which is to include the parish more, we have already developed strategic steps, so that they will recognise more the opportunities that the EU offers' (interview 42).

5.4.3 The incentive structure for actors to engage with EU policy making

Positive and negative perceptions of the EU

More clearly than the other two groups, actors from anti-poverty groups have a rather positive view of the EU: 63.0 per cent of them say they could only see advantages, 25.9 per cent see both advantages and disadvantages and 11.1 per cent do not know. Particularly German actors have very positive assessments of the European integration process: 'There are risks ... But in sum the European integration process is not only without alternatives, it is also for the better' (interview 44; similarly interview 36; interview 39; interview 40).

Many actors (29.6 per cent) see the exchange of good practices and the mutual learning that can entail as an advantage coming from the EU. It allows a larger horizon and for learning processes about similar challenges and problems. These exchanges show:

> ... that many issues that we are dealing with and that people are struggling with, such as conditions of poverty, are not only local or national issues, but are European issues. So I think there is a lot to learn from the possibility of mutual learning and from different practices which exist in different states. There are massive opportunities and advantages in the possibility of communicating at the European level about policies and strategies to fight poverty. There is an added value there both for the people suffering from poverty and for the organisation (interview 37; similarly interview 36; interview 45; interview 47; interview 49; interview 50; interview 51; interview 55).

Ideational factors are mentioned by 18.5 per cent of the actors as positives coming from the EU. In particular, they underline how, at the EU level, issues are considered that national governments tend to neglect: 'The EU Commission seems to care more about fighting poverty than national or regional governments do. So I am glad that the Commission has a position on the issue and often puts the spotlight on disadvantaged people, for example, the Roma' (interview 36; similarly interview 38; interview 45; interview 52; interview 54). The fact that the Commission picks up these issues helps organisations to put their governments under pressure:

> Yes, there are huge opportunities. The European Roma integration strategy is one significant one. Although the UK government is basically not engaging, or not willing to produce strategies. But it still represents an opportunity, it highlights the issue for us, it helps us argue our concerns and push for the laws which we seek more effectively (interview 52; similarly interview 54).

An additional three actors say that they are putting their governments under pressure, in case of non-compliance with EU law (interview 44; interview 48; interview 57).

Finally, five actors (18.5 per cent) mention EU funding as a positive. They report how EU funding had allowed them to implement projects which they otherwise could not have done. They also point out that having access to EU funding was one reason to be a member of an umbrella organisation, so as to have better access to information (interview 37; interview 45; interview 47; interview 54). At the EU level, dependence on EU funding is particularly clear: 'We wouldn't exist if the EU didn't exist and our existence at the moment is very much related to the support that we get from the Commission, from the financial support' (interview 60).

As regards the disadvantages, 11.1 per cent find that the institutional diversity of welfare arrangements across Member States poses a serious problem. It would hardly allow for common positions and often not for the defence of German interests as anti-poverty actors see them:

> The problem is that there are four welfare systems. Maybe two of them have some similar features, but the south European and East European are so different, that even within the organisation, you can hardly communicate. ... That means that it is difficult to develop a coherent, generalisable and common position. As a consequence, you have to differentiate your strategy as you cannot achieve a truly common position. That is a huge, main problem (interview 47; similarly interview 34; interview 44).

For 22.2 per cent, another major hindrance to becoming more engaged with the EU seems to be the procedures of EU funding, the bureaucratic demands of which are mentioned by both regional and national actors. Particularly for smaller organisations, the time required to draft a grant proposal and to administer it if successful in the application is repeatedly felt to be too demanding (interview 40; similarly interview 42; interview 45):

> As the co-ordinating organisation, you have a lot of bureaucracy before you even get the funding. Additionally you have difficulties to bill things and do that in a timely manner. And then it has happened every now and then that exams were being made after five years or that the money only arrived after three years and the like. For small organisations, it is really difficult (interview 48; similarly interview 42).

In fact, these bureaucratic demands are felt so strongly that they provoke 'major annoyance within the organisation which, in the end, means that ever fewer EU projects are implemented because simply they are way too complicated, way too bureaucratic' (interview 38). Another difficulty with EU funding that actors mention is the necessity of co-financing EU funding by local, regional or national bodies. Whilst the importance of CSO actors not becoming dependent on EU project funding is acknowledged, co-funding simply is not always available and, for this reason, organisations often cannot participate in EU programmes or budget lines (interview 37). The difficulty of being dependent to a large degree on EU funding becomes clear in this quotation from a European actor:

> The reality for a long time has been that what we wanted to do as an organisation and what we could get the money for from the Commission was the same. So there was a nice unity between what we wanted to do and what the money was available for. In terms of using Commission funding, it can engage you a little bit more in rigid processes because you have to tell a year in advance, in quite

a lot of detail, how you're going to spend the money. In terms of the content of what we said, I don't feel that there was a big influence from the fact that we get public money or Commission money for it. In this period it's a little bit more difficult, from the first Barroso Commission, you had a breakdown in this, and so the process to engage directly with our members and everything is much harder. And the reality is that the funding we get from the Commission is clear, we can find funding whenever we want. But the funding from them is to engage with these EU processes. And the reality is that there is less space for engagement in those processes, and so there can be a degree of frustration (interview 60).

A more substantial reason for 22.2 per cent not to become more engaged with EU affairs is a critical appraisal of current EU economic and social policies, so far as they exist. These are perceived to be biased and to have negative consequences for the poor. Indeed, 'many policies which come from the EU level are not necessarily in the interest of our organisation' (interview 44). A European actor explains: 'We're working with an unbalanced treaty, so it's inevitable that European co-operation has been unbalanced. The need for a more balanced treaty is not understood by the majority … If you allow a European Union to continue that is unbalanced, then we will get the results that we are getting' (interview 60). Others mention the implications of policies such as those in the Lisbon Strategy (2000), particularly the development of activation policies, low-pay sectors and promoting flexible work contracts, which would be negatively perceived within anti-poverty organisations (interview 50). Others are concerned about the long-term effects of either the lack of Western-type social-protection schemes in the newer, Eastern Member States (interview 48), or of the current austerity policies, particularly on Southern Member States: 'The current EU-wide austerity programme is causing massive social dislocation and unrest – most obviously within Greece and Spain. It is not clear that integration on the current EU model can be sustained' (interview 54). In both cases, actors fear migration towards the wealthier Member States, along with financial burdens on their protection schemes (*see also* interview 46).

Differences in work environments

Only two actors within anti-poverty organisations, one regional and one European, think that it does not matter, workwise, at which governance level one is working: 'I don't think it's that much different really, and the processes that you need to use are very similar' (interview 60). Mostly, however, actors of anti-poverty organisations see differences between the EU level and domestic politics. Four actors (three regional, one national, 14.8 per cent) point to the different degrees of abstraction one finds at different levels of governance:

There is certainly some degree of abstraction, a certain meta level in the communication in Brussels. At the local and regional levels, it is very important to establish the local or regional link when communicating – what are the concrete local consequences? It's less about for example, talking in an abstract manner about the EU strategy 2020 (interview 37; similarly interview 34; interview 40; interview 46).

A different political culture is another element that 18.5 per cent (three national, two regional actors) mention. Three actors state that at the regional and national levels, they are much more confrontational and less inclined to accept compromises than at the EU level, where their own interests would not necessarily rank first but where other interests would be acknowledged and a more consensual strategy would be chosen (interview 49). One actor explains that the more confrontational approach may be chosen domestically because one enjoys a publicity there which one does not have at the EU level (interview 44). Also, one has to communicate differently at the EU level because of different communication styles throughout the EU, in order to avoid misunderstandings (interview 34; similarly interview 50). Another actor suggests that the engagement with the EU is less hostile so as to win over its representatives as political allies:

> Quite often when we are approaching national actors, for instance, government departments, unfortunately it's quite often a confrontational relationship. … But in terms of our engagement – the small amount of engagement we have had with the EU – our engagement isn't as hostile. We're looking to persuade them to come over and support us, to engage their support to help us challenge the government on issues which we need to challenge them on (interview 52).

It is noted by 14.8 per cent that EU politics is more complex than national politics (interview 46; interview 57). Often, a consequence seems to be that the contact with EU actors is less straightforward and less regular:

> A difference is that at the EU level, we know much less how the discussions, processes and decision-making work, who could be a contact person or political ally, and therefore our engagement is not as strong. On the regional and federal level, our steering committee members know better whom they should contact and how to go about things (interview 45; similarly interview 46).

As a consequence, 'there's just more confidence in working with the national government – it's more immediate and more doable' (interview 55).

Finally, 11.1 per cent (two national, one regional actor) comment on the kind of work they are engaged in at the EU level as opposed to the national or regional level. They think that the difference is that at the EU level there is much more of a focus on network-building and lobbying rather than on concrete service-delivery or the implementation and further development of policies: 'It is much more a loose exchange of experiences and a place to discuss things, where mutual learning is an important aspect, whilst the national level is much more about making concrete steps in policy development and regulation' (interview 45; similarly interview 37).

Is it easier or harder to be heard at the EU level than domestically?

Reflecting the above, 22.2 per cent of the anti-poverty actors I interviewed find it easier to make their voices heard at the EU level than domestically whilst 48.1 per cent find it more difficult; 11.1 per cent find both equally easy or difficult and 18.5 per cent don't know (*see* graph 9 in the appendix). Two main elements are mentioned by those regional and national actors who find it easier to be heard at the EU level than domestically. One is that there are fewer hierarchies, making it much easier for citizens to get in touch with, say, Commission officials: 'That is not a problem at all. Brussels is a village' (interview 42; similarly interview 37). The other element is more substantial and relates to actors finding it easier to create substantial interest in their issues from EU institutions:

> In regard to these issues, homelessness, working with the poor, it is sometimes easier to be listened to at the EU level. There were many decisions in this regard by the EP last year, also by the Committee of the Regions, that homelessness should be abolished. As a consequence, there were many new programmes, building programmes, in many states. Sadly not in Germany (interview 48; similarly interview 45).

However, two actors also mention that whilst it is quite easy to have access to the European Commission, the latter was mostly interested in the views of larger networks rather than of single organisations: 'Our experience shows that the positions of European networks have a bigger weight than that of individual national actors' (interview 43; similarly interview 44). This is, of course, difficult in terms of lobbying in a situation in which the lowest common denominator of European anti-poverty networks is, and will continue to be in the foreseeable future, dramatically below German social standards. Indeed, most actors do find it more difficult to be heard at the EU level than domestically, a main reason being the institutional diversity of welfare arrangements between Member States.

Another factor that appears repeatedly is the higher degree of abstraction that exists at the EU level, making it difficult to establish a link to a concrete situation at the local or regional level, particularly since the effects of EU policies only become visible at the domestic level a few years later (interview 38):

> It is much further away, a bit out of reach. The EU still is unknown to most people, myself included. Of course one knows a few bright heads from the EP. But to get them to listen to local issues – when MEPs speak it feels as if they are speaking of a different world (interview 40).

The difference is that 'it will be easier to establish a link with an MP who knows there is a disadvantaged area in his or her constituency because the link is there' (interview 51; similarly interview 44; interview 35; interview 57). A consequence is that there is no 'institutionalised form of exchange. For example, with our regional representatives, we have regular discussions whereas with MEPs we don't have that. It's a lack of routines so far as the political process is concerned' (interview 50). Finally, besides those already mentioned one reason why it is more difficult to be heard at the EU level is language barriers (interview 38; interview 47; interview 49).

An important way of being heard in Brussels is the European Commission's consultation regime. How do anti-poverty actors evaluate it? When asked directly, 44 per cent say they are either happy (29.6 per cent) or rather satisfied (11.1 per cent) with the consultations, whilst 11.1 per cent say they are rather unsatisfied and 40.7 per cent cannot tell, due to lack of experience with it.[12] Those actors who have a positive view of the consultations consider that these opportunities are 'very open and oriented towards participation' (interview 44; similarly interview 37; interview 43; interview 35; interview 60), 'really supporting the participation of civil society organisations in a broad way' (interview 47) and 'quite good' if 'compared to what is going on at the national level' (interview 57). Therefore, actors 'don't feel it's been hard to engage with them' (interview 52). In fact, one has 'all the possibilities. As a citizen, you can speak to any topic, and you also can get in touch with the related Commission officials comparatively quickly, that is not a problem at all. Brussels is a village' (interview 42).

So far as the online consultations of the Commission are concerned, around half of the anti-poverty actors (51.9 per cent), from all governance levels, have some experience with them. Those with positive evaluations find the consultations to be 'very convenient' (interview 38) and 'good and important for us in order to participate' in EU policy making (interview 46). Others are more critical and question the deeper motivation of the Commission for engaging in the online consultations: 'Afterwards, the Commission picks up the points it deems interesting. Then one can say that formally, there was a broad participation. But the reality is different. The Commission picks up those arguments which are in line with what it had wanted to do anyway, but now has got a legitimation to do' (interview 34). Another – regional – actor mentions that whilst all participation opportunities could be improved, the real issue was whether or not the organisations had the resources to really participate in improved consultations (interview 50).

Constituency interest in the EU

Not many actors from anti-poverty groups say that there is, in their constituency, a real and vivid interest in EU affairs. Only two actors from the regional level explain that it had also been members who had signalled they wanted the organisation to be more involved with EU affairs (interview 37) or who were actually becoming more involved: 'We try, and increasingly it happens. Of course it is the politically most distant level for members. What we do is to inform them all who is involved and when it will reach them at the regional level. And that way we increasingly manage to involve them in lobbying' (interview 46).

---

12. The remaining 4.2 per cent are missing.

At the national level, three actors state that there is a vivid interest in EU affairs and regular requests that relate to them, not least when organisations are looking for contacts in other countries with whom they could, potentially, co-operate (interview 44); this is also the case in regard to implementation issues:

> Very often, somewhere on the local or the regional level, a problem pops up which is in some way linked to Europe. And then colleagues approach us and we try to solve the problem together. Indeed, things that are relevant in regard to the EU do not only get noticed by us in Brussels, but also during implementation at the working level (interview 43).

The third national actor notes that whilst the EU certainly was an issue, the resources would simply not be there to become more profoundly engaged (interview 51).

Three actors mention that the importance of the EU had increased for their organisation of late. The Lisbon Strategy (2000), the Convention process and the financial crisis are mentioned as boosters for a stronger European engagement: 'The development from a market union to a political union obviously is noticed. Everyone feels that the decisions that are taken in Brussels ever more affect people locally' (interview 42). As a result of the increased importance of the EU for social-welfare providers, some of the organisations have developed more active strategies for being involved: 'We as Caritas really got involved more actively since 2000. Before, the organisation did not have an EU strategy. ... There only was a willingness to participate, but not a strategy as we have it today. This has been a huge development for us which was not imaginable back then' (interview 42). Others do not share this optimism: 'There were times, a few years back, where we devoted more energy to really get engaged with these European networks. But we have reduced that a bit because we noticed that it's not that easy' (interview 43).

Indeed, more actors raise critical points as regards their involvement with EU affairs. At the regional level, actors seem mainly to focus on lobbying regional-level addressees. Even at AGMs, the EU is hardly an issue (interview 42; interview 48; interview 57). For some, this is so because there are (more) interesting national funding opportunities (interview 36); because 'issues to do with the EU don't come up in our work' (interview 57; similarly interview 40), not least because the EU does not have strong competence in the field of anti-poverty policy (*ibid.*; similarly interview 37); because 'we find so much to hold our attention here that that occupies us full-time' and 'because we're working on a national level' (interview 59); or because there simply is resistance to becoming involved with EU affairs and, more precisely, with EU funding, because this is perceived as being overly bureaucratic and demanding (interview 40).

Actors from the national level report quite similar, if not identical, issues when explaining why the EU was not so much of an issue in their respective organisations: 'Europe only plays a subordinate role. Particularly in the field of social policy, where the EU still does not have many competences, national politics obviously has a much greater role than European politics' (interview 43; similarly interview 47). Actors report that the EU does not come up as an issue from either members or from representatives (interview 38; interview 34; interview 45; interview 47; interview 51), so that it would mostly stay within headquarters (interview 35); that there was 'more confidence in working with the national government – it's more immediate and more doable' (interview 55); that in order to get involved in EU issues, one would have to do it regularly to acquire the necessary competence, both linguistic and substantial, and that members in general did not have this competence (interview 38; similarly interview 49); that resources were lacking to get engaged with the EU and that therefore, actors were concentrating on domestic lobbying (interview 53; similarly interview 49); or that the UK simply was 'divorced from the European approach in a lot of ways' (interview 56).

Difficulties in mobilising members are also recognised at the EU level in the field of anti-poverty policy:

> The reality is that it can be a limited number of individuals, no matter how big our national network might be. So in some cases it can be several hundred organisations. But very often the work is carried out by a limited number of individuals. It's hard to mobilise large numbers within the countries to follow some of the detailed policies that we follow. And I know from my own experience when I was a member, when I was working for a member organisation within Ireland, you're very happy that somebody is taking on this work, you give some support to it. But often within the daily challenges that local organisations are facing, it's often hard to devote time to look at policies like the European Employment Strategy, to reflect on and look at the national reform programmes under the Europe 2020 strategy. For several years now you don't really have an EU inclusion strategy that works within Member States. There's a lot of activity exchanged at the European level. So it's quite hard to engage a lot of people to these processes unless there are real processes linked at local and national level (interview 60).

For anti-poverty groups, resources seem to be a very important issue, more precisely, limited and insufficient resources – 51.8 per cent volunteered this without being explicitly asked. Lack of resources is generally a problem at the national level: 'The EU issue is there, but we lack the resources to get more engaged. It is currently not possible for us to pursue this in a more pro-active, more informed way because of these limitations. We clearly lack the resources to do so' (interview 51; similarly interview 53). For some, therefore, becoming involved with the EU 'seems much more of a luxury for people who are better resourced' (interview 55). As a result, groups choose to focus on domestic politics and lobbying: 'Most of our issues have been involved at Westminster level and we have been more looking to have more resources focused on that before we would even look at anything at an EU level' (interview 53). A number of actors regret that they are not able to do more at the EU level: 'If we had the resources it would be a big opportunity. … And this would definitely be an interest in trying to effect change at the EU level to help look after older people, we just don't have the resources at this time to manage that' (*ibid.*). Some actors have considered whether or not to have an office in Brussels but decided it was too expensive (interview 41). Others actually did once have an office but had made the decision to close it: 'We did have an office in Brussels until the end of 2006, with two and a half staff working on EU affairs. We then came to the entrepreneurial decision to shut it down because it was not effective, and that is also our view on lobbying in Brussels' (interview 44). Others suggest that having an office in Brussels would not be a worthwhile investment of resources (interview 49). Still others would like to participate in EU policy processes, or at least in EU funding, but do not have the necessary resources even for the latter: 'I find the administrative requirements are difficult. I can hardly see how we could administer projects because the requirements for the budget management of such projects are very time-consuming' (interview 45).

The above is also mirrored when anti-poverty actors reflect their role in the EU. Their motivation to participate in EU policy making is more idealistic when compared to the other two groups – they wish to learn from others, disseminate information and build a common language against poverty, even though the institutional diversity and the lack of resources render that difficult. Accordingly, 44.4 per cent of them say, in the interviews, that they see as their roles to inform about the EU and to influence related discourses whereas only 22.2 per cent mention as a role that of a lobbyist. In the survey, 74.1% of the anti-poverty actors say that information and exchange is highly relevant to their EU-related work, and 44.4% think that contributing to democracy is highly relevant for their EU-related work, a figure which is considerably higher than for the other two groups. In contrast, 'only' 59.3% consider lobbying important for their EU-related work, a considerably lower figure than for the other two groups, though this is certainly also linked to the lower degree of legal integration in the field (*see* graphs 11–16).

Chapter Six

What we can learn about Representation by CSOs in EU Policy Making

As set out in the introduction, the present study is located at the intersection of two research agendas, that is, the (re)configuration of political representation in Western democracies and the role CSOs (can) play therein on the one hand, and the democratic deficit of the EU and potential ways of alleviating it on the other. As regards the first agenda, the political egalitarianism on which the institutions of modern representative democracy rest is today challenged by a number of diversification processes, i.e. the diversification of actors, arenas, competences and geographical levels. As regards the latter, nation-states have started to delegate tasks up- and downwards. Indeed, European integration and wider processes of globalisation seem to increasingly undermine the traditional notions of '*demos*' and 'sovereignty' that lie at the heart of modern concepts of representative democracy (Goodhart 2007). Overall, these and more diversification processes are contributing to the dilution of traditional representative politics (Warren and Castiglione 2004).

The second agenda reflects the deficiencies in democratic representation, in the EU. Fundamentally, the deficit arises because the EU as a whole has, so far, not developed the kind of thick identity that allows for mutual trust and solidarity between citizens who recognise each other as members of the same polity (Offe 1998). The lack of a European *demos*, in turn, implies a lack of the intermediary structures that are necessary for the channelling of democratic representation, that is, political parties and media. The EU therefore has a limited ability to engage in partisan, majoritarian politics, which needs a shared public sphere to take place in, and lacks the capacity to directly linking citizens to an EU government (Scharpf 2009). In consequence, there has been stagnation in regard to the development of both the EP and European party federations towards European equivalents of the corresponding national representative institutions. Acceptance of the EP in terms of electoral turnout has decreased over the years, ever fewer citizens are voting, and European political parties are still at an embryonic stage. The representative institutions familiar from the Member States for achieving democratic representation are thus lacking to a large degree.

In this context, representation by CSOs has been perceived by many as a response to both challenges. It has been argued that it could make up for some of the deficiencies of traditional democratic representation, i.e. by mobilising people in the first place, but also by bringing weak interests into the political process (Young 2002) or by representing certain ideas (Dryzek and Niemeyer 2008). As regards the second challenge, functional representation in the EU has, by some, been perceived as an additional source of legitimacy-generation, given the lack of democratic legitimacy through the standard model of representative democracy at the EU level. Here, 'partnership' with relevant 'stakeholders' as a means of representing citizens has become a guiding theme of the EU in the last 20 years (Kohler-Koch and Finke 2007; Saurugger 2010). Some even hoped that CSOs could contribute to the creation of a European demos.

This study has combined these two research agendas by investigating empirically how CSOs engage in political representation, and using the multi-level system of the EU and its search for more democracy as its example. It has done so by focusing on how CSO actors themselves perceive of their interest representation in regard to the EU. This perspective was adopted to get a better sense of how the involved actors understand their interest representation and their involvement in EU affairs, what drives it and what blocks it (*see* Chapter 2.2).

This chapter summarises the results of the previous three empirical chapters in relation to the six research questions identified in the first chapter (6.1). The chapter concludes by discussing whether CSOs can compensate for the alleged failure of traditional forms of democratic representation in the EU, by means of reducing either an institutional and/or a social deficit (6.2). It suggests that the CSOs investigated in this study, at present and in their majority, do not seem apt to work against the social deficit of the EU, but that agricultural groups seem to legitimately work against the institutional deficit whereas the legitimacy of the contribution of the two other groups against the institutional deficit seems somewhat constrained by their umbrella organisations displaying a structural remoteness from their social constituencies.

6.1. Summary of empirical findings

1. What conceptions of representation do actors have and who do they represent?

Agricultural groups clearly see themselves as representing a constituency rather than an issue, with no variation between levels of governance. They do not seem particularly concerned with taking into account interests other than those of farmers. At most, the interests of 'people living in rural areas' are also considered. For most of these actors, representation is achieved when legislation is influenced to the advantage of farmers: 'The goal is achieved when our demands are implemented by the legislator'. It comes as no surprise, therefore, that most agricultural actors perceive themselves as classical lobbyists. However, some of them have a more process-oriented view of when representation is achieved – namely, never fully – and three would even consider that representation is achieved when one has made one's voice heard – whether or not that voice ultimately influences legislation. Finally, for agricultural actors, the legitimacy of representation, is provided through the democratic structure of farmers' groups and the mandate given by members to their representatives. Another factor a number of actors mention is that the high level of organisation within their potential constituency confers legitimacy on them.

Agricultural organisations quite clearly mirror a delegate type of representation. They represent a constituency, namely, their members, with the representatives understanding themselves mainly as lobbyists for their members. Legitimacy is located on the input side by the representatives of these organisations.

Actors in environmental groups show two kinds of understanding of representation. One is that of representing *members*, the other that of representing a *public interest*, or, as some would put it, 'the environment'. The representatives of environmental groups primarily conceive of their activities as lobbying and, for the majority of the interviewees, representation is achieved when legislation or a government programme has been influenced. However, 40.9 per cent of the actors say that influencing a discourse is a way of achieving representation. The main aim of actors with this perspective is awareness-raising. As regards the legitimacy of representation activities, almost two thirds think that the legitimacy of their representation derives from their members and the democratic mandate members give to representatives, who decide positions together with members, whereas 40.9 per cent think that their legitimacy derives from a wider democratic societal mandate. Additionally 45.4 per cent mention 'expertise' as conferring legitimacy on their activities.[1] Thus, legitimacy-generation seems to be divided between the input and the output sides.

How actors conceive of representation is therefore less clear for 'cause' groups such as environmental organisations than for the 'members' groups. They display elements of delegate and of gyroscopic representation. In gyroscopic representation, the represented selects a representative with similar policy preferences whom (s)he trusts will stay committed to his or her known principles and where therefore no on-going communication is needed. The delegate elements appear in those instances where actors see themselves as being representatives of a constituency, that is, of members, rather than of an issue. The gyroscopic elements show in those instances where governance structures are not used or absent all together. Several actors either indicated that they had no links with the European level but, nonetheless, expressed satisfaction with the representation by their European umbrella; or that the purpose of being a member of the European umbrella was to provide it with legitimacy, trusting it was doing good work but not necessarily being involved in the work. The mixture of delegate and gyroscopic representation also shows in the understanding of legitimacy that actors have, which is divided between the input and the output side: many actors see the source of legitimacy as a democratic mandate from the membership or the wider society; others see its source in the expertise that these CSOs have. The same ambiguity appears where a slight majority of the actors sees themselves as lobbyists who, based on a democratic mandate, seek to change legislation; whilst for a large minority, the main aim is to influence a discourse – again, based on their expertise.

---

1.   Actors could choose two options.

Finally, three-quarters of the anti-poverty actors associate representation with 'advocacy for the weak'. When asked directly who or what it is they represent, 55.6 per cent say they represent members and 74 per cent 'poor people'.[2] These findings suggest that the large majority thinks of itself as representing a constituency rather than an issue, even though that is not necessarily the same constituency for everybody. Actors are divided mainly between those who see influence on legislation or on policy programmes as the point at which representation has been achieved (48.1 per cent) and those who see influencing a discourse as the point of representation (37 per cent). Actors are also rather divided between a traditional perception of their organisations' role as lobbyists versus that of, ideally, acting as channels through which those affected by poverty and disadvantage can be involved in policy discussions and policy making. Indeed, 80.8 per cent of the anti-poverty actors say they either regularly or irregularly involve the poor in their lobbying activities. As regards the generation of legitimacy, 44.4 per cent think it is having a democratic mandate from their members that provides their activities with legitimacy and 22.2 per cent that legitimacy comes from a societal mandate; while for 25.9 per cent, legitimacy comes from involving the poor. Additionally, for 44.4 per cent, legitimacy is generated via expertise[3]. For the majority, therefore, legitimacy seems to rest on the input side. However, a considerable number of actors (also) locate it on the output side.

The 'weak interests' groups in some respects resemble the 'cause' groups in their understanding of representation. As the former, they also have elements of both delegate and gyroscopic representation. Again, the gyroscopic elements show in those instances where governance structures are not used (see below). A number of regional actors did not seem particularly aware of what EAPN was doing at the European level and yet said they were 'happy' or 'rather satisfied' with the way they were represented by it. Membership in EAPN, therefore, sometimes seems to have more a symbolic nature than a practical application. The mixture of delegate and gyroscopic representation also shows in the understanding of legitimacy that actors have. As for the 'cause' groups, actors are torn between locating legitimacy on the input and on the output side. In the former case, actors see its origin in a democratic mandate from members of the organisation, from the wider society or from involving the poor directly; in the latter, they see it in the expertise that comes from working with the poor. What differentiates 'weak interests' groups from 'cause' groups is that they do not think of themselves as representing an issue but as representing a constituency, be it their own organisational members or be it 'the poor', whose advocates they perceive themselves to be.

Do these three groups constitute three distinct ways of conceiving of representation? I think the data suggests yes. Two kinds of groups ('members' and 'weak interests') see themselves as representing a people rather than an issue (as 'cause' groups do), however the constituency differs in important ways. The

---

2. Respondents could choose two answers.

3. Respondents could choose two answers.

interests of members groups are rather narrowly defined, in this case to represent the articulated interests of farmers. By contrast, the constituency of weak interests groups is, by definition, much broader, which is also reflected in where actors see the legitimacy of their activities stemming from. Whereas for 'members' groups, legitimacy exclusively comes from the democratic mandate given by their members, 'anti-poverty' actors additionally draw on a wider societal mandate as well as on involving the poor themselves, with an important minority locating legitimacy on the output side.

What we do not find amongst the three groups is *claims-making* of the prominent 'Bono-kind', that is, where self-chosen representatives claim to represent others without having undergone some sort of democratic process (see below). This suggests that this type of claims-making occurs *outside* of organised interest representation, whereas in the latter, official representatives do have a mandate of one kind or another *before* they start making claims in the name of the organisation, rather than making a claim and then waiting to see whether or not it is accepted by some audience.

2. What are the organisational structures and processes by which CSOs organise representation?

In agricultural organisations, there are straightforward chains of delegation in place that the members and their representatives use regularly and extensively. Farmers send their democratically elected delegates to the relevant committees across all levels of governance. Control happens in these committees as well as in AGMs but also more informally and via direct contact. The high level of mobilisation and involvement of farmers is also mirrored in the efforts to mobilise the existing constituency, for example, for debates, demonstrations or actions against e.g. cheap supermarket chains.

The situation does not seem to change significantly at the EU level. Actors from both the national and the regional levels are regularly involved in EU affairs, both outside of and via their European umbrella organisation. As regards representation by the latter, the high level of satisfaction with COPA-COGECA signals that the views of its domestic members are regularly taken into consideration, diminished only by the necessities of lowest common denominator policies that are the result of consensus-seeking strategies at the EU level. Overall, therefore, there is low organisational autonomy from the constituency, both domestically and at the EU level. This means that the higher levels of governance cannot make decisions without the consent of the lower levels.

The attempts, of agricultural organisations, to reach out to a larger public, are rather limited. Only a little more than a third of them offer membership to potential new members, and only 14.3 per cent of the websites invite visitors to join a campaign, sign a petition, send a mail to an MP or go to a demonstration. This comparatively low percentage may be explained by the very high level of organisation that exists already, by membership being limited to farmers and the fact that recruitment is mostly done face-to-face. The only form of direct interaction that exists is to invite attendance at public events – 78.6 per cent of the organisations advertise public events on their websites. Agricultural groups do make quite an effort to have informative websites. However, for the most part these are addressed explicitly at the press. All of this suggests that these groups do not really seek to grow in size or interact with the larger public. In that sense, agricultural CSOs resemble a traditional interest group with a quite restricted membership base.

As for the environmental CSOs, all the organisations have a democratic structure in place, in the sense that they have AGMs at which their main policy positions are discussed and boards are elected. However, not all of the organisations follow entirely democratic processes throughout the year – four organisations (18.2 per cent) stand out as not involving their members regularly between AGMs. In regard to exercising control, which is traditionally achieved through these AGMs, a couple of actors point out that control is likely to function not in traditional ways but rather orally or through individual members leaving the organisation in protest. Outside of the official governance structures, just over 90 per cent either regularly or irregularly seek to mobilise their constituencies for their activities. There are two main kinds of mobilisation: on the ground, with concrete projects of environment protection; and political mobilisation, by means of campaigning, lobbying parliament, events with politicians and experts or larger demonstrations. At the EU level, the mobilisation of members seems, first and foremost, to mean having them participate in the governance of the umbrella organisation, rather than mobilising them politically.

Environmental actors seem quite active when it comes to reaching out to the larger public. Over three quarters address the press as well as the larger public on their websites and 54.5 per cent use social media to connect to a larger public. Environmental groups also actively seek to enlarge their constituencies: 81.8 per cent of the organisations use their websites to invite individuals to join the organisation and 54.5 per cent of the actors mention that their organisation deploys active recruitment strategies to attract new members. The same percentage invites the public to participate in a campaign, sign a petition, send a mail or go on a demonstration. Finally, a clear majority (59.1 per cent) offers the opportunity to volunteer in their organisation. These findings suggest that these 'cause' groups are oriented towards the larger public and actively seek to enlarge their constituency and support.

Finally, a very large majority of anti-poverty groups have democratic structures in place and also use them, though less consistently than the agricultural groups, throughout the different levels of governance. The regional and local members of weak interests groups do not engage with EU affairs as much as those of members groups do across all levels of governance. As a result, what the few EU policy officers/staff of weak interests groups do in regard to EU affairs can sometimes seem somewhat disconnected from the constituency – not because the constituency's preferences were disregarded but because these preferences are not necessarily that pronounced or clear. It also seems as if procedures are less formalised in regard to EU issues than in regard to domestic issues. This is also the case for the control of representatives who do not necessarily function along electoral lines but rather more informally. Most (81.5 per cent) of the actors say that they mobilise their constituency either regularly or irregularly. Additionally, 80.8 per cent indicate that they regularly or irregularly involved the poor themselves. A number of actors point out that whether or not mobilisation is successful very much depends on the topic and, more precisely, on whether people are themselves affected by the issue in question. Mobilisation generally takes the form of consultations, committees, training, projects, lobbying and events.

As regards the involvement of the larger public, all of the anti-poverty organisations investigated have a website, and approximately half of them use social media. Two thirds of the 'weak interests' groups also maintain active relationships with the press and 55.6 per cent offer the opportunity of volunteering in the organisation and thereby getting to know it better as well as actively supporting it. In contrast, only 44.4 per cent of them offer individuals the opportunity to become a member and 70.4 per cent say their organisation has no active recruitment strategy. These latter findings are perhaps not so surprising given that for an important range of actors (confessional social service providers), the constituency is structurally limited to begin with. To the difference of 'cause' groups, 'weak interests' groups do not appear as oriented towards the larger public and resemble more the 'members' groups in terms of where the focus of their attention mainly goes.

3. To what degree are CSOs Europeanised?

Unsurprisingly, given the material and legal incentives provided by CAP for farmers, the overwhelming majority of them says that dealing with EU processes enjoyed a high importance in their organisation. 91.7 per cent say that the EU is regularly an issue in their work and 92.9 per cent deem it 'very important' to be present in Brussels to achieve organisational goals. Agricultural groups are thus highly Europeanised.

Of the environmental actors, 35 per cent think the importance of dealing with EU processes in their organisation is high; while 50 per cent say the EU is regularly an issue in their own work. On the one hand, there seems to be the recognition that it is either 'very' (36.4 per cent) or 'rather important' (54.5 per cent) to be present in Brussels to achieve organisational goals, mirroring the legal impact Brussels has for environmental policy. Indeed, in some organisations, there is an increased awareness of the importance of the EU and an effort to adapt the organisation's strategies to that. On the other hand, a considerable number of actors suggest that the individual members of environmental organisations are not all that interested in EU affairs. Indeed, several national actors point out that it is difficult to get regional and local members involved in EU affairs and that, so far as interest representation in EU policy making is concerned, that task is mostly located within the headquarters of organisations. Environmental actors therefore seem moderately Europeanised.

Anti-poverty actors evaluate the importance of dealing with EU processes in their organisation as rather low: only 19.2 per cent judge the EU 'important', 30.8 per cent evaluate its importance as 'medium' whilst 50 per cent say its importance is 'rather low' or that the EU is 'not important at all'. Also, for more than half of the actors the EU comes up 'rarely' (34.6 per cent) or 'never' (19.2 per cent) in their daily work. Indeed, even at AGMs, the EU is rarely an issue. The main organisational reason that actors mention for this rather low EU profile is a lack of resources and time. This is reflected when 40.7 per cent of the 'weak interests' actors think it is 'very important' to be present in Brussels in order to achieve organisational goals and 33.3 per cent think this is 'rather important'. Clearly, the actors cannot match, in their daily work, the importance they attribute to the EU. Anti-poverty actors thus display a comparatively low degree of Europeanisation.

4. Who are CSOs addressing when they engage in political representation in EU affairs and with which strategies?

All the regional agricultural groups are organised under the same national umbrella organisation and lobby through it. Domestically, they turn to regional ministries, heavily to national ministries, and less so to MPs. As regards the EU level, all the organisations have very strong ties to the European umbrella organisation, COPA-COGECA, and are generally satisfied with its work. Two thirds of the actors are in regular touch with the Commission. A very large majority (83 per cent) say they lobby MEPs directly.

Only a quarter of the environmental actors mention the national umbrella as a channel they use for lobbying EU policies.[4] For many, the link they have with the national umbrella seems to be rather weak or indeed non-existent. Most actors mention the national ministry as a venue for influencing EU policies; some also mention regional ministries (in Germany) whilst MPs seem to be of lower importance. As regards the EU level, half the actors refer to the European umbrella structure, the EEB, as relevant for their interest representation. Some say that they are more successful back home because they know the people there and their networks were more close-knit; they also say that they cannot afford to lobby well in Brussels. In this context, being a member of a European umbrella appears like a middle-way solution. However, about two-thirds say that they use a European umbrella organisation other than the EEB to influence EU policies – despite being members of the EEB. Which umbrella is used depends mainly on the issue but there also is some discontent with the functioning of the EEB. Some consider it as being a rigid and bureaucratic structure and view it as communicating badly. As regards the European Commission, two-thirds say that they address it directly to try and influence EU policies. Finally, 40 per cent of the environmental actors mention MEPs as one channel of their EU-lobbying activities.

As for the anti-poverty groups, and so far as state institutions are concerned, regional ministries (30.8 per cent), national ministries (38.5 per cent) and MPs (25.9 per cent) are mentioned as a domestic way of trying to influence EU policies.

4.　This low figure must also be explained by the (three) British organisations I was able to interview which do not have a national umbrella organisation.

Additionally, 53.8 per cent mention the national umbrella structure. Those who have strong and regular links tend to come from the federal level and from larger organisations. Where involvement is weak, a lack of resources often seems to be the reason. As regards EU institutions, almost two thirds of the anti-poverty actors say that they directly lobby the European Commission when seeking to influence EU policies whereas almost one third says they lobby MEPs directly. 42.3 per cent mention their own office in Brussels as one strategy to influence EU policies. In contrast, only 23.1 per cent mention the European umbrella structure, EAPN, of which all the organisations investigated here are members. Again, often actors lack the resources to get involved with EAPN, but also they sometimes cannot see the relevance of what EAPN is doing for their own work. Repeatedly, the lowest common denominator positions one finds at the EU level do not seem to make much sense to actors seeking to pursue their (often exclusively German) interest of defending welfare standards. Finally, 26.9 per cent indicate that they are going through another European umbrella than EAPN to pursue their EU-related goals.

When asked whether they would resort to confrontational or to consensus-seeking strategies in Brussels, or whether they would decide the strategy on a case-by-case basis, none of the actors said they would opt for confrontational strategies only whilst some thought they would only employ consensual strategies and the majority opted for a case-by-case decision. This is in line with other findings that suggests that there is little evidence of CSOs adopting confrontational strategies in Brussels (Imig and Tarrow 2001; Beyers 2004). Instead, the default strategy for these groups seems to be an 'access' strategy.

5. Does the institutional environment of the EU affect the activities of CSOs and their interest representation strategies?

The impact of the involvement in EU policy making for agricultural organisations remains rather unclear. This is likely related to the fact that agricultural groups cannot apply for EU funding that would directly support their organisational work, but is instead tied to agricultural policy, thereby leading actors to refuse the idea that there is a direct impact on the organisations. However, actors certainly recognise the importance of EU funding and of the common legal framework for their work.

Of the environmental actors, almost 82 per cent say that being involved in EU policy making affects the work of their organisation. For almost a third, EU funding has an impact on their organisation, given its demands in terms of proposal-writing and accounting, which lead to a professionalisation of organisations. A number of actors also said that they had become more international; that the EU had a greater presence in the organisation; and that their reputation had improved in reaction to receiving EU funding.

Being involved in EU policy making affects anti-poverty groups, not least through receipt of EU funding, say 63 per cent of the related actors. A first impact that is noted is that the way they work has become more target-driven and that they have adopted a different 'quality standard' in terms of evaluation of projects as well as a different understanding of administration. Some of the anti-poverty actors suggested they were now doing work they would not have done without EU funding. However, they also asserted that they only applied for EU funding in areas which belonged to their principle fields of concern anyway, suggesting the EU had not substantially re-oriented their work. Another point which got mentioned repeatedly is that their work has become more internationalised and gained in reputation. Finally, some actors say they have benefited from mutual learning and exchange processes with CSOs from other Member States. In general, these sorts of impacts seem to mainly occur at the national level and for larger regional organisations whereas interviewees of smaller regional, let alone local organisations did not seem to feel an EU-induced impact on their work.

Overall, it seems that being involved in EU affairs strongly affects CSOs (for dissimilar findings, see Grote and Lang 2003; Beyers and Kerremans 2007). Where there is no awareness of such an impact, this might be due to organisational changes relating to the EU having occurred before the interviewee was hired – EU policy officers or EU project coordinators who likely got their position because of previously introduced changes in the organisation. In how far being involved with the EU also affects the balance groups strike between the logic of membership and the logic of influence (Schmitter and Streeck 1999) is less clear, given this study is not looking at a longer time horizon. However, the trend towards professionalisation as well as the rare usage of 'voice' strategies of interest representation in general, and at the EU level in particular, point towards the logic of influence by which organisations 'adapt their aims and methods to the actual decision-making processes on which they wish to exert an impact' (Schmitter and Streeck 1999: 19) as being predominant.

6. What are the incentives and disincentives for CSOs to become engaged with EU policy making?

Agricultural actors note that policy making becomes more complex at the EU level, not least due to the institutional diversity among Member States, which increases the need for consensus-building and for co-operative strategies. The main advantages they identify are a single market, common regulation, the existence of the CAP and the financial security that comes with it. Disadvantages are associated with policies of the lowest common denominator and of being governed from far away in Brussels. Their satisfaction with the consultation opportunities the Commission offers, and therefore the chances of getting their voice heard, is quite mixed. A clear majority of the actors – 57.2 per cent – are rather unsatisfied or unsatisfied with these opportunities, not least in relation to the issue of a lack of representativity of these consultations. Still, agricultural actors tend to have a rather positive appraisal of the EU, given that half of them could only see advantages, 14.3 per cent only disadvantages and 35.7 per cent both advantages and disadvantages.

Turning to the environmental CSOs, actors note that politics in the EU is more oriented towards consensus and less confrontational; that policy positions are more abstract as a response to institutional diversity; and that actors have fewer contacts with EU institutions than with domestic ones. As a result of these differences, almost two thirds find it harder to make their voices heard at the EU level. They cite a number of reasons for why this is so: the higher number of lobbyists; because they have fewer contacts at the EU level, making it more difficult to influence policies; the complexity of the EU's political system, making EU politics more time-intensive to follow than domestic politics; a lack of resources as well as difficulties with EU funding procedures; and language problems. Environmental actors also have a mixed evaluation of the Commission consultation practices, in particular the online consultations. Whilst it is acknowledged that the Commission tries to balance different views and bring all the interests to the table, many actors make critical comments about the online consultations. Mostly, and across levels of governance, they wonder about the impact on policies and legislation the consultations have. A number of actors also find that the results of the consultations can be skewed in favour of economic interests or in favour of what the Commission wants, the latter being reflected in the way questionnaires are constructed. The main positive that is mentioned is the common political framework for the protection of the environment and nature. As a result of this positive evaluation of what the EU could offer and the negatives associated with the difficulties many experience of exploiting this potential to the full, their appraisal of the EU is rather mixed, with 42.9 per cent who could only see advantages, 52.4 per cent both advantages and disadvantages and 4.8 per cent only disadvantages.

Anti-poverty actors, finally, note the complexity of the EU political system as well as the multitude of different interests within it; they also see a different political culture in the EU, which is less adversarial than in the national context and instead more consensus-driven. Finally, they note that there are fewer direct contacts with EU officials than is the case domestically. The negatives actors note are the institutional diversity which renders common positions difficult and at best produces undesired lowest common denominator policies, the bureaucratic demands of EU funding that are particularly harsh on smaller CSOs, and current EU economic and social policies which are perceived as detrimental for social protection schemes. So far as the online consultations of the Commission are concerned, around half of the anti-poverty actors (51.9 per cent), have some experience with them, with mixed evaluations. Those with positive evaluations find the consultations to be a convenient and important tool for participation. More critically minded actors support the idea – also mentioned by environmental actors – that the Commission would only pick up the points it deems interesting and which are in line with what it had wanted to do anyway. These difficulties notwithstanding, the majority of actors has a rather positive view of the integration process and mentions positive aspects such as ideational factors – putting pressure on domestic governments via reminding them of European commitments, or possibilities for mutual learning processes and funding opportunities. Overall, their appraisal of the EU is quite positive, with 63 per cent who could only see advantages, 25.9 per cent both advantages and disadvantages and 11.1 per cent who did not know.

6.2 The contribution of CSOs to EU policy making

In this last section, I will discuss what the implications of the foregoing are for interest representation by CSOs and democracy in the EU. In doing so, I will ask whether CSOs can compensate for the alleged failure of traditional forms of democratic representation in the EU. More specifically, are they a) capable of reducing an institutional deficit by enhancing the representation of a broad range of interests or even of b) reducing a social deficit by contributing to the building of a European demos? Or, on the contrary, does being involved in EU policy making perhaps reduce the democratic potential of CSOs?

Before I deal with these questions, it is of order to come back to the chosen perspective and to address its obvious limitations as well as advantages. As explained in Chapter 2.2, I have adapted an abductive approach and a subjective perspective in this study. The former implies that no theories were tested and that I do not seek to make universal generalisations from the data gathered either, thereby being neither a deductive nor an inductive study. The latter means that this study focuses on CSO actors' perspectives rather than on 'hard facts', thereby giving these actors a lot of weight. The first choice is due to the perception a) of the EU very much being a 'moving object', and b) of non-electoral representation equally being a very fluid process which very much depends on the concrete circumstances and environment in which it occurs. Both work against generalisations across time and space. The second choice was made because what is missing in much of the scholarship are micro accounts that explore the questions of how CSO actors perceive of their activities and why they assign relevance to the EU and how they get engaged with it – or not (but see Heidemann 2012). One way of getting at actors' perceptions of interest representation and of the EU lies in a 'subjective' approach (Crotty 1998) whereby the views of actors become the analytical focal point. Conceptually, the reason to choose such an approach is rooted in the premise that 'opportunity is, ultimately, what people make of it' (Kurzman 2004: 117).

The advantages of adapting a subjective perspective I hope have become clear in the empirical chapters. Focusing on actors' perceptions provides incredibly rich accounts of how they interpret their own role, and of which kinds of activities they engage in and are important to them and why. It also allows us to understand why some strategies in their view might work better than others. Similarly, only if we address actors' perceptions and views about the EU will we be able to see whether or not the Europeanisation of CSOs also implies that their actors are also interested in EU democracy. Obviously, given actors' views are not contrasted with 'hard facts' or, e.g. the views of other involved actors, such as politicians, this study relies on limited objectivity. However, this need not mean that there is no objectivity and therefore no explanation is possible (Bevir and Rhodes 2006). Explanation is grounded on the meaning actors give to their actions. Given I have interviewed a certain number of actors, one can see rather easily which views are representative and which are not, the mere number of interviews providing a 'reality check'. However, such an explanation is limited to the particular time and space, based on a subjective interpretation and, as such, is provisional whereas generalisations must be avoided. With these limitations in mind, let us now see how we can answer the above listed questions.

Those who perceive of the democratic deficit in the EU as being an institutional deficit aim at improving the links between domestic processes of authorisation and accountability on the one hand and EU decision-making on the other. Traditionally, this literature has mostly looked at the EP and at how to improve the quality of democratic representation by it. More recently, the related literature has also addressed both the Council of the EU as well as the European Commission in order to see how this institutional legislative triangle could be better authorised and held to account. Others, being aware of the deficiencies of the more traditional representative actors at the EU level, have focused on CSOs and their potential to represent EU citizens in EU policy making (Friedrich 2010; Kohler-Koch 2010; Ruzza 2007). They argue that CSOs might have a contribution to make to input legitimacy as a complementary layer to outlets of representative democracy, not least by functioning as 'transmission belts' that bring the interests and values of citizens to the EU and vice versa. To assess whether or not CSOs can or indeed do take on such a role, we need to first of all know whether they are Europeanised, at all, and whether they engage with the European institutions.

As summarised above, it seems that only agricultural groups can be seen as highly Europeanised. They consider the EU has a high importance in their organisation; the EU regularly is an issue in their work; they broadly inform about EU policies and also deem EU affairs in general, as well as interest representation in Brussels in particular, as highly relevant to their work. Neither the environmental nor the anti-poverty groups are as highly Europeanised, with the environmental organisations finding themselves in the middle between the two other groups and the anti-poverty groups displaying a comparatively low degree of Europeanisation. Agricultural groups also seem to lobby on all fronts, regionally, nationally and at the EU level, whereas the efforts of the other two groups are more limited.

Why do these groups Europeanise (or not)? As discussed in Chapter 1.3.2, the literature either focuses on the institutional *environment* of the organisations (legislative activity, access, fit/misfit), or on the organisations *themselves* (resources and strategic use of those resources). If we leave to one side that legislative activity is obviously a strong incentive to become engaged with the EU, my findings mainly support the thesis of the importance of resources for engagement with EU affairs. Institutional differences between the EU political system and the respective domestic political system are recognised and mentioned, but do not seem to keep actors from becoming engaged with the EU. The thesis that actors would seek to compensate weak domestic access by going European and do not go European when they can reach their goals back home is also not backed by the findings. However, resource-poor CSOs might engage with local, regional and national politics, where they can and do get engaged as they see fit, but they lack the resources to become involved with EU affairs. This tends to be the case for a number of anti-poverty and environmental groups, at both the sub-national and the national levels, while it is not the case for agricultural groups, which, due to their membership fees, enjoy sufficient resources to engage with EU affairs across all the different levels of governance. The modalities of EU funding seem to reinforce the differences in resource-endowment of the various kinds of groups: only those groups that can afford to pay for the audit, which is necessary in order to apply for EU funding in the first place, and the deployment of staff for the development of grant proposals and the implementation of EU projects in advance of receiving EU funding, can actually apply for funding; whereas the resource-poorer groups do not fulfil these necessary preconditions and therefore will not apply for or receive EU funding. However, resources on their own – nor any of the other proposed factors – cannot explain why groups get engaged with the EU (or not).

Given the low legal incentive in the anti-poverty field as well as the poor resource-endowment of many anti-poverty groups, one would expect their engagement with the EU to be substantially lower than it actually is, if one only took resources and the legislative activity of the EU into account. It therefore seems that we also need to take the deeper motivations that drive actors into consideration, when seeking to explain why they Europeanise. For, not only are some interests easier to organise than others and not only do some groups have more resources for their interest representation than others; but also, some groups have less desire to transcend national boundaries than others and, instead, exclusively seek to defend their own interests. For example, agricultural groups are mainly engaged in EU policy making in order to defend their material interests; contributing to EU democracy is of comparatively low importance to them (*see* graphs 11–16 in the appendix). Lobbying to influence EU policies is also quite important for environmental actors, who, nevertheless, have a similarly low level of interest in contributing to EU democracy as agricultural actors – a result that is rather surprising, given that environmental problems are often truly transnational in implication and need to be dealt with at that level. Finally, whilst anti-poverty actors display the lowest degree of Europeanisation, it remains rather high given the low level of legal incentives for them and their lack of resources. Apparently they nonetheless wish to influence EU policy making in order to create a common social sphere, a suggestion that is supported by the finding that almost half of them consider that contributing to EU democracy is a relevant aspect of their EU-related work (*see* graph 15 in the appendix). This finding suggests that idealistic motivations can be quite strong incentives to get involved with the EU.

However, the story cannot stop there. If CSOs are to be 'transmission belts' of citizens in EU policy making, if they are to compensate for the deficiencies of traditional representative actors in representing citizens, then we need to be sure that they are actually re-presenting citizens or, in other words, that they represent a social constituency, rather than being self-authorised claims-makers. Along those lines, I argued in Chapter 1.2, that in order for their contribution to EU policy making to be legitimate, CSOs need a reliable link to their social constituency. Such a reliable link not only presupposes the existence of governance structures which allow members (and sometimes supporters) to be involved. It also implies the actual involvement, of the constituencies, in the development of policy positions as well as a good degree of acceptance of those positions and satisfaction with the representation by the higher levels of governance. We must therefore ask whether these conditions seem satisfied in the context of this study?

The contribution of agricultural CSOs to EU policy making when assessed against these criteria is highly legitimate. These groups have straightforward chains of delegation in place that the members and their representatives use regularly and extensively, and at all levels of governance. Furthermore, there is a high degree of satisfaction with the representation by their European umbrella organisation, diminished only by the necessities of lowest common denominator policies that are the result of consensus-seeking strategies at the EU level. Their interest representation in EU affairs is highly legitimate, therefore.

The environmental groups in their very large majority also have democratic governance structures in place. However, they are not always used to the full when it comes to EU interest representation it seems. In consequence, not all the satisfaction with the European umbrella was based on involvement with it, but on the desire to provide it with legitimacy, trusting it was doing good work. The legitimacy of the contribution of environmental groups to EU policy making therefore seems compromised by the somewhat limited engagement of their constituencies in the process.

Finally, as regards the anti-poverty actors, the picture resembles that of the environmental groups. These groups also have governance structures in place, but do not always seem to use them in full when it comes to the EU. This holds particularly true for the sub-national level of governance which only gets engaged with the EU to a very limited degree. Particularly regional actors did not always seem aware of what their European umbrella was doing and yet said they were 'happy' or 'rather satisfied' with the way they were represented by it. Membership in EAPN, therefore, sometimes seems to have more a symbolic nature than a practical application. Overall, therefore, the legitimacy of the contribution, by anti-poverty actors, to EU policy making also seems confined. In sum, whereas the interest representation in EU affairs by agricultural groups, seems highly legitimate, there seems to be a degree of structural remoteness of the European umbrellas from their grassroots constituencies for both 'cause' and 'weak interests' groups (see also Johansson 2012; Kröger 2013), thereby limiting the legitimacy of their input into EU policy making. However, this remoteness is not caused by the absence of participatory governance structures, but by them not being used to the full. This suggests that groups functioning on a delegate model of representation are in a position to complement traditional representative actors in EU policy making by representing a social constituency whereas groups which operate at least to some degree according to a gyroscopic logic face more difficulties in achieving legitimacy as defined in this study.

Not everybody interested in the matter looks at the democratic deficit of the EU from an institutional perspective. Quite a few analysts argue that the deficit is societal more than anything else, a perspective which is best known as the *no-demos-thesis* (see Höreth 1999). According to this perspective, the EU lacks the fundamental features of nation-states that enable citizens to collectively govern themselves, namely a *demos*, and therefore also a public sphere for debate, political parties that would mediate between the citizens and the state, and an authoritative channel of democratic representation. In sum, citizens from such a perspective cannot be represented at the EU level because there is no common *demos* (*see* Chapter 1.3.3). In such a situation, some have seen CSOs as perhaps being able to bring about and foster the kind of trust that a political community in-the-making (Fossum and Trenz 2006) requires: trust in the reciprocity of the rule-conforming behaviour of others and in mutual solidarity (Putnam 1993: 182–3), not least by contributing to the creation of a European public sphere, the Europeanisation of the national demoi and the construction of a common European interest. I will now look at how the empirical findings of this study relate to these expectations, always bearing in mind that given the limited amount of data, the way it was generated, and the subjective perspective chosen, these findings cannot and should not be generalised.

It is difficult to imagine how CSOs could perform a demos-creating function if they were hardly Europeanised or did not engage with EU policy making at all. As we have seen, the groups studied are Europeanised to different degrees and address European institutions to different degrees. Agricultural groups from this perspective are best equipped to contribute to demos-creation whereas anti-poverty groups are least equipped to do so.

What can we say about the efforts, of these CSOs, to reach out to a larger public and to thereby contribute to the creation of a European public sphere? Related efforts even at the domestic level seem rather limited for both the agricultural and the anti-poverty groups, though the latter make more efforts than the former in this regard. In both cases, this suggests that these groups do not really seek to grow in size which is not entirely surprising, particularly for the agricultural groups, as their respective constituencies are both limited. Environmental actors, in contrast, seem quite active when it comes to reaching out to the larger public, and also actively seek to enlarge their constituencies.

What happens to the efforts of relating to a larger public at the EU level? As pointed out, the existence of a public sphere is generally considered a central element of a functioning democracy. The findings show that access strategies are consistently more used than voice strategies, particularly insofar as the latter concern forms of protest. Whilst a majority of actors mention the media as addressees of their work in the domestic sphere, hardly anyone mentions them for the EU level. The number of actors who consider protest a highly relevant form of influencing policies is comparatively low in general and even lower at the EU level than domestically. This is quite likely to be a strategic choice of CSOs given they are aware that the vibrant public sphere one needs in order to exert pressure via 'voice' strategies does hardly exist at the EU level. Based on the admittedly limited amount of evidence I gathered in regard to the creation of a European public sphere, it therefore seems difficult to come to the conclusion that the studied CSOs massively contribute to the creation of a European public sphere.

In a next step, what we need to know is how far CSO actors are interested in creating a common interest. This is best expressed in their efforts to join forces and work together under the head of a European umbrella organisation, given it is here that actors are forced to seek common solutions to problems which might sometimes be common, but at other times might not be. Only if groups would undertake the effort of cooperating with groups from other Member States could this (but need not) be interpreted as contributing to the creation of a European demos. As we have seen, agricultural groups have very strong ties to the European umbrella organisation, COPA-COGECA, and are generally satisfied with its work. However, they do regret its common denominator policies and lobby outside of COPA-COGECA whenever they think this serves their interests better. Therefore, one might conclude that they only engage with COPA-COGECA as long and as much as it serves their material interests.

As regards the environmental groups, half the actors refer to the European umbrella structure, the EEB, as relevant for their interest representation. Where actors chose other, mainly domestic lobbying channels, this is linked to better networks and the lack of resources to be more present in Brussels. In this context, being a member of a European umbrella appears like a middle-way solution. However, about two-thirds of the environmental actors say that they use a European umbrella organisation other than the EEB to influence EU policies, and namely an umbrella organisation with a narrower focus – birds – than that of the EEB, suggesting once more the difficulty to find common grounds beyond very vague lowest common denominator positions.

So far as anti-poverty actors are concerned, whereas the satisfaction rate with the work of the European umbrella, EAPN, is rather high, many actors, particularly, but not only, of the subnational levels of governance do not seem aware of what EAPN is doing. Often, CSOs lack the resources to get involved with EAPN, but also they sometimes cannot see the relevance of what EAPN is doing for their own work. Repeatedly, the lowest common denominator positions one finds within EAPN do not seem to make much sense to actors seeking to pursue their (often exclusively German) interest of defending welfare standards. Instead, they lobby EU institutions separately or with other European umbrellas which have a more narrowly defined interest.

Overall, we do find significant levels of involvement with the European umbrella organisations studied here. The 'members' groups, in particular, have a high level of involvement with their European umbrella, whilst for 'cause' and 'weak interests' groups, the involvement is less. And yet, for all three kinds of groups, there seems to be a structural hindrance to more cooperation: the heterogeneity between groups and their interests. This hindrance clearly operates in (re-)distributive policy-areas such as agricultural or anti-poverty policy. In both cases, many actors mention the lowest common denominator policies of the European umbrella, which means that groups lobby outside the joint structure in order to pursue their individual interests. In agricultural policy, this has much to do with regional differences in farming and the status of agriculture in the national culture and economy, whereas in anti-poverty policy, it is linked to enormous differences in welfare standards. If lobbying individually is not as accentuated in agricultural policy as it is in anti-poverty policy, then this is likely so for two reasons. First, agricultural policy is almost fully integrated, rendering it plausible to join forces when seeking to influence it. And second, the organisational landscape in the agricultural field is substantially less diverse than in the anti-poverty field. In the former, there are only two main European umbrella organisations, which, in fact, co-operate as COPA-COGECA; whereas in the latter, there are a variety of European umbrellas which seek to defend specific anti-poverty interests, with EAPN taking the role of an umbrella of European umbrellas, which, by definition, can only be rather broad in its lobbying efforts since it seeks to represent and cover a large variety of interests and issues. The implication is that national groups, whilst members of EAPN and happy to also be represented by it, tend to organise their lobbying efforts separately in order to a) be able to articulate their *own* interests and b) be more concise in their demands. In fact, this dynamic also exists for non-distributive policies, such as environmental policy. Given its high degree of integration and the lack of redistributive policies involved, one might have expected to find a very high degree of involvement with the European umbrella (EEB). And yet, actors repeatedly suggest that they mainly lobby through other channels, either directly or via other European umbrellas that do not assemble as many different groups and therefore are less heterogeneous in their aims and in the interests they defend. Overall, the results suggest the difficulty, for non-sectoral CSOs in particular, of overcoming the boundaries of their national constituencies. European umbrellas therefore rather seem to serve as ways of receiving information about EU policies and, likewise, feeding information from the grassroots into the umbrella than as engineers of a European *demos*, so far (Wonka 2009: 196).

Finally, this study addressed which activities (lobbying, networking, funding, information and exchange, services, protest, contributing to democracy) are most important for CSOs when engaging with the EU and when engaging domestically. It also asked actors which positives and negatives they perceive in the EU. As argued in Chapter 2.2, it is of utmost importance to also take ideational factors into account when seeking to understand why groups engage with the EU (or not). From the related data, I gained a sense of why CSOs get engaged with the EU – is it a mostly rent-seeking interest or does it go beyond lobbying *strictu sensu*? If it was the former, this could be legitimate, but would not work in favour of creating a common European interest and thereby contributing to the creation of a European demos (and vice versa).

Agricultural groups are mainly engaged in EU policy making in order to defend their material interests; contributing to EU democracy is of comparatively low importance to them (*see* graphs 11–16 in the appendix). These priorities also became apparent when the respective actors mentioned the main advantages of the EU, i.e. the existence of a single market, common regulation, the existence of the CAP and the financial security that comes with it. Agricultural actors tend to have a rather positive appraisal of the EU which, however, seems mostly linked to gains they get from it as farmers.

Lobbying to influence EU policies is also quite important for environmental actors, who, nevertheless, have a similarly moderate level of interest in contributing to EU democracy as agricultural actors – a result that is rather surprising, given that environmental problems are often truly transnational and need to be dealt with at that level. The main advantage of the EU that these actors mention is the common political framework for the protection of the environment and nature while their overall appraisal of the EU is rather mixed.

Whilst anti-poverty actors display the lowest degree of Europeanisation, it is surprisingly high given the low level of legal incentives for them and their lack of resources. Also, almost half of them consider that contributing to EU democracy is a relevant aspect of their EU-related work (*see* graph 15 in the appendix). This finding suggests that idealistic motivations can be quite strong incentives to get involved with the EU. The advantages these actors see in the EU are also more idealistic than those of the other two groups, namely a less adversarial political culture, the possibilities for mutual learning processes or more support, by European institutions, for anti-poverty causes than actors receive from their national governments.

Overall, then, we can draw three conclusions from the findings presented in this study as regards the issue of supranational *demos*-creation. First, they suggest that those groups that find it easiest to Europeanise their activities, and where the legitimacy of representation is highest, show the least interest in contributing to EU democracy, whilst those who are the least Europeanised, and where the legitimacy of representation is lowest, are considerably more interested in European democracy.

Second, they imply that identity does not necessarily follow function, as neo-functionalist theory would have us expect (Risse 2005). Whilst all the groups are Europeanised to a considerable degree, for most of them this does not seem to imply that they become more attached to EU democracy than to domestic democracy. One might, of course, object that simply by participating in EU policy making they contribute to rendering it more democratic, by making it a pluralistic regime. However, what is needed, amongst other things, for the creation of a *demos*, namely the integration of different interests into the same political process and the creation of a common interest, only happens to a limited degree.

Third, the results confirm the message of earlier research that certain CSOs are ill-suited to provide the kind of Europeanisation of their constituencies that would seem necessary for the creation of a supranational polity (Warleigh 2001). However, this is not because internal democratic structures are not in place but because they are not used by more than a few key national policy officers. Many CSOs do not seem to mediate between the state and society, as hoped by some scholars or Commission officials – not between the EU and national peoples anyway. Overall, therefore, the idea of CSOs univocally contributing to the creation and the representation of *one* European *demos* must be rejected. What is sure is that much more research is needed on both the transnational activities of CSOs and on the domestic face of their Europeanisation, in order to be able to evaluate of what nature their activities and orientations are – supranational, domestic, *demoicratic*, all of these or combinations of them.

Finally, some analysts have focused not so much on either the institutional or the social deficit, but have been more interested in what I call the domestic deficit, i.e. the potentially negative impacts of increasing European integration on domestic democratic processes (Bartolini 2005; Bellamy and Kröger 2014; Scharpf 1999; Schmidt 2005). Mostly, this literature has been interested in national parliaments, courts, governments, political parties or the overall political system, and less so in CSOs. However, this need not mean that the EU cannot equally have detrimental effects on the capacity, of CSOs, to legitimately represent a constituency or an issue and given the resources required to be present in Brussels, one might expect CSOs to be affected in some way or other by their engagement with the EU. The limited research that exists in this direction has concerned itself with the issue of the professionalisation, of CSOs, in response to being active at the EU level. Indeed, keeping a close contact to their constituencies may take second place to the more functional objectives of being part of the policy-making process and to the kind of professionalisation this requires. Can we find any such traces in the interest representation strategies or the activities more generally of the three groups under study here?

Being involved in EU affairs seems to mainly impact those CSOs which receive EU-funding. The requirements of EU-funding are such that they lead CSOs to professionalise their work so far as quality standards and project evaluation are concerned. However, these sorts of impacts seem to mainly occur at the national level and for larger regional organisations whereas interviewees of smaller regional, let alone local organisations did not seem to feel an EU-induced impact on their work. In how far being involved with the EU also affects the balance groups strike between the logic of membership and the logic of influence is less clear, given this study is not looking at a longer time horizon. However, the trend towards professionalisation as well as the rare usage of 'voice' strategies of interest representation in general, and at the EU level in particular, point towards the logic of influence by which organisations 'adapt their aims and methods to the actual decision-making processes on which they wish to exert an impact' (Schmitter and Streeck 1999: 19) as being predominant. More long-term studies would be required to evaluate the extent to which being involved in EU policy making affects CSOs in their work, substantially and strategically. The limited amount of data in regard to this issue does not allow for stronger conclusions.

To conclude, while the results of this study point in a rather pessimistic direction as regards the capacity, of CSOs, to reduce the social deficit of the EU, this need not mean that groups cannot help the more representative actors to uphold the standard of political equality in the different phases of EU policy making. Indeed, we know from theory that political representation is more than the formal processes of authorisation and accountability (*see* the discussion in Chapter 1.2). Ongoing public debate about competing political programmes between and beyond elections is crucial for democratic representation because it allows interaction between the represented and the representatives and for the former to influence the choices about public policies of the latter, and CSOs have a valuable role to play in this process. Particularly in the context of the EU with the documented deficiencies of the traditional representative actors, CSOs have a contribution to make to input legitimacy as a complementary layer to outlets of representative democracy – by supporting political competition, by contributing to greater publicity and to public control of elected representatives.

Appendix

List 1 — Coding of interviews

Interview 1: Representative of the Deutscher Raiffeisenverband, 1 March 2012

Interview 2: Representative of the Hessischer Bauernverband, 30 April 2012

Interview 3: Representative of the Landesbauernverband Sachsen-Anhalt, 24 April 2012

Interview 4: Representative of the Bauernverband Mecklenburg-Vorpommern, 19 April 2012

Interview 5: Representative of the Landesbauernverband in Baden-Württemberg, 8 May 2012

Interview 6: Representative of the Bayerischer Bauernverband, 2 May 2012

Interview 7: Representative of Ulster Farmer's Union, 28 February 2012

Interview 8: Representative of NFU Regional Board, 27 April 2012

Interview 9: Representative of the British farmers' office in Brussels, 13 March 2012

Interview 10: Representative of COPA-COGECA, 5 April 2012

Interview 11: Representative of COPA-COGECA, 29 March 2012

Interview 12: Representative of Grüne Liga, 24 January 2012

Interview 13: Representative of Bundesvereinigung Boden, 9 February 2012

Interview 14: Representative of Forum Ökologisch-Soziale Martkwirtschaft e.V., 26 January 2012

Interview 15: Representative of Bund Heimat und Umwelt in Deutschland, 22 February 2012

Interview 16: Representative of Landesheimatbund Sachsen-Anhalt, 19 June 2012

Interview 17: Representative of Öko-Institut e.V., 27 January 2012

Interview 18: Representative of Naturschutzbund Deutschland e.V. (NABU), 17 February 2012

Interview 19: Representative of Naturschutzbund Hamburg e.V., 7 May 2012

Interview 20: Representative of Deutsche Umwelthilfe, 2 February 2012

Interview 21: Representative of Naturschutzbund Bayern, 7 May 2012

Interview 22: Representative of Naturschutzbund Nordrhein-Westphalen, 20 April 2012

Interview 23: Representative of Bund für Umwelt und Naturschutz Deutschland (BUND), 30 January 2012

Interview 24: Representative of Landesbund für Vogelschutz, Bavaria, 24 April 2012

Interview 25: Representative of Deutscher Naturschutzring (DNR), 23 January 2012

Interview 26: Representative of Bundesverband Bürgerinitiativen Umweltschutz e. V. (BBU), 5 March 2012

Interview 27: Representative of Wildlife and Countryside Link (WCL), 3 February 2012

Interview 28: Representative of Royal Society for the Protection of Birds (RSPB), 6 March 2012

Interview 29: Representative of the European Environmental Bureau (eeb), 2 May 2012

Interview 30: Representative of the European Environmental Bureau (eeb) / Friends of the Earth, 27 January 2012

Interview 31: Representative of Deutscher Gewerkschaftsbund, 17 April 2012

Interview 32: Representative of Zentrale Wohlfahrtsstelle der Juden in Deutschland e.V., 17 February 2012

Interview 33: Representative of Caritas Köln, 24 April 2012

Interview 34: Representative of Diakonisches Werk Württemberg e.V., 7 May 2012

Interview 35: Representative of Deutsches Rotes Kreuz, 10 February 2012

Interview 36: Representative of Caritas, 2 April 2012

Interview 37: Representative of Diakonisches Werk Worms-Alzey Stadtteilbüro Wormser Süden, 26 April 2012

Interview 38: Representative of Lawaetz-Stiftung, 8 May 2012

Interview 39: Representative of Caritas Osnabrück, 24 April 2012

Interview 40: Representative of Caritas, Brussels office, 17 February 2012

Interview 41: Representative of Der Paritätische, 2 May 2012

Interview 42: Representative of BAG Schuldnerberatung, 25 January 2012

Interview 43: Representative of Kompetenzzentrum Europa der Caritas in Baden-Württemberg, 8 May 2012

Interview 44: Representative of BAG Wohnungslosenhilfe, 27 February 2012

Interview 45: Representative of Diakonie Niedersachsen, 23 April 2012

Interview 46: Representative of Armut-Gesundheit e.V., 27 February 2012

Interview 47: Representative of Diakonie Hamburg, 23 May 2012

Interview 48: Representative of Soziale Stadtentwicklung und Gemeinwesenarbeit, 13 February 2012

Interview 49: Representative of the Irish Traveller, 31 January 2012

Interview 50: Representative of Age Scotland, 30 January 2012

Interview 51: Representative of Church Action on Poverty, 20 February 2012

Interview 52: Representative of the Single Parent Action Network, 13 February 2012

Interview 53: Representative of the Child Poverty Action Group, 1 February 2012

Interview 54: Representative of Church Action on Poverty, 23 April 2012

Interview 55: Representative of Runnemede, 21 February 2012

Interview 56: Representative of ATD Fourth World, 31 January 2012
Interview 57: Representative of the European Anti-Poverty Network (EAPN), 17 May 2012
Interview 58: Representative of the European Anti-Poverty Network (EAPN), 30 May 2012

List 2 — Interview questions

1) Understanding of representation

a) What do you understand by 'representation'?
b) When do you think is representation achieved?
c) Who or what does your organisation represent?
d) What makes for your organisation to be a legitimate representative of these interests?

2) Mobilisation of members / supporters

a) How do you attract members and supporters?
b) How do you entertain your relationship with them?
c) Do you mobilise members / supporters for some of your activities?

3) Decision-making

a) How do topics get on the agenda?
b) Which procedures are there in your organisation to find positions on EU policy processes?
c) How regularly are these procedures used?
d) Can members participate in them? And other supporters? And if so, how?
e) Do they in fact participate in them?
f) What kind of control is there in regard of EU-related activities and positions?
g) Can members hold the organisation to account, and if so, how?
h) How does your organisation link to the national umbrella structure?
i) How do your positions feed into EU-positions of the EU-umbrella structure? Do you feel well represented by it?

4) European institutions

a) Which contacts do you have to the European Commission?
b) How do you perceive of the consultation opportunities that the Commission offers?
c) Is your organisation currently funded by the Commission, amongst others?
d) Which contacts do you have to the EP?

e) How do you perceive of the consultation opportunities that the EP offers?
f) Has working with European institutions in any way changed the way you organise your work or the activities you pursue?

5) Political environment

a) With which other actors are you in touch with in order to influence policies?
b) Do you perceive differences between being involved in EU politics and domestic politics?
c) Is it easier or more difficult for your CSO to be heard at the EU rather than the domestic level? Why?
d) Which opportunities and benefits, threats and costs do you see coming from European integration?

List 3 — Questionnaire

1) Personal information

What is your position in the organisation and your principle field of work?

How long have you been working for it?

Do you share a biographical background with the interests you are representing?

2) Organisational Resources

> What, approximately, is your annual budget?
>
>

> How many staff are working on EU issues?
>
>

> Do you consider this to be sufficient?
>
>

> Has the percentage of staff (also) devoted to EU issues / processes increased, decreased or remained stable over the last decade?
>
>

> What percentage of your time approximately do you spend on EU issues?
>
>

3) Activities

In your organisation, what importance does dealing with EU processes have?			
High	Medium	Rather low	None

How important is being present at EU-level to achieve the organisational goals?			
Very important	Rather important	Rather unimportant	Not important

When you seek to influence EU policies, which channel do you commonly use?			
	Very important	Rather important	Rather unimportant
National NGOs			
National MPs			
National ministries			
European NGOs			
MEPs			
European Commission			

Which of these strategies do you pursue with regard to EU policies?		
Consensual	Conflict-driven	From case-to-case

In your dealings with the EU, can you range the following in terms of their importance for your work:			
	Highly relevant	Medium relevance	No relevance
Lobbying			
Networking			
Funding			
Information and exchange			
Service delivery			
Protest			
Contribution to EU-democracy			
Any other:			

When acting domestically, can you range the following in terms of their importance for your work:			
	Highly relevant	Medium relevance	No relevance
Lobbying			
Networking			
Funding			
Information and exchange			
Service delivery			
Protest			
Contribution to democracy			
Any other:			

Graph 4: Degree of Europeanisation

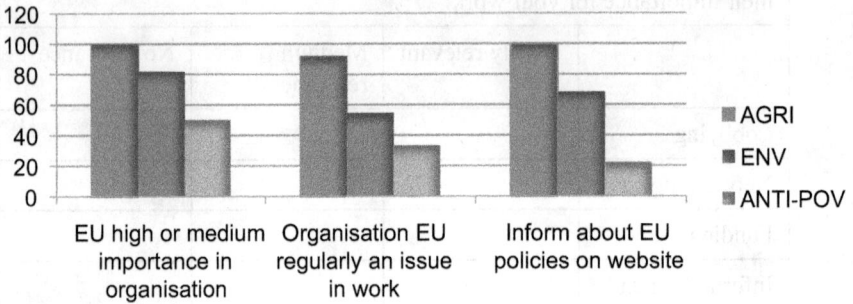

Graph 4: First column: In your organisation, what importance does dealing with EU processes have (high – medium – rather low – none)? Second column: Is the EU an issue in your work (regularly – irregularly – rarely – never)? Third column: Do organisations inform about the EU / EU policies on their website (yes – no, researched by author)?

Graph 5: When you seek to influence EU policies, which channels do you commonly use (very important – rather important – rather unimportant)?

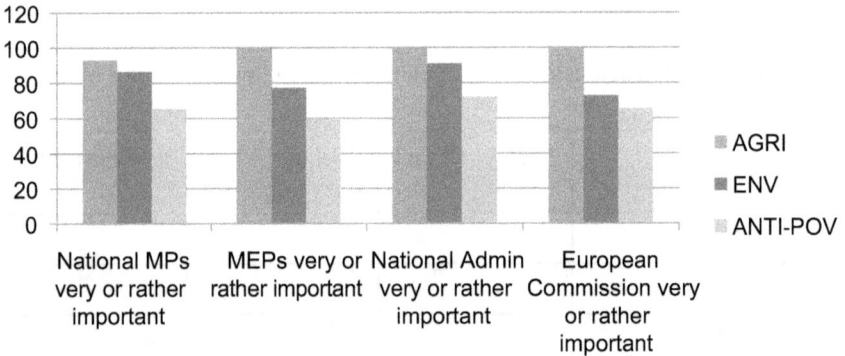

Graph 6: When you seek to influence EU policies, which channel do you commonly use? First column: National NGOs (very important – rather important – rather unimportant); second column: European NGOs (very important – rather important – rather unimportant).

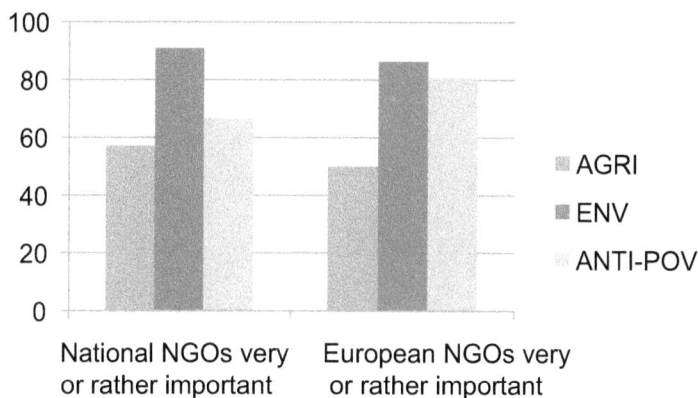

Graph 7: How strong are your links with the European umbrella organisation?

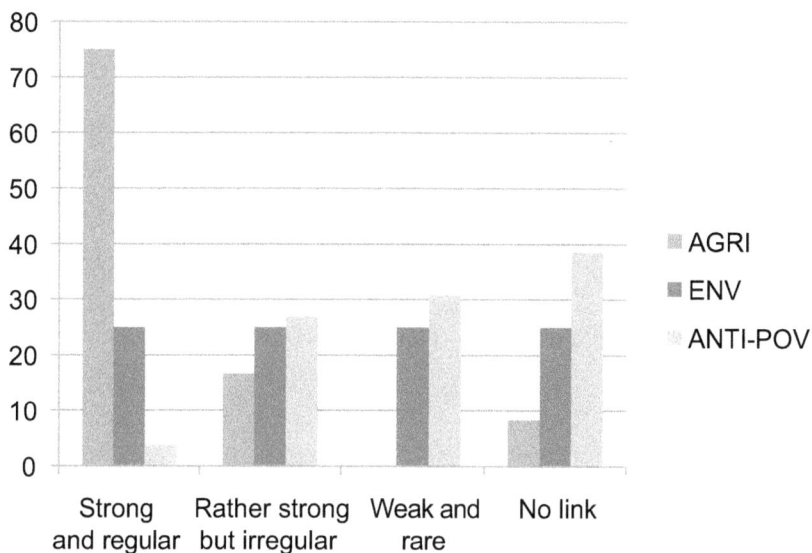

Graph 8: Level of satisfaction of CSO with representation by European umbrella structure

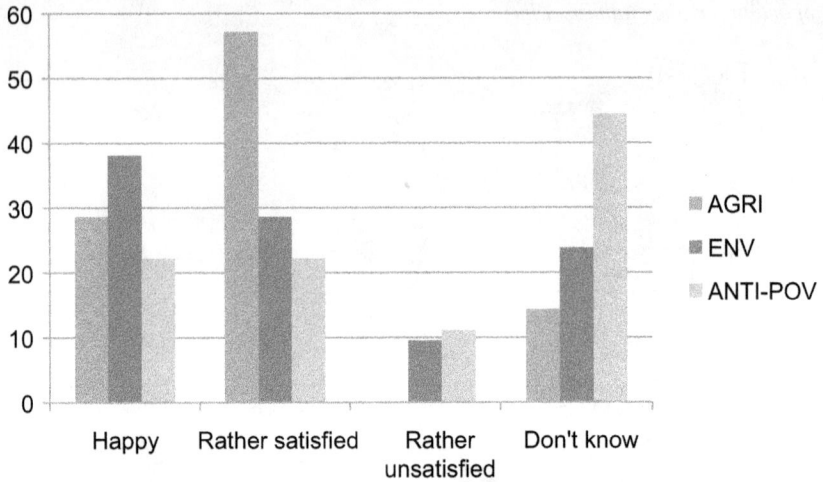

Graph 9.1: Is it easier or more difficult to get your voice heard at the EU level than at the national level?

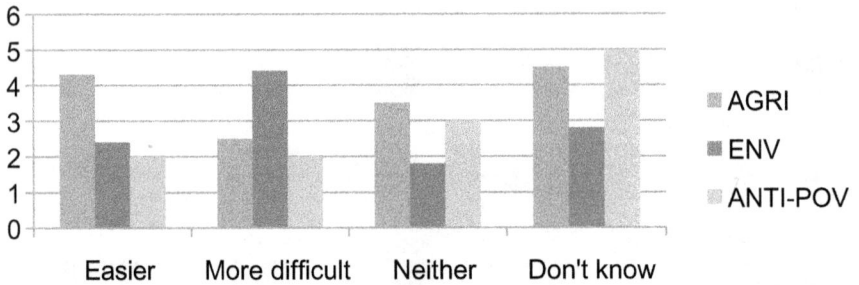

Graph 9.2: Advantages and disadvantages coming from the European integration process

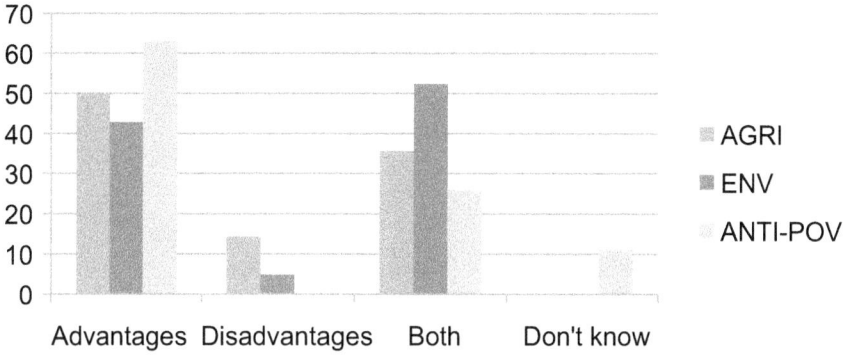

Graph 10: Does being involved in EU policy making affect the workings of the organisation?

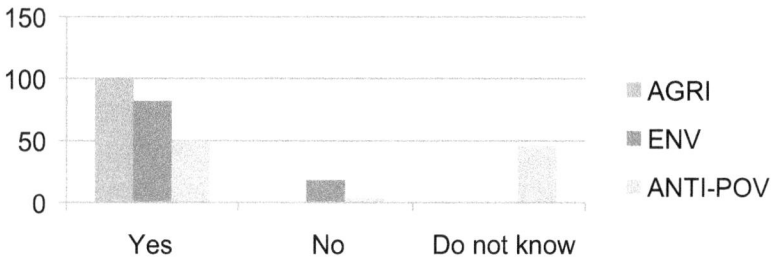

Graph 11: In your dealings with the EU, can you range the following in terms of their importance for your work: Lobbying

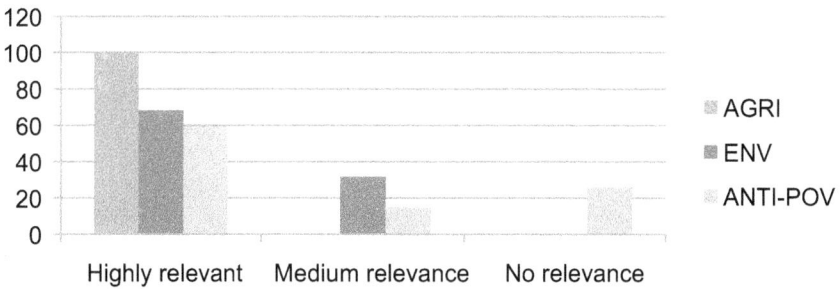

Graph 12: In your dealings with the EU, can you range the following in terms of their importance for your work: Networking

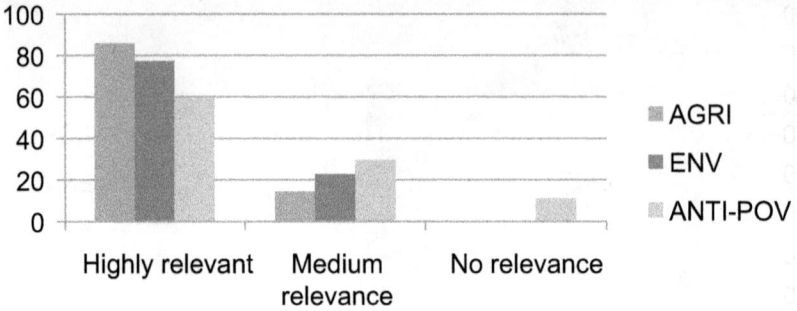

Graph 13: In your dealings with the EU, can you range the following in terms of their importance for your work: Information and exchange

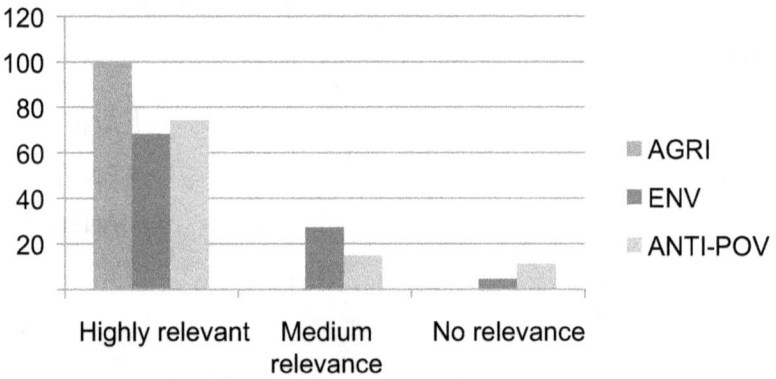

Graph 14: In your dealings with the EU, can you range the following in terms of their importance for your work: Protest

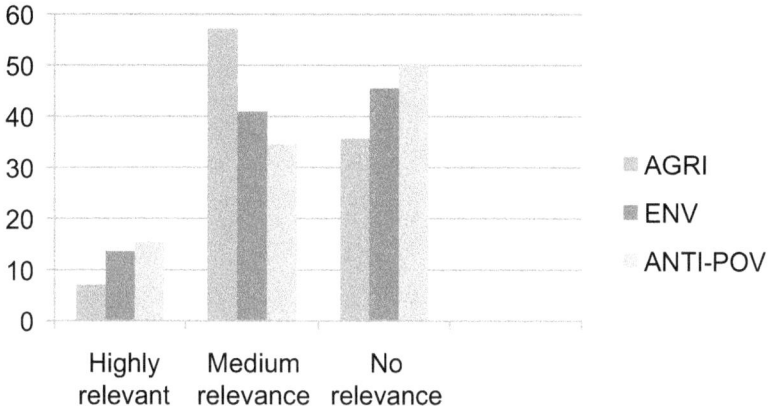

Graph 15: In your dealings with the EU, can you range the following in terms of their importance for your work: Contribution to EU-democracy

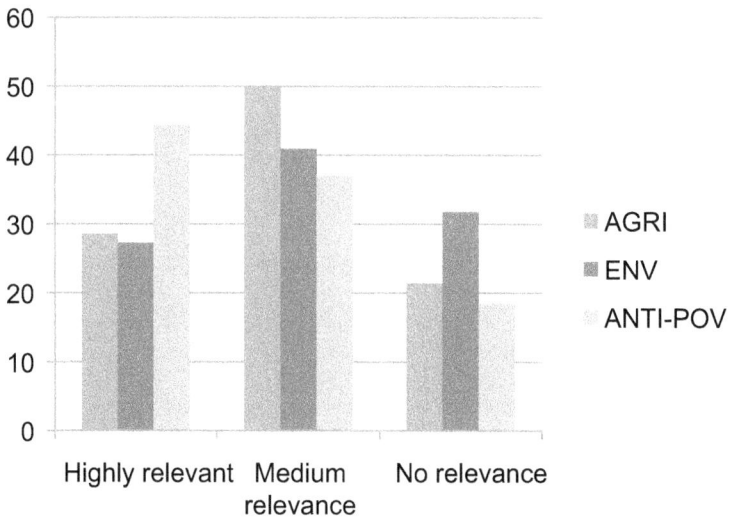

Graph 16: When acting domestically, can you range the following in terms of their importance for your work: Contribution to democracy

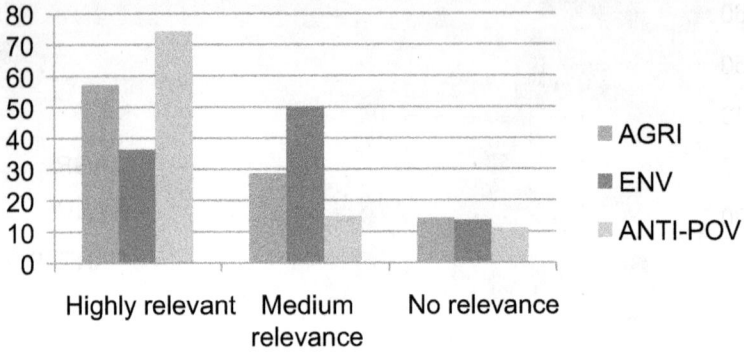

References

Altides, C. and Kohler-Koch, B. (2009) 'Multi-level accountability via civil society associations?' paper presented at the conference 'Bringing Civil Society In: The European Union and the rise of representative democracy', Robert Schuman Centre for Advanced Studies – European University Institute (EUI), Florence, 13–14 March 2009.

Arnull, A. and Wincott, D. (2002) *Accountability and Legitimacy in the European Union*, Oxford: Oxford University Press.

Auel, K. and Benz, A. (2005) 'The politics of adaptation: The Europeanisation of national parliamentary systems', *The Journal of Legislative Studies*, 11(3–4): 372–393.

Bartolini, S. (2005) *Restructuring Europe: Centre formation, system building and political structuring between the nation-state and the European Union*, Oxford: Oxford University Press.

Bauer, M.W. (2002) 'Limitations to agency control in EU policy making: the commission and the poverty programmes', *Journal of Common Market Studies*, 40(3): 381–400.

Baumgartner, F.R. *et al.* (2009) *Lobbying and Policy Change: Who wins, who loses, and why*, Chicago: University of Chicago Press.

Bellamy, R. and Castiglione, D. (2010) 'Democracy by delegation? Who represents whom and how in European governance', *Government and Opposition*, 46(1): 101–125.

Bellamy, R. and Kröger, S. (2014) 'Domesticating the democratic deficit? The role of national parliaments and parties in the EU's system of governance', *Parliamentary Affairs*, 67(2): 437–457.

Bennet, L. *et al.* (2011) 'Public Engagement vs. Institutional Influence Strategies: Comparing Trade and Environmental Advocacy Networks at the National and EU levels in Germany and the UK', paper prepared for the ECPR Conference, Reykjavik, August 2011.

Benz, A. (2003) 'Compounded Representation in EU Multilevel Governance', in Kohler-Koch, B. (ed.) *Linking EU and National Governance*, Oxford: Oxford University Press, 82–110.

Berger, P.L. and Luckmann, T. (1969) *Die gesellschaftliche Konstruktion der Wirklichkeit: Eine Theorie der Wissenssoziologie*, Frankfurt am Main: Fischer.

Bevir, M. and Rhodes, R.A.W. (2006) 'Defending interpretation', *European Political Science*, 5(1), 69–83.

Beyers, J. (2002) 'Gaining and seeking access: the European adaptation of domestic interest associations', *European Journal of Political Research*, 41(5): 585–612.

—— (2004) 'Voice and access: the political practices of European interest associations', *European Union Politics*, 5(2): 211–240.

— (2008) 'Policy issues, organisational format and the political strategies of interest organisations', *West European Politics*, 31, 1188–1211.

Beyers, J., Eising, R. and Maloney, W. (2008) 'The politics of organised interests in Europe: lessons from EU studies and comparative politics', *West European Politics*, 31(6): 1103–1128.

Beyers, J. and Kerremans, B. (2007) 'Critical resource dependencies and the Europeanization of domestic interest groups', *Journal of European Public Policy*, 14(3): 460–481.

Binderkrantz, A. (2005) 'Interest group strategies: navigating between privileged access and strategies of pressure', *Political Studies*, 53(4): 694–715.

— (2009) 'Membership recruitment and internal democracy in interest groups: do group-membership relations vary between group types?', *West European Politics*, 32(3): 657–678.

Börzel, T. A. and Risse, T. (2003) 'Conceptualizing the domestic impact of Europe', in Featherstone, K. and Radaelli, C. (eds.) *The Politics of Europeanization*, Oxford: Oxford University Press, 57–80.

Bouwen, P. (2002) 'Corporate lobbying in the European Union: the logic of access', *Journal of European Public Policy*, 9(3): 365–390.

— (2007) 'Competing for consultation: European civil society and conflict between the European commission and the European parliament', *West European Politics*, 30(2): 265–284.

Bovens, M. (2007) 'Analysing and assessing public accountability: a conceptual framework', *European Law Journal*, 13(4): 447–468.

Broscheid, A. and Coen, D. (2003) 'Insider and outsider lobbying of the European Commission: an informational model', *European Union Politics*, 4(2): 165–189.

Brzinski, J.B., Lancaster, T.D. and Tuschoff, T. (1999) *Compounded Representation in Western European Federations*, London/Portland, OR: Frank: Cass.

Burke, E. (1968) *Reflections on the Revolution in France*, London: Penguin Books.

Butler, I.d.J. (2008) 'Non-governmental organisation participation in the EU law-making process: the example of social non-governmental organisations at the commission, parliament and council', *European Law Journal*, 14(5): 558–582.

Castiglione, D. and Warren, M.E. (2008) 'Rethinking Democratic Representation: Eight Theoretical Issues', paper prepared for the workshop on Rethinking Representation, Bellagio, 30 September–3 October 2008.

Checkel, J. (2001) 'Why comply? Social learning and European identity change', *International Organization* 55(3): 553–588.

Cheneval, F. and Schimmelfennig, F. (2012) 'The case for demoicracy in the European Union', *Journal of Common Market Studies*, 51(2): 334–350.

Christiano, T. (1996) *The Rule of the Many*, Boulder: Westview Press.

Christiansen, T., Jorgenson, K., & Wiener, A. (1999) 'The social construction of Europe', *Journal of European Public Policy* 6(4): 528–544.

Coen, D. and Richardson, J. (2009) (eds.) *Lobbying in the European Union: Institutions, actors and issues*, Oxford: Oxford University Press.

Collingwood, V. (2006) 'Non-governmental organisation, power and legitimacy in international society', *Review of International Studies*, 32, 439–454.

Collingwood, V. and Logister, L. (2005) 'State of the art: addressing the INGO "legitimacy deficit"', *Political Studies Review*, 3, 175–192.

Constantelos, J. (2004) 'The Europeanization of interest group politics in Italy: business associations in Rome and the regions', *Journal of European Public Policy*, 11(6): 1020–40.

Cowles, M.G. (2001) 'The transatlantic business dialogue and domestic business-government relations', in Green Cowles, M.G., Caporaso, J.A. and Risse, T. (eds.) *Transforming Europe: Europeanization and Domestic Change*, Ithaca, NY: Cornell University Press, 159–79.

Cram, L. (1993) 'Calling the tune without paying the piper? Social policy regulation: the role of the commission in European community social policy', *Policy and Politics*, 21(1): 135–46.

— (2001) 'Whither the commission? Reform, renewal and the issue-attention cycle', *Journal of European Public Policy*, 8(5): 770–786.

— (2007) 'In the Shadow of Hierarchy: The Commission and the Community Method', paper presented at the CONNEX Workshop 'How Much is Known about the "Community Method"', Science Po, Paris, 29 November 2007.

Crotty, M. (1998) *The Foundations of Social Research: Meaning and perspective in the research process*, Thousand Oaks, CA: Sage.

Crum, B. and Fossum, J.E. (2009) 'The multilevel parliamentary field: a framework for theorizing representative democracy in the EU', *European Political Science Review*, 1(2): 249–271.

Curtin, D. (2003) 'Private interest representation or civil society deliberation? A contemporary dilemma for European Union governance', *Social & Legal Studies*, 12(1): 55–75.

Dahl, R.A. (1998) *On Democracy*, Yale University Press.

Daly, M. (2006) 'EU social policy after Lisbon', *Journal of Common Market Studies*, 44(3): 461–481.

Dawson, M. (2009) 'EU Law "Transformed"? Evaluating Accountability and Subsidiarity in the "Streamlined" OMC for Social Inclusion and Social Protection', European Integration Online Papers, 1(13).

Decker, F. (2002) 'Governance beyond the nation-state: reflections on the democratic deficit of the European Union', *Journal of European Public Policy*, 9(2): 256–272.

Della Sala, V. and Ruzza, C. (2007) (eds.) *Governance and Civil Society: Policy perspectives*, Manchester: Manchester University Press.

Dinan, D. (2014) 'Governance and institutions: the unrelenting rise of the European parliament', *Journal of Common Market Studies*, 52, Annual Review, 109–124.

Disch, L. (2011) 'Toward a mobilization conception of democratic representation', *American Political Science Review*, 105(1): 100–114.

Dovi, S. (2002) 'Preferable descriptive representatives: or will just any woman, black, or Latino do?' *American Political Science Review*, 96(4): 745–754.

Draft Constitutional Treaty of the European Union (2004): Article 47–1 §1.4

Dryzek, J. (2000) *Deliberative Democracy and Beyond: Liberals, critics, contestations*, Oxford: Oxford University Press.

— (2010) *Foundations and Frontiers of Deliberative Governance*, New York: Oxford University Press.

— and Niemeyer, S. (2008) 'Discursive representation', *American Political Science Review*, 102(4): 481–93.

Duina, F. G. and Blithe, F. (1999) 'Nation-states and common markets: the institutional conditions for acceptance', *Review of International Political Economy*, 6(4): 494–530.

Dür, A. and de Bièvre, D. (2007) 'Inclusion without influence? NGOs in European trade policy', *Journal of Public Policy*, 27(1): 79–101.

Dür, A. and Mateo, G. (2012) 'Who lobbies the European Union? National interest groups in a multilevel polity', *Journal of European Public Policy*, 19(7): 969–987.

Dür, A. and Mateo, G. (2013) 'Gaining access or going public? Interest group strategies in five European countries', *European Journal of Political Research*, 52(5): 660–686.

Eising, R. (2007) 'Institutional context, organizational resources and strategic choices: explaining interest group access in the European Union', *European Union Politics*, 8(3): 329–362.

Eising, R. and Kohler-Koch, B. (2005) 'Interessenpolitik im europäischen Mehrebenensystem'. In: *ibid.* (eds.) *Interessenpolitik in Europa*, Baden-Baden: Nomos, 11–78.

Eriksen, E. O. and Fossum, J. E. (2000) 'The EU and Post-National Legitimacy', *ARENA Working Papers* – WP 00/26.

— (2002) 'Democracy through strong publics in the European Union', *Journal of Common Market Studies*, 40(3): 401–24.

European Commission (2000) *'The Commission and NGOs: building a stronger partnership'*, COM (2000) 11 final.

— (2001) *'European Governance: A White Paper'*, COM (2001) 428 final.

— (2002) 'Communication from the Commission: Towards a Reinforced Culture of Consultation and Dialogue – General Principles and Minimum Standards for Consultation of Interested Parties by the Commission', COM (2002) 704 final.

Fairbrass, J. (2003) 'The Europeanization of business interest representation: UK and French firms compared', *Comparative European Politics*, 1(3): 313–334.

Fairbrass, J. and Warleigh, A. (2013) *Influence and Interests in the European Union: The new politics of persuasion and advocacy*, London: Routledge.

Falkner, G. (2007) 'The EU's Social Dimension', in Cini, M. (ed.) *European Union Politics*, 2nd ed., Oxford: Oxford University Press, 271–285.

Follesdal, A. and Hix, S. (2006) 'Why there is a democratic deficit in the EU: a response to Majone and Moravcsik', *Journal of Common Market Studies*, 44(3): 533–62.

Fossum, J.E. and Trenz, H.-J. (2006) 'The EU's fledgling society: from deafening silence to critical voice in European constitution-making', *Journal of Civil Society*, 2(1): 57–77.

Fraser, N. (2005) 'Reframing justice in a globalizing world', *New Left Review*, 36, November–December 2005, 69–88.

Friedrich, D. (2011) *Democratic Participation and Civil Society in the European Union*, Manchester: Manchester University Press.

Friedrichs, J. and Kratochwil, F. (2009) 'On acting and knowing: how pragmatism can advance international relations research and methodology', *International Organization*, 63, Fall 2009, 701–31.

Garzon, I. (2006) *Reforming the Common Agricultural Policy: A history of paradigm change*, Basingstoke: Palgrave Macmillan.

Goodhart, M. (2007) 'Europe's democratic deficits through the looking glass: the European Union as a challenge for democracy', *Perspectives on Politics*, 5(3): 567–584.

Goodin, R.E. (2003) 'Democratic Accountability: The third sector and all. harvard: the hauser center for nonprofit organizations', Working Paper No. 19.

Grant, W. (2007) 'Policy instruments in the common agricultural policy', paper prepared for the workshop on 'Governing the EU: policy instruments in a multi-level polity' at the Centre d'Etudes Européennes, Sciences Po, Paris 21–22 June 2007.

Greenwood, J. (1997) *Representing Interests in the European Union*, Basingstoke: Palgrave Macmillan.

— (2007) 'Review article: Organized civil society and democratic legitimacy in the European Union', *British Journal of Political Science*, 37(2): 333–357.

— (2011) *Interest Representation in the European Union*, 3rd edition, Basingstoke: Palgrave Macmillan.

— (2012) 'The European citizens' initiative and EU civil society organisations', *Perspectives on European Politics and Society*, 13(3): 325–336.

Greer, A. (2005) *Agricultural Policy in Europe*, Manchester: Manchester University Press.

Grethe, H. (2006) 'Environmental and Agricultural Policy: What Roles for the EU and the Member States?' Keynote paper for the conference Subsidiarity and Economic Reform in Europe, November 8–9, 2006, Brussels.

Grimm, D. (1995) 'Does Europe need a constitution?' *European Law Journal*, 1(3): 282–302.

Grote, J.R. and Lang, A. (2003) 'Europeanization and organizational change in national trade associations: an organizational ecology perspective', in Featherstone, K. and Radaelli, C. (eds.) *The Politics of Europeanisation*, Oxford: Oxford University Press, 225–254.

Habermas, J. (1992) *Faktizität und Geltung: Beiträge zur Diskurstheorie des Rechts und des demokratischen Rechtsstaats*, Frankfurt am Main: Suhrkamp.

Habermas, J. (2001) 'Why Europe needs a constitution', *New Left Review*, 11, September–October, 5–26.

Hallstrom, L.K. (2004) 'Eurocratising enlargement? EU elites and NGO participation in European environmental policy', *Environmental Politics*, 13(1): 175–193.

Halpin, D.R. (2006) 'The participatory and democratic potential and practice of interest groups: between solidarity and representation', *Public Administration*, 84(4): 919–940.

Harris, T. (2007) 'Constructionism in sociology', Holstein, J. and Gubrium, J. (eds.) *The Handbook of Constructionist Research*, Thousand Oaks, CA: Sage, 231–250.

Heidemann, K.A. (2012) 'The view from below: exploring the interface of Europeanization and Basque language activism in France', *Mobilization: An International Journal*, 17(2): 195–220.

Held, D. (1995) *Democracy and the Global Order: From the modern state to cosmopolitan governance*, Cambridge: Polity Press.

Hendriks, C.M. (2009) 'The democratic soup: mixed meanings of political representation in governance networks', *Governance: An international journal of policy, administration, and institutions*, 22(4): 689–715.

Hix, S. (2002) 'Why the EU should have a single president, and how she should be elected'. paper for the Working Group on Democracy in the EU for the UK Cabinet Office, October 2002. http://personal.lse.ac.uk/hix/Working_Papers/Why%20the%20EU%20Should%20Have%20a%20Single%20President.pdf (accessed 22 January 2013).

Hix, S. and Noury, A. (2009) 'After enlargement: voting patterns in the sixth European parliament', *Legislative Studies Quarterly*, 34(2): 159–74.

Hobolt, S.B. (2014) 'A vote for the President? The role of Spitzenkandidaten in the 2014 European parliament elections', *Journal of European Public Policy*, 21(10): 1528–1540.

Hobson, C. (2008) 'Revolution, representation and the foundations of modern democracy', *European Journal of Political Theory*, 7(4): 449–471.

Hooghe, L. and Marks, G. (2001) *Multi-Level Governance and European Integration*, Oxford: Rowman and Littlefield.

Höreth, M. (1999) 'No way out for the beast? The unsolved legitimacy problem of European governance', *Journal of European Public Policy*, 6(2): 249–68.

Hüller, T. (2007) 'Assessing EU strategies for publicity', *Journal of European Public Policy*, 14(4): 563–581.

Hüller, T. (2010) *Demokratie und Sozialregulierung in Europa: Die Online-Konsultationen der EU-Kommission*, Serie Staatlichkeit im Wandel, Frankfurt am Main: Campus.

Hunold, C. (2005) 'Green political theory and the European Union: the case for a non-integrated civil society', *Environmental Politics*, 14(3): 324–343.

Hurrelmann, A. and DeBardeleben, J. (2009) 'Democratic dilemmas in EU multilevel governance: untangling the Gordian knot', *European Political Science Review*, 1(2): 229–247.

Imig, D.R.I. and Tarrow, S.G. (2001) *Contentious Europeans: Protest and politics in an emerging polity*, Lanham: Rowman and Littlefield.

Jachtenfuchs, M. (1997) 'Democracy and Governance in the European Union'. *European Integration Online Papers*, 1(2), http://eiop.or.at/eiop/texte/1997-002a.htm (accessed 3 February 2013).

Joerges, C. and Neyer, J. (1997) 'Transforming strategic interaction into deliberative problem-solving: European comitology in the foodstuffs sector', *Journal of European Public Policy*, 4(4): 609–625.

Johansson, H. (2012) 'Whom do they represent? Mixed modes of representation in EU-based CSOs', in Kröger, S. and Friedrich, D. (eds.) *The Challenge of Democratic Representation in the European Union*, Basingstoke: Palgrave Macmillan, 74–91.

Kay, A. (2000) 'Towards a Theory of the Reform of the Common Agricultural Policy', *European Integration online Papers*, 4 (9).

Kendall, J. (2010) 'The limits and possibilities of third sector Europeanization', *Journal of Civil Society*, 6(1): 39–65.

Kielmannsegg, P. Graf (2003) 'Integration und Demokratie', Jachtenfuchs, M. and Kohler-Koch, B. (eds.) *Europäische Integration*, 2, Auflage, Opladen: Leske und Budrich, 49–84.

Kitschelt, H. (1986) 'Political opportunity structures and political protest: anti-nuclear movements in four democracies', *British Journal of Political Sciences*, 16(1): 57–85.

Klüver, H. (2012) 'Biasing politics? Interest group participation', *EU Policy making, West European Politics*, 35(5), 1114–1133.

— (2010) 'Europeanization of lobbying activities: when national interest groups spill over to the European level', *Journal of European Integration*, 32(2): 175–191.

Klüver, H. and Saurugger, S. (2013) 'Opening the black box: the professionalization of interest groups in the European Union', Interest groups & Advocacy 2, 185–205.

Kohler, M. (2014) 'European governance and the European parliament: from talking shop to legislative powerhouse', *Journal of Common Market Studies*, 52(3): 600–615.

Kohler-Koch, B. (2009) 'The three worlds of European civil society – what role for civil society for what kind of Europe?' *Policy & Society*, 28(1): 47–57.

— (2010) 'Civil society and EU democracy: "astroturf" representation?' *Journal of European Public Policy*, 17(1): 100–116.

Kohler-Koch, B. and Finke, B. (2007) 'The institutional shaping of EU-society relations: a contribution to democracy via participation?' *Journal of Civil Society*, 3(3): 205–221.

Kohler-Koch, B. and Quittkat, C. (2013) *De-Mystification of Participatory Democracy: EU-governance and civil society*, Oxford: Oxford University Press.

Kohler-Koch, B., Quittkat, C. and Buth, V. (2008) Civil Society Organisations under the Impact of the European Commission's Consultation Regime. Paper presented at the CONNEX Final Conference, Workshop 5: Putting EU civil society involvement under scrutiny. Mannheim University, 6–8 March 2008, Mannheim.

Kratochwil, F. (2007) 'Of communities, gangs, historicity and the problem of Santa Claus: replies to my critics', *Journal of International Relations and Development*, 10(1): 57–78.

Kröger, S. (2006) 'When Learning Hits Politics Or: Social Policy Coordination Left to the Administrations and the NGOs?' *European Integration online Papers* 10(3).

— (2007a) 'The end of democracy as we know it? The legitimacy deficits of bureaucratic social policy governance', *Journal of European Integration*, 29(5): 565–582.

— (2007b) 'Mittendrin und doch außen vor? Die Armutspolitik der Europäischen Kommission (1975-2006)', in Fischer, R., Karrass, A. und S. Kröger (eds.), *Die Europäische Kommission und die Zukunft der EU: Ideenfabrik zwischen europäischen Auftrag und nationalen Interessen*, Budrich: Opladen, 251–273.

— (2008a) 'Nothing but consultation: the place of organised civil society in EU policy making across policies', European Governance Papers (EUROGOV) No. C-08-03, http://edoc.vifapol.de/opus/volltexte/2011/2471/pdf/egp_connex_C_08_03.pdf (accessed 12 February 2016).

— (2008b) *Soft Governance in Hard Politic:. European coordination of anti-poverty policies in France and Germany*, Wiesbaden: VS Verlag.

— (2009) 'The Open Method of Coordination: under-conceptualisation, over-determination, de-politicisation and beyond', *European Integration online Papers*, 1(13).

— (2012) 'Democracy promoter or interest defender? How the European Commission influences non-electoral representation by civil society organizations', in Kröger, S. and D. Friedrich (eds.), *Representation in the European Union: Coping with present challenges to democracy?* Palgrave Macmillan: Houndmills, 226–240.

— (2013) 'Creating a European demos? The representativeness of European umbrella organizations', *Journal of European Integration*, 35(5): 583–600.

Kröger, S. and Friedrich, D. (2013a) 'Introduction: the representative turn in EU studies', *Journal of European Public Policy*, 20(2): 155–170.

— (2013b) 'Democratic representation in the EU: two kinds of subjectivity', *Journal of European Public Policy*, 20(2): 171–189.

Kuhn, T. (1970) *The Structure of Scientific Revolutions*, Chicago, IL: Chicago University Press.

Kurzman, C. (2004) 'The poststructuralist consensus in social movement theory', in Goodwin, J. and Jasper, J. (eds.) *Rethinking Social Movements: Structure, meaning and emotion*, New York: Rowan and Littlefield, 111–120.

Kymlicka, W. (1995) *Multicultural Citizenship: A liberal theory of minority rights*, Oxford: Oxford University Press.

Ladrech, R.J. (1994) 'Europeanization of domestic politics and institutions: the case of France', *Journal of Common Market Studies*, 32(1): 69–88.

Lijphart, A. (1999) *Patterns of Democracy: Government forms and performance in thirty-six countries*, New Haven: Yale University Press.

Lister, S. (2003) 'NGO legitimacy: technical issue or social construct?' *Critique of Anthropology*, 23(2): 175–192.

Lord, C. (2010) 'The Aggregating Function of Political Parties in EU Decision-Making', *Living Reviews in European Governance* 5(3), http://europeangovernance-livingreviews.org/Articles/lreg-2010-3/ (accessed 12 February 2016).

Lord, C. and Pollak, J. (2010) 'The EU's many representative modes: colliding? Cohering?' *Journal of European Public Policy*, 17(1): 117–136.

Lynggaard, K. (2004) 'The Common Agriculture Policy and the Study of Continuity and Change', paper for presentation at The Danish Association for European Studies, Annual Meeting, Denmark 24–25 September.

van Maanen, J. (1983) *Qualitative Methodology*, London: Sage.

McLaverty, P. (2002) 'Civil Society and democracy', *Contemporary Politics*, 8(4): 303–318.

Mahoney, C. (2004) 'The power of institutions: state and interest-group activity in the European Union', *European Union Politics*, 5(4): 441–466.

—   (2008) *Brussels Versus the Beltway: Advocacy in the United States and the European Union*, Washington, D.C.: Georgetown University Press.

Maia, R.C.M. (2012) 'Non-electoral political representation: expanding discursive domains', *Representation*, 48(4): 429–443.

Mair, P. (2006) 'Ruling the void? The hollowing of Western democracies', *New Left Review*, 42, November–December 2006, 25–51.

—   (2007) 'Political parties and party systems', in Graziano, P., Vink, M.P. (eds.) *Europeanization: New research agendas*, Palgrave Macmillan: Basingstoke, 154–166.

Majone, G. (1998) 'Europe's "democratic deficit": the question of standards', *European Law Journal*, 4(1): 5–28.

—   (2006) 'The common sense of European integration', *Journal of European Public Policy*, 13(5): 607–626.

Maloney, W. (2008) 'The Professionalization of representation: biasing participation', in Kohler-Koch, B. de Bièvre, D. and Maloney, W. (eds.) *Opening EU Governance to Civil Society: Gains and challenges*, Connex Report Series, 5, 69–86.

—   (2009) 'Interest groups and the revitalisation of democracy: are we expecting too much?' *Representation*, 45(3): 277–287.

Manin, B. (1997) *The Principles of Representative Government*, Cambridge: Cambridge University Press.

Mansbridge, J. (1999) 'Should blacks represent blacks and women represent women? A contingent "yes"', *Journal of Politics*, 61(3): 628–57.

— (2003) 'Rethinking representation', *American Political Science Review*, 97(4): 515–528.

— (2004) 'Representation revisited: introduction to the case against electoral Accountability', *Democracy and Society*, 2(1): 1, 12–13.

Marks, G. (1993) 'Structural policy and multilevel governance in the EC', in Cafruny, A. and Rosenthal, G. (eds.) *The State of the European Community: The Maastricht debate and beyond*, Boulder: Lynne Rienner, 391–411.

Martensson, M. (2007) 'Mixed representation and legitimacy in the European Union', *Journal of European Integration*, 29(3): 285–302.

Maurer, A. and Wessels, W. (2001) (eds.) *National Parliaments on their Ways to Europe: Losers or latecomers?* Baden-Baden: Nomos.

Mény, Y. (2002) '*De la démocratie en Europe:* old concepts and new challenges', *Journal of Common Market Studies*, 41(1): 1–13.

Michalowitz, I. (2004) 'Analysing structured paths of lobbying behaviour: why discussing the involvement of "civil society" does not solve the EU's democratic deficit', *Journal of European Integration*, 26(2): 145–173.

Michel, H. (2008) 'Incantations and uses of civil society by the European Commission', in Jobert, B. and Kohler-Koch, B. (eds.) *Changing Images of Civil Society: From protest to governance*, London: Routledge, 107–119.

Miklin, E. (2014) 'EU politicisation and national parliaments: visibility of choices and better aligned ministers?', *The Journal of Legislative Studies*, 20(1): 78–92.

Mill, J. S. (1861) Considerations on representative government, http://www.gutenberg.org/files/5669/5669-h/5669-h.htm (accessed 12 February 2016).

Moravcsik, A. (2002) 'In defence of the democratic deficit: reassessing legitimacy in the EU', *Journal of Common Market Studies*, 40(4): 603–624.

Moravcsik, A. (2006) 'What can we learn about the collapse of the European constitutional project?' *Politische Vierteljahreszeitschrift*, 47(2): 219–241.

Moravcsik, A. (2008) 'The myth of Europe's democratic deficit', *Intereconomics: Journal of European Public Policy*, 331–340.

Nanz, P. and Steffek, J. (2004) 'Global governance, participation and the public sphere', *Government and Opposition*, 39(2): 314–335.

Näsström, S. (2010) 'Democracy counts: problems of equality in transnational democracy', IN Tallberg, J. and Jönsson, C. (eds.) *Transnational Actors in Global Governance: Patterns, explanations and implications (Democracy Beyond the Nation State? Transnational Actors and Global Governance)*, Basingstoke: Palgrave Macmillan, 343–383

Natali, D. (2005) 'Comparing Participation in Hard and Soft Modes of Governance on Pensions: Is the OMC more open than the Legislative Process?' paper presented at the 3rd Annual ESPAnet Conference, Fribourg, 22–24 September 2005.

Nedergaard, P. (2006) 'Market failures and government failures: a theoretical model of the common agricultural policy', *Public Choice*, 127(3–4): 385–405.

Neto, O. A. and Strøm, K. (2006) 'Breaking the parliamentary chain of delegation', *British Journal of Political Science*, 36(4): 619–643.

Neuhold, C. (2005) The European Parliament: a venue for "civil society interests"? paper presented at the CONNEX Workshop 'The institutional shaping of EU-society Relations', University of Mannheim, Mannheim, 12–15th October 2005.

O'Flynn, I. (2010) 'Democratic theory and practice in deeply divided societies', *Representation*, 46(3): 281–293.

O'Neill, J. (2001) 'Representing people, representing nature, representing the world', *Environment and Planning*, 19(4): 483–500.

Obradovic, D. and Vizcaino, J.M.A. (2006) 'Good governance requirements for the participation of interest groups in EU consultations'. In: Obradovic, D. and Pleines, H. (eds.) *The Capacity of Central and East European Interest Groups to Participate in EU Governance*, Stuttgart: Ibidem Publishers, 67–108.

Offe, C. (1998) 'Demokratie und Wohlfahrtsstaat: Eine europäische Regimeform unter dem Streß der europäischen Integration', in Streeck, Wolfgang (ed.): *Internationale Wirtschaft, nationale Demokratie. Herausforderungen für die Demokratietheorie*, Frankfurt am Main / New York: Campus, 99–136.

Olson, M. (1965) *The Logic of Collective Action: Public goods and the theory of groups*, Cambridge, MA: Harvard University Press.

Papadopoulos, Y. (2006) 'Conceptualising accountability in network and multi-level governance', Committee on Concepts and Methods Working Paper Series.

Papadopoulos, Y. (2010) 'Accountability and multi-level governance: more accountability, less democracy?' *West European Politics*, 33(5): 1030–1049.

Persson, T. (2007) 'Democratizing European chemicals policy: do consultations favour civil society participation?' *Journal of Civil Society*, 3(3): 223–238.

Peruzotti, E. 'Representation, accountability and civil society', paper presented at Civil society and democratic innovation in Latin America: The politics of social accountability and control, LASA XXV International Congress, Las Vegas, 2004.

Peruzotti, E. (2006) 'Civil society, representation, and accountability: restating current debates on the representativeness and accountability of civic associations', in Jordan, L. and Van Tuijl, P. (eds.) *NGO Accountability: Politics, principles and innovations*, London: Earthscan.

Pesendorfer, D. (2006) 'EU environmental policy under pressure: chemicals policy change between antagonistic goals?' *Environmental Politics*, 15(1): 95–114.

Phelps, J. (2007) 'Much ado about decoupling: evaluating the environmental impact of recent European Union agricultural reform', *Harvard Environmental Law Review*, 31, 279–320.

Phillips, A. (1995) *The Politics of Presence*, Oxford: Oxford University Press.

Piattoni, S. (2012) 'The committee of the regions and the upgrading of subnational territorial representation', in Kröger, S. and Friedrich, D. (eds.) *The Challenge of Democratic Representation in the European Union*, Houndmills: Palgrave Macmillan.

Pitkin, H.F. (1967) *The Concept of Representation*, Berkeley: University of California Press.

Pitkin, H.F. (2004) 'Representation and democracy: uneasy alliance', *Scandinavian Political Studies*, 27(3): 335–342.

Pleines, H. (2012) 'Representing workers or presenting EU prescriptions? Trade unions from post-socialist member states in EU multi-level governance', in Kröger, S. and Friedrich, D. (eds.) *The Challenge of Democratic Representation in the European Union*, Basingstoke: Palgrave Macmillan, 241–158.

Plotke, D. (1997) 'Representation is democracy', *Constellations*, 4(1): 19–34.

Pollack, M.A. (1997) 'Representing diffuse interests in EC policy making', *Journal of European Public Policy*, 4(4): 572–590.

Puntscher Riekmann, S. and Wydra, D. (2013) 'Representation in the European state of emergency: parliaments against governments?' *Journal of European Integration*, 35(5): 565–582.

Putnam, R. (1988) 'Diplomacy and domestic politics: the logic of two-level games', *International Organization*, 42(3): 427–60.

Putnam, R. D. (1993) *Making Democracy Work: Civic traditions in modern Italy*, Princeton: Princeton University Press.

Quittkat, C. und Finke, B. (2008) 'The EU commission consultation regime', in Kohler-Koch, B., De Bièvre, D. and Maloney, W.A. (eds.) *Opening EU-Governance to Civil Society: Gains and challenges*, Mannheim, 183–222.

Radaelli, C.M. (2003) 'The Europeanization of public policy', in K. Featherstone and Radaelli, C.M. (eds.) *The Politics of Europeanization*, Oxford: Oxford University Press, 26–56.

Rancière, J. (2006) 'Democracy, republic, representation', *Constellations*, 13(3): 297–307.

Raunio, T. (2009) 'National parliaments and European integration: what we know and agenda for future research', *The Journal of Legislative Studies*, 15(4): 317–334.

Raunio, T. and Hix, S. (2000) 'Backbenchers learn to fight back: European integration and parliamentary government', *West European Politics*, 23(4): 142–168.

Rehfeld, A. (2005) *The Concept of Constituency: Political representation, democratic legitimacy and institutional design*, Cambridge: Cambridge University Press.
— (2006) 'Towards a general theory of political representation', *Journal of Politics* 68(1): 1–21.
— (2009) 'Representation rethought: on trustees, delegates, and gyroscopes in the study of political representation and democracy', *American Political Science Review*, 103(2): 214–230.
— (2011) 'The concepts of representation', *American Political Science Review*, 105(3): 131–141.
Reif, K.-H. and Schmitt, H. (1980) 'Nine second-order national elections – a conceptual framework for the analysis of European election results', *European Journal of Political Research* 8(1): 3–44.
Risse, T. (2005) 'Neofunctionalism, European identity, and the puzzles of European integration', *Journal of European Public Policy*, 12(2): 291–309.
Risse, T., Green Cowles, M. and Caporaso, J. (2001) 'Europeanization and domestic change: introduction', in Green Cowles, M., Caporaso, James A. and Risse, T. (eds.) *Transforming Europe: Europeanization and domestic change*, Ithaca: Cornell University Press, pp. 1–20.
Rittberger, B. (2009) 'The historical origins of the EU's system of representation', *Journal of European Public Policy*, 16(1): 43–61.
Rumford, C. (2003) 'European civil society or transnational social space? Conceptions of society in discourses of EU citizenship, governance and the democratic deficit: an emerging agenda', *European Journal of Social Theory*, 6(1): 25–43.
Ruzza, C. (2005) 'EU Public Policies and the Participation of Organized Civil Society', Working Papers del Dipartimento di studi sociali e politici, Università degli studi di Milano, 23 November 2005.
— (2007) 'Conclusion. Linking governance and civil society'. In: Della Sala, V. and Ruzza, C. (eds.), *Governance and Civil Society in the European Union: Exploring policy issues*, Manchester: Manchester University Press, 139–154.
— (2010) 'Identifying uncivil society in Europe: towards a "new politics of the enemy?"' In Liebert, Ulrike and Hans-Jörg Trenz (eds.) *The New Politics of European Civil Society*, London: Routledge, 143–162.
Ruzza, C. and Bozzini, E. (2008) 'Organized civil society and European governance: routes of Contestation', *European Political Science*, 7, 296–303.
Sabel, C.F. and Zeitlin, J. (2008) 'Learning from difference: the new architecture of experimentalist governance in the EU', *European Law Journal*, 14(3): 271–327.
Sánchez-Salgado, R. (2007) 'Giving a European dimension to civil society organizations', *Journal of Civil Society*, 3(3): 253–269.
Saurugger, S. (2005) 'Europeanization as a methodological challenge: the case of interest groups', *Journal of European Comparative Policy Analysis*, 7(4): 291–312.

— (2007) 'Differential impact: Europeanizing French non-state actors', *Journal of European Public Policy*, 14(7): 1079–1097.

— (2008) 'Interest groups and democracy in the European Union', *West European Politics*, 31(6): 1274–91.

— (2010) 'The social construction of the participatory turn: the emergence of a norm in the European Union', *European Journal of Political Research*, 49: 471–495.

Saward, M. (1998) *The Terms of Democracy*, Oxford: Polity Press.

— (2005) 'Governance and the transformation of political representation', in Newman, J. (ed.) *Remaking Governance: Peoples, politics and the public sphere*, Bristol: Policy Press, 179–196.

— (2006) 'The Representative Claim', *Contemporary Political Theory*, 5(3): 297–318.

— (2009) 'Authorisation and authenticity: representation and the unelected', *The Journal of Political Philosophy*, 17(1): 1–22.

— (2010) *The Representative Claim*, Oxford / New York: Oxford University Press.

Scharpf, F. (1999) *Governing in Europe: Effective and democratic?* Oxford: Oxford University Press.

— (2009) 'Legitimacy in the multilevel European polity', *European Political Science Review*, 1(2): 173–204.

Schattschneider, E. E. (1942) *Party Government*, New York: Holt, Reinhart and Winston.

Schmidt, V.A. (1999) 'European "federalism" and its encroachments on national institutions', *Publius*, 29(1): 19–44.

Schmidt, V.A. (2006) *Democracy in Europe: The EU and national polities*, Oxford: Oxford University Press.

— (2013) 'Democracy and legitimacy in the European Union revisited: input, output *and* "throughput"', *Political Studies*, 61(1): 2–22.

Schmitt, H. and Thomassen, J. (1999) *Political Representation and Legitimacy in the European Union*, Oxford: Oxford University Press.

Schmitter, P. (2000) *How to Democratize the European Union...And Why Bother?* Oxford: Rowman and Littlefield.

— (2002) 'Participation in governance arrangements: is there any reason to expect it will achieve "sustainable and innovative policies in a multi-level context"?' in Grote, J. and Gbikpi, B. (eds.) *Participatory Governance: Political and societal implications*, Leske and Budrich: Opladen, 51–70.

— (2007) 'Can the European Union be legitimized by governance?' *European Journal of Legal Studies*, 1(1), http://www.ejls.eu/issue/1/ (accessed 4 May 2011).

— (2009) 'Re-representing representation', *Government and Opposition*, 44(4): 476–490.

Schmitter, P.C. and Streeck, W. (1999) 'The organization of business interest: studying associative action of business in advanced industrial societies'.

Discussion paper 99/1, Max Planck Institute for the Study of Societies, Cologne, Germany.

Seale, C. F. (1999) 'Quality in qualitative research', *Qualitative Inquiry*, 5(4): 465–78.

Severs, E. (2010) 'Representation as claims-making: quid responsiveness?' *Representation* 46(4): 411–423.

Sigalas, E. and Pollak, J. (2012) 'Political parties at the European level: do they satisfy the condition of programmatic convergence?' in Kröger, S. and Friedrich, D. (eds.) *The Challenge of Democratic Representation in the European Union*, Basingstoke: Palgrave Macmillan, 23–40.

Slob, A. and Smakman, F. (2007) 'A voice, not a vote: evaluation of the civil society dialogue at DG trade'. final report, commissioned by the European Commission, Brussels, February 2007.

Smismans, S. (2003) 'European civil society: shaped by discourses and institutional interests', *European Law Journal*, 9(4): 482–504.

— (2004) *Law, Legitimacy and European Governance: Functional participation in social regulation*, Oxford: Oxford University Press.

— (2009) 'The representativeness of organised civil society: generally desired…until defined', paper presented at Bringing Civil Society In: The European Union and the rise of representative democracy, European University Institute, Florence, 13–15 March 2009.

— (2012) 'Interest *representation* in the EU, is there any? A top-down perspective', in Kröger, S. and Friedrich, D. (eds.) *The Challenge of Democratic Representation in the European Union*, Basingstoke: Palgrave Macmillan, 209–225.

Steffek, J. and Nanz, P. (2008) 'Emergent patterns of civil society participation in global and European governance', in Steffek, J. *et al.* (eds.) *Civil Society Participation in European and Global Governance: A cure for the democratic deficit?* Basingstoke: Palgrave Macmillan, 1–29.

Steffek, J., Piewitt, M. and Rodekamp, M. (2010) 'Civil society in world politics: how accountable are transnational CSOs?' *Journal of Civil Society*, 6(3): 237–258.

Stewart, J. (1992) *Accountability to the Public*, London: European Policy Forum.

Sudbery, I. (2003) 'Bridging the legitimacy gap in the EU: can civil society help to bring the union closer to its citizens?' *Collegium* 26(Spring), 75–95.

Tarrow, S. (1994) *Power in Movement: Social movements, collective action and politics*, Cambridge: Cambridge University Press.

Taylor, L. (2010) 'Re-founding representation: wider, broader, closer, deeper', *Political Studies Review*, 8(2): 169–79.

Trenz, H.J. (2009) 'European civil society: between participation, representation and discourse', *Policy and Society*, 28(1): 35–46.

Urbinati, N. (2000) Representation as advocacy: a study of democratic deliberation, *Political Theory*, 28(6): 758–86.

Urbinati, N. (2004) 'Condorcet's democratic theory of representative government', *European Journal of Political Theory*, 3(1): 53–75.

Urbinati, N. (2006) *Representative Democracy: Principles and genealogy*, Chicago: University of Chicago Press.

Urbinati, N. and Warren, M.E. (2008) 'The concept of representation in contemporary democratic theory', *Annual Review of Political Sciences*, 11, 387–412.

Vedder, A. (2003) 'Non-state actors' interference in the international debate on moral issues – legitimacy and accountability', in Vedder, A. (ed.) *The WTO and Concerns Regarding Animals and Nature*, Nijmegen: Wolf Legal Publishers.

Warleigh, A. (2000) 'The hustle: citizenship practice, NGOs and "policy coalitions" in the European Union – the cases of auto oil, drinking water and unit pricing', *Journal of European Public Policy*, 7(2): 229–43.

— (2001) 'Europeanizing civil society: NGOs as agents of political socialization', *Journal of Common Market Studies* 39(4), pp. 619–39.

Warren, M.E. (2001) *Democracy and Association*, Princeton: Princeton University Press.

Warren, M.E. and Castiglione, D. (2004) 'The transformation of democratic representation', *Democracy and Society*, 2(1): 5–22.

Wedeen, L. (2004) 'Concepts and commitments in the study of democracy', in Shapiro, I., Smith, R.M. and Masoud, T.E. (eds.) *Problems and Methods in the Study of Politics*, Oxford: Oxford University Press, 274–306.

Williams, M. (1998) *Voice, Trust, and Memory: Marginalized groups and the failings of liberal representation*, Princeton: Princeton University Press.

Wonka, A. (2009) 'Europeanized convergence? British and German business associations' European lobbying strategies in the formulation of REACH', in Grote, J.R., Lang, A. and Schneider, V. (eds.) *Organised Business Interests in Changing Environments*, Houndmills: Palgrave Macmillan, pp. 179–199.

Young, I. (2002) *Inclusion and Democracy*, Oxford: Oxford University Press.

Zeitlin, J., Pochet, P. and Magnusson, L. (2005) (eds.) *The Open Method of Coordination in Action: The European employment and social inclusion strategies*. Brussels: P.I.E.-Peter Lang.

Zeitlin, J.H. (2009) 'The open method of coordination and national social and employment policy reforms: influences, mechanisms, effects', in Heidenreich, M. and Zeitlin, J.H. (eds.) *Changing European Employment and Welfare Regimes: the influence of the open method of coordination on national reforms*, London: Routledge, 214–245.

Index

www.ingramcontent.com/pod-product-compliance
Lightning Source LLC
Chambersburg PA
CBHW072117020426
42334CB00018B/1632